The Church We Want

THE CHURCH WE WANT

African Catholics Look to Vatican III

Editor

AGBONKHIANMEGHE E. OROBATOR

ORBIS BOOKS
www.orbisbooks.com

Founded in 1970, Orbis Books endeavors to publish works that enlighten the mind, nourish the spirit, and challenge the conscience. The publishing arm of the Maryknoll Fathers and Brothers, Orbis seeks to explore the global dimensions of the Christian faith and mission, to invite dialogue with diverse cultures and religious traditions, and to serve the cause of reconciliation and peace. The books published reflect the views of their authors and do not represent the official position of the Maryknoll Society. To learn more about Maryknoll and Orbis Books, please visit our website at www.maryknollsociety.org.

Versions of these essays appeared previously in *The Church We Want: Foundations, Theology and Mission of the Church in Africa. Vol. 2 of TCCRSA Research Project* (Nairobi, Kenya: Paulines Publications Africa, 2015), Agbonkhianmeghe Orobator, editor, and *Theological Reimagination: Conversations on Church, Religion, and Society in Africa. Vol. 1 of TCCRSA Research Project* (Nairobi, Kenya: Paulines Publications Africa, 2014), Agbonkhianmeghe Orobator, editor.

Manufactured in the United States of America.

Library of Congress Cataloging-in-Publication Data

Names: Orobator, A. E., editor.
Title: The church we want : African Catholics look to Vatican III / edited by Agbonkhianmeghe E. Orobator.
Description: Maryknoll : Orbis Books, 2016. | Includes bibliographical references and index.
Identifiers: LCCN 2016003367 (print) | LCCN 2016012879 (ebook) | ISBN 9781626982031 (pbk.) | ISBN 9781608336685 (ebook)
Subjects: LCSH: Church renewal—Catholic Church—Congresses. | Catholic Church—Africa—Congresses.
Classification: LCC BX1746 .C5153 2016 (print) | LCC BX1746 (ebook) | DDC
282/.6—dc23
LC record available at http://lccn.loc.gov/2016003367

Contents

ACKNOWLEDGMENTS

I offer my sincere gratitude to the following people who played significant roles in the publication of this volume. The idea to publish this volume by Orbis Books originally came from Joe Healey, MM, who remains unwavering in his support for theological research and scholarship in Africa. Jim Keane, Robert Ellsberg, Bernadette Price, and their colleagues at Orbis worked hard to ensure the timely publication of this volume. The key success factor of the Theological Colloquium on Church, Religion, and Society in Africa (TCCRSA) was the commitment of several scholars from different parts of Africa and beyond, who made a heroic commitment to the life-span of the project, writing and revising papers for presentation and publication. My colleagues and support staff at Hekima University College and the Provincial Office of the Eastern Africa Province of the Society of Jesus were admirable in providing logistical support and assisting with the organization and planning for the duration of TCCRSA.

Theological research of this nature requires substantial financial resources. Generous gifts from a European family foundation and the General Office of the Jesuits in Rome, as well as several individual friends and partners, made the project and this publication possible. In the midst of so many commitments, finding a suitable place to edit and produce this volume also proved a daunting task. The generous offer of the Wade Chair by the Jesuit Community of Marquette University, Milwaukee, Wisconsin, provided the ideal space for research and writing. Along with this offer came the assistance of Nicholas Elder, my research assistant, who did an amazing job. The hospitality and support of the Rector, Rev. Jeff LaBelle, SJ, and members of the Jesuit Community at Marquette University; the chair of the theology department, Professor Robert Masson; my colleague, Professor Joseph Ogbonnaya, and the rest of the theology faculty made my year at Marquette University intellectually stimulating and productive. I owe a debt of gratitude to all these people for their support, encouragement, and assistance in the publication of this book.

As always, my final and profound word of gratitude goes to Kijana wa Zamani Joe Healey; my brother, Chuks Afiawari, SJ; and my soulmate, Oghomwen n'Oghomwen Anne Arabome, SSS.

Asanteni sana!

Milwaukee, January 2016

Preface

ABOUT A THEOLOGICAL RESEARCH PROJECT

Theological Colloquium on Church, Religion, and Society in Africa (TCCRSA)

The Theological Colloquium on Church, Religion, and Society in Africa (TCCRSA) is a three-year theological research project on the currents of the fiftieth anniversary of Vatican II. A primary objective of the colloquium was to develop, model, and sustain a new and innovative methodology and process of theological reflection, research, and study at the service of the African Church and the World Church. From 2013 to 2015 the colloquium convened a community of African Catholic scholars doing theology or using Roman Catholic theological/ethical (re)sources in their academic disciplines to identify, analyze, and study a wide variety of issues in the African Church and society. Each annual gathering focused on a particular theme:

- **Year I (2013):** African Theology in the Twenty-First Century: Identity and Profile, Contexts, and Models
- **Year II (2014):** The Church We Want: Theological Voices from Within and Outside the Church at the Service of Ecclesia in Africa
- **Year III (2015):** An Agenda for Vatican III: Ideas, Issues, and Resources from Africa for the World Church

Each colloquium served as a forum for conversation, listening, presentation of commissioned papers and responses, and joint working/research sessions among participants, who came from a wide range of backgrounds: the theological academy and allied disciplines; the ecclesial hierarchy; and civil society/practitioners.

The colloquium aimed for a pan-African participation. Participants included representatives of different linguistic communities (French-, Portuguese-, and English-speaking), different genders (women and men), geographical areas (North Africa and sub-Saharan Africa: east, west, central, and south), generations (established theologians and young/new scholars), and ecclesial communities (laity, religious, clergy, and bishops). It also included African theologians in the Diaspora. For the duration of the project sixty theologians and scholars participated in the colloquiums.

Regarding process and methodology, each colloquium combined plenary, panel, and palaver sessions. A plenary session allowed for one speaker to deliver a commissioned paper on a topic of major significance in African Christianity/theology that may not have previously received serious theological consideration. A panel discussion comprised three or four panelists discussing a point of relevance in African Christianity/theology. During a palaver session, two speakers presented position papers on an issue of concern/contention in African Christianity/theology. In addition, during each session all participants engaged in open conversations to contribute to and clarify the understanding of the topic under consideration.

An important component of TCCRSA is the publication of select materials presented at the colloquiums. To date, two volumes have been published: *The Church We Want: Foundations, Theology and Mission of the Church in Africa* (Nairobi, Kenya: Paulines Publications Africa, 2015) and *Theological Reimagination: Conversations on Church, Religion, and Society in Africa* (Nairobi, Kenya: Paulines Publications Africa, 2014). The third and final volume is scheduled to appear in 2016. This present anthology is a selection of essays from all three volumes for a global audience and for the purposes of introducing current trends and issues in African theological scholarship.

To judge by the manner in which the project has unfolded, one can say that TCCRSA has achieved significant goals and objectives. The project has created a new community of African scholars at the service of church and society. They understand their task as critically identifying, exploring, and studying emerging ideas and issues in theology in Africa and the world church. This community is an inclusive platform that facilitates constructive theological conversation, engagement, and interaction between theologians and the hierarchy/leadership of the Roman Catholic Church in Africa and beyond. It also builds the capacity, reinforces the confidence, and enhances the methodological competence of a new, young generation of African theologians. The publication of edited volumes has generated a new set of materials and resources for theological education and learning in Africa. In sum, TCCRSA has successfully initiated a new way of doing conversational, cross-disciplinary, collaborative, and multigenerational theology.

As a pioneering multiyear, multilevel theological research project in African theology TCCRSA is envisaged to have a wide-ranging, long-lasting, and positive impact on the study of theology, religion, church, and society in Africa and beyond.

Agbonkhianmeghe E. Orobator, SJ
Convener and Principal Researcher

Introduction

Reading the Times for Signs of the Future

Agbonkhianmeghe E. Orobator

Four significant events in the life of the church coincided with the Theological Colloquium on Church, Religion, and Society (TCCRSA), the research project at the origin of this anthology of essays: the election of Pope Francis (2013), the two-phased Synod on the Family (2014–2015), the Year of Consecrated Life (2014–2016), and the Jubilee Year of Mercy (2015–2016). These interrelated and overlapping events are noteworthy for at least two reasons. First, taken together, they remind us that the church is a living body. Far from being an entity that is fossilized in history, the church embodies a community that, in the words of Francis, "goes forth" (*Evangelii Gaudium*, no. 46). This forward movement is an outcome of the church's historical past and a reflection of its present reality. Each one of these ecclesial moments connected with Pope Francis, his personality and pontificate, carries significant associations relative to the contents of this volume. Second, the various ways in which the essays in this volume refer to these events confirm the importance of paying attention to the environment of theological discourse. The environment provides sources and shapes the discourse. To ignore it is to risk producing a sanitized theology that neither stimulates action nor breathes the gospel of life into the broken conditions of human existence in the world. A brief consideration of the theological and ecclesiological pertinence of each event can shed light on the perspective adopted in this collection of essays.

The election of Pope Francis has inaugurated a new era for the world church. The fascination that he elicits globally owes not only to his bold and creative ideas but also to his singular capacity to personify these ideas in powerful actions and striking gestures. On one level, Francis incarnates a sort of living theology, where text takes flesh in context and challenges and spurs "readers" into action. His deeds are his words. On another level, his exercise of pastoral leadership permits critical inquiry and encourages further analysis, debate, and conversation about issues of critical importance in the church, including those that the pope has declared off-limits, like ordained ministry for women. The contributors here take their cue from this Theologian-in-Chief in examining the various dimensions of theology, the church in Africa, and the world church with boldness and creativity, because the theological enterprise is a never-ending rigorous quest for truth, meaning, and value for our times.

The Synod on the Family stirred contention and controversy around a handful of issues, revealing gaping fault lines that separate proponents of varying shades of moral and doctrinal proclivities. When we probe beyond the private and public disagreement that oftentimes characterized the synodal debates, one of the enduring lessons of the event is Francis's refreshing teaching on the fundamental meaning of synod as a process, a journeying or walking together of all members of the church. Synodality is not an episodic occurrence in the life of the church; it is "a constitutive dimension of the Church."[1] For Francis, synodality is the way of being church, that is, a collaborative search or discernment of the divine path for God's people, by God's people. Thus, "A synodal Church is a Church which listens, which realizes that listening 'is more than simply hearing.' It is a mutual listening in which everyone has something to learn."[2] Arguably, under previous pontiffs, effective synodality fell into desuetude. Its present revival under Francis constitutes a teaching example of what it means to retrieve a positive element from the tradition of the church as an expression of what "God expects of the Church of the third millennium."[3] The pope's lesson on the synod still needs to be heeded and practiced in all its dimensions, especially the aspect of synodality as an inclusive process that embraces not only members of the official hierarchy journeying together but also members of the theological magisterium, and the *sensus fidelium*. Safeguarding this process from appropriation by a privileged few represents an ongoing task for theological projects such as the one depicted in this volume.

---

[1] Address of His Holiness Pope Francis on the 50th Anniversary of the Institution of the Synod of Bishops, October 17, 2015, http://w2.vatican.va.

[2] Ibid.

[3] Ibid.

In his proclamation of the Year of Consecrated Life, Francis identifies the common ideals, spirit, and mission that unite the church as a community of disciples of the risen Christ. For the pope, the Year of Consecrated Life is a year of the whole Christian people. Consequently, the responsibility for evangelization and renewal devolves not exclusively on religious and consecrated people but on the entire church as the people of God, according to the understanding of Vatican II's *Lumen Gentium.* In this way, the triple movement of looking to the past with gratitude, living the present with passion, and embracing the future with hope becomes an ecclesial vocation in which all share and participate actively as the faithful pilgrim people of God.

Finally, in this Year of Mercy (2015–2016), in addition to discovering mercy as the name and face of the compassionate God (see Luke 6:36), we perceive yet another constitutive dimension of the theological self-understanding of the church as a purveyor of mercy. The echoes of this mark of the church hark back not only to Pope John XXIII's vision of the church as dispenser of "the medicine of mercy" and, earlier, Martin Luther's metaphor of the church as "hospital for the incurably sick," but fundamentally to the raison d'être of the mission of Jesus of Nazareth, who sought out the sick and the vulnerable as a matter of evangelical preference (Mark 2:17). Under the banner of mercy, the church becomes a home where all are welcome, without an antecedent need to pass a litmus test for dogmatic conformity or moral exemplariness, devised by self-appointed and self-righteous judges of orthodoxy.

As mentioned, the essays in this volume reflect various aspects of these ecclesiological moments directly or indirectly. Although the conversation that takes place in this volume happens in the context of the church in Africa, the scope is intended to be much wider, encompassing developments and moments of theological pertinence in the world church. Thus church, as understood here, is not an insulated reality, no matter how successfully it may reflect and respond to the needs of the local community. Church is envisaged as a growing and open community, a concrete incarnation of a much larger reality, from which the local community is never detached. The aim of the contributors is to elicit a greater appreciation and deeper knowledge of the specific and unique issues of critical importance in the African church, and the affinity that these issues bear to the concerns of the global ecclesial community. The dynamic movements between the local and the universal offer one key for reading and understanding the approaches and subjects that the contributors focus on in this volume. Conscious of their task to gather the conversations of the local community into a coherent whole, they offer them as a part of a larger conversation happening in the world church.

This volume is divided into three parts. The essays in part 1 take an incisive look at the phenomenon called "the Francis effect" and the challenges it poses to the church in Africa and the world church. Part 2 contains a critique of the church in Africa and aspects of Christian identity, theological method, and ecclesial leadership. Part 3 moves the conversation to the future of Vatican III and identifies some of the issues that should claim the attention of the church as it scans its context and environment in order to discern the imperatives of mission in the world. The common aim of these three parts is to provide a critical understanding of present reality and create paths toward growth, transformation, and change in the church.

Overview of Essays

What is the role of a bishop as a theologian? How does a bishop do theology? In keeping with his down-to-earth and engaging style of ministry, Bishop Kevin Dowling thinks the answer is to enter into and be comfortable in the mess of ordinary people's lives. His account is a poignant illustration of Francis's idea of a hurting, bruised, and dirty church that is not averse to "sharing the hardships of history" (*Evangelii Gaudium,* no. 49).[4] This invitation extends to theologians and the hierarchy of the church. Dowling offers a powerful narrative of his vocation as a bishop called to witness to the gospel through faithful service and compassionate accompaniment of the people of God broken by poverty and ravaged by disease. The concomitant lesson for the world church is unambiguous: pay attention to the signs of the times through which God speaks to and calls church leaders and theologians to task. Dowling highlights two key principles in the exercise of theological and ecclesiastical leadership: subsidiarity and collegiality, the same aspects that Francis considers paramount in his model of church-as-synod. Both qualities of theological and ecclesiastical leadership yield a third element, namely, discernment. This third principle enables the church to recognize God's revelations and actions through respectful listening to the people of

---

[4] Ibid.

God and paying attention to their material poverty and spiritual starvation. This principle accords with Francis's idea of a listening church grounded in deep compassion and respect for people. Listening allows for an inclusive conversation that begins with the people and goes through the various levels of leadership, including theologians and bishops. For Dowling, whether a person is a theologian, a bishop, or both, the requisite virtues are the same: listening, discernment, and dialogue. The ability to incarnate these virtues in pastoral praxis makes a bishop a theologian.

Stan Chu Ilo proposes a provocative perspective of "the Francis effect" set in the context of church and leadership in Africa. Had an African cardinal been elected pope, would he have demonstrated the same boldness, creativity, and innovation of Francis in his reform and transformation of the church? Ilo answers in the negative. One could argue that Ilo exaggerates the point at issue and is needlessly strident in his sweeping judgment of a hypothetical African pope. But his analysis of African Catholicism should draw no such criticism. For him, African Catholicism is trapped in a theological warp presided over by leaders who seldom demonstrate the requisite boldness, vision, depth of history, and adequate judgment of prevailing context. Their understanding and practice of church are miles apart from the ecclesiology and theology that produced Pope Francis. Yet all is not lost, according to Ilo. Francis offers us a path and a strategy forward, one that is grounded in the familiar ecclesiology of Vatican II. This ecclesiological path is encapsulated in a "triple-A ecclesiology" that prioritizes the practice of accountability, accompaniment, and action. In various ways, other authors, such as Kambanda, Mayemba, Mwaura, Hadebe, and Arabome, validate the analysis and proposal of Ilo regarding the kind of ecclesial leadership that befits the church in Africa and the world church.

Pope Francis's call for a more incisive presence of women in the church provides the cue for Josée Ngalula's three-pronged analysis of the progress, prospects, and shortfalls in regard to the role and participation of women in the church. As do Akossi-Mvongo and Arabome, she detects a major problem, namely, the disconnect between rhetoric that affirms the dignity and role of women in church and practices that deny their dignity and limit their participation. Ngalula explains this gap by what she terms "theological illiteracy," a condition that manifests as ignorance of those biblical and magisterial texts that uphold the dignity and equality of women. This illiteracy or ignorance selectively shuts out positive affirmations of women's role in the church while retaining those that go in a contrary direction and promote sexism and cultural gender discrimination. Interestingly, Ngalula demonstrates how the *sensus fidelium* creates its own dynamics of change and transformation of ecclesial traditions and practices in favor of gender equality and human dignity. In conceptualizing the role and participation of women in ministry, the defining factor is not gender but competence and skills attained through sustained formation and training. She criticizes the uncritical and unscriptural binding of the particularity of masculinity to the image of God and the church as condition sine qua non for participation in ordained ministry. Her critique is vital considering, as Hadebe and Mwaura do, the dangers of distorted masculinities. Her insightful analysis opens up conversation and debate on many fronts about the desired incisive presence of women in the church.

Bienvenu Mayemba compares and contrasts two theological and pastoral thinkers: Jorge Mario Bergoglio (Pope Francis) of Argentina and Jean-Marc Ela of Cameroon. He traces in detail the sociopolitical, cultural, religious, and theological formative influences that underpin their theological visions and approaches. In line with Ilo, Mayemba notes the pivotal significance of Vatican II for understanding Francis's vision and theology of the church. Theologically, both Vatican II and liberation theology account for the way he leads and perceives the church. The outcome is exemplified in love and mercy embodied in a church for the poor and an understanding of liberation deeply embedded in revelation and salvation. Viewed this way, both in its self-understanding and outward manifestation, the church is best modeled as good Samaritan and prophet. Evidently, in the era of "the Francis effect," there is no dearth of comparisons between Francis and other figures of history. Ela, however, is not Francis; Francis is not Ela. Mayemba's correlation of the influences on both men is interesting, not least for highlighting the essential aspects of their understanding of the nature and mission of the church in contemporary society.

Anne Arabome takes a critical look at Francis's *Evangelii Gaudium* through the prism of women's lives in Africa. Echoing and reinforcing Hadebe's analysis, her argument is compelling: women are the face of poverty and therefore command specific focus within the corpus of *Evangelii Gaudium* and beyond that in the gospel of Jesus of Nazareth. Poverty manifests in the lives of women in various forms. Besides material deprivation, it inflicts disease on women, in much the same way that oppression, gender-based violence, and exclusion taint the dignity of women in Africa. Arabome exposes the complicity between society and church in the exclusion of women, which itself is both a cause and an aggravator of poverty. Among her antidotes, listening, compassion, and mercy stand out, elements, as indicated above, that form the pillars that Francis envisions for ecclesiology and characteristics of the church. Perhaps more striking is her proposal for a synod of women, for women, and by women, a radical step worthy of the title of this book—toward Vatican III. This proposal merits further study in the context of the world church and what Francis calls a more incisive presence of women in the church.

Bishop Antoine Kambanda examines the context of the resignation of Emeritus Pope Benedict XVI and the providential guidance of the Holy Spirit that ushered in a new spirit in the church under Pope Francis. This new spirit stimulates enthusiasm and hope. In Kambanda's view, Francis exercises an important influence on the practice of authority and leadership in the church. Besides the conception of authority as service and solidarity—in other words, "sleeping like a cow," as Kambanda metaphorically depicts—a critical element of this influence is attentiveness to the presence, voice, and actions of the Spirit in the people of God. Essentially, the qualities of pastoral leadership that Francis has inspired for the church can be condensed into three areas: compassion in listening, love and concern for the poor, and pastoral service of the people. These qualities of pastoral leadership find useful applications in the postgenocide context of Rwanda and the contemporary context of the church in Africa and the world.

In the first essay in part 2 Laurenti Magesa takes up the matter of the African continent's and its church's identity. In the maze and haze of globalization as well as competing perceptions, visions, and interpretations of reality, Africa contemplates its identity at the crossroads of doubt, uncertainty, and confusion. The question of Christianity and African identity is by no means simple, and has dogged theological reflection in Africa since the era of missionary Christianity in the nineteenth century. As theologians and historians of African Christianity would concede, the answer to the question of identity is not prefabricated; it is to be desconstructed and (re)constructed. Later, in part 3, Katongole and Healey show this process in various ways in their essays as a process that unfolds in a radical departure from the old ways of being African and Christian. Thus the unpredictable dynamics of this process carry a risk for Africa and Christianity: a dying unto self that permits the resurrection and creation of a novel reality.

This nascent reality synthesizes elements of the old and new and the local and the global, and it is truly African and fully Christian. Similarly, due attention must be paid to the language in which the African communicates and ritualizes his or her story and identity and existential concerns and experiences.

Teresa Okure brings her exegetical expertise to bear as she plumbs the depths of scripture and uncovers the rich foundations of the theology and practice of church. Her analysis anchors the foundation of the church in the divine work of reconciliation embodied in pure love. This experience was lived as covenant by the early Christians, at the core of which is Jesus Christ, from whom we learn to become a New Testament church. The new covenant sealed in the body and blood of Jesus Christ makes believers children of God and outlines a program of life for the disciples of Christ. The principal components of this program include reconciliation, self-sacrificial love, inclusiveness, and a diversity of ministries. The ultimate rule for the practice of church as new covenant is Jesus Christ, not the self-preserving bureaucratic institution that Francis also criticizes in *Evangelii Gaudium*. Becoming the church of Christ—that Eucharistic church anchored in the new covenant of love—requires a strict adherence to the program and rule of Jesus Christ. This is a task not only for the hierarchy and theologians but also for all Christians without exception as God's children and Jesus' siblings.

In the context of ecumenical rapprochement, Elochukwu Uzukwu focuses his analysis on the church as a community grounded in the plan of the Triune God. The principal mission of the church is to live and witness to the unity of God's people. In reality, as we know, the church is a divided community. Such division deviates from the will of Jesus Christ that all may be one. Uzukwu is searching for new ideas on which to anchor a new ecumenical relationship in a post-missionary church. Like Okure, he identifies diversity and differentiation as the foundational experience of the New Testament churches. The central and concrete manifestation of this experience is koinonia, communion. In its most foundational identity, the ecclesia is a visible koinonia. Understood as such, the division among Christian traditions constitutes an inexcusable scandal. Koinonia is a manifestation of inculturation and contextualization in the same way that Healey under-stands these terms in his essay in part 3. Because of this koinonia, the church is able to live its unique identity as a particular entity that is part of the symphony of ecclesiologies or churches. Koinonia allows the church to with-stand the centrifugal forces of diversity and difference without calcifying its identity and self-understanding into a totalitarian, centralized institution. The mandate to work toward visible unity expressed in Vatican II is still as pertinent as it was fifty years ago. In Africa, one clear resource is the gift and practice of African religion and spirituality. This *ressourcement*, as Uzukwu calls it, allows Christianity in Africa to rediscover itself as a religion of peace, harmony, hospitality, and relationality.

Paul Béré seeks to answer the question, What role does biblical exegesis play in the theological research and scholarship of African theologians? He focuses on the Old Testament in his review of African theology's historical trajectory. His discovery points to the absence of scripture as a key source of theological scholarship in African theology of Catholic extraction in contrast to the significant emphasis on scripture in Protestant theologies. The issue is not as simple as it might seem; deep fissures and tensions exist between practitioners of exegesis and proponents of biblical theology as well as between them and fundamental theologians. The situation raises the challenge of how to bridge the gap and create conditions for a sustained, penetrating study of scripture as an indispensable tool and component of theological discourse. A useful starting point is the recognition of the multiple and wide senses in which the Word of God functions as a medium of revelation and the ability to distinguish specific methodologies and foci of exegesis and biblical theology, deconstruct the cultural conditionings in the study of the Bible, and pay critical attention to context and broader interdisciplinary conversations.

Nader Michel presents a condensed account of the history and evolu-tion of the Coptic Orthodox Church from its origins in the apostolic times to the present. Centuries of political and religious intrigues have shaped this church whose existence many in the West and sub-Saharan Africa are hardly aware of. In this sense, Michel's essay is a brilliant introduction to an ancient ecclesiological tradition that warrants deeper and further studies. The issues that Michel raises are multiple and fascinating. Particularly striking is the historical movement of the Coptic Church through isolationist mentality, withdrawal from the wider Christian community, negotiating tight political complexities, surviving the threat of sectarianism, and opening to ecumenical actions and initiatives. His essay illuminates the contestations, conflicts, and claims that define the religious, social, and political landscape of Egypt and weaves a narrative of ecclesiological withdrawal and engagement, decline and revival, self-preservation and daring proclamation, despair, and hope. In the context of present-day Egyptian society and the global tension that has polarized Christianity and Islam, Michel's narrative of the Coptic Orthodox Church demonstrates that it is possible to find seeds of hope toward a future of genuine interreligious tolerance and ecumenical dialogue, as well as increased participation of Christians in public political life. As in politics, there are positive signs of a nascent ecclesiological Arab Spring.

Philomena Mwaura refutes the idyllic portrayal of family that fails to take account of its inherent weaknesses, especially in regard to the experience of women. Theological evaluation of the family is not enough; sociological analysis and anthropological study are equally important for understanding the meaning and function of the family. Her account of the family presents a multifaceted and complex reality shaped by a combination of socioeconomic, cultural, and political factors. In particular, following the same approach adopted by Arabome (in part 1) and Hadebe (in part 3), she analyzes the common thread of violence and abuse in the family that is the shared experience of many women in Africa. In light of the recent Synod on the Family, she raises critical questions for the church in formulating the gospel of the family. Considering present circumstances, family is a task for the church, not a ready-made sanguine metaphor available for constructing innocuous ecclesiological models. On all of this, as Arabome and Hadebe also point out, the church does not have the answers. Hence it needs to listen and learn from the lived experience of people. Even while detailing the complex nature and dynamic integration of change and continuity in the family, Mwaura's account still paints a conservative or traditional portrait of the family. For this reason, Hadebe's analysis of sexual minorities need to be noted by church and society as important components in the evolution of the meaning and practice of family.

In the first essay in part 3, Emmanuel Katongole makes a powerful case for a critical redefinition of what constitutes pressing and contested moral issues beyond narrow ideological concerns. For him, the pressing and contested moral issues identified ought not to be addressed or dealt with in abstraction from particular cultural, social, and theological contexts. In the same way that Mwaura argues for a sociological and anthropological appreciation of the meaning of family, Katongole points out that the sociological reality of the African church is the best index for an accurate assessment of the challenges, mission, theology, and practice of the church. This approach has the advantage of eliminating an unhelpful and rigid distinction between the social and the ethical or moral in identifying and analyzing the context of the mission of the church. Looking ahead to Vatican III he identifies seven pressing moral challenges for the church in Africa. Far from being an interesting thought experiment on the profile and mission of a futuristic church, these issues constitute real-life concerns that call the church to action here and now as the sacrament and bearer of the liberating and transforming gospel of the Jesus Christ.

Leading Zambian-born British theologian Tina Beattie draws amply on her personal experience as a theologian and a mother to break the silence on maternal mortality and suffering, a subject that theological discourse and analysis have hardly broached. Her essay is a disturbing revelation of the intricate intersection of religion, motherhood, and poverty that silences women's wisdom and suffering. Beattie's deconstruction of silence also reveals the insidious mechanism of its imposition by culture, economic systems, and patriarchy in church and society. A concrete example of the silencing of women in church is the effective exclusion of women from church forums, like the Synod on the Family, that decide on the sexuality and maternal and reproductive rights of women. Equally unsettling is the profusion of maternal rhetoric versus the reality of maternal deaths, which Arabome, Katongole, Healey, Hadebe, Ngalula, and Akossi all highlight. Considering the abundance of maternal imagery of God in scripture, Beattie argues that the silencing of women is as oppressive as the silencing of the divine is repulsive. Yet doing good is neither the sole preserve of benevolence and philanthropy nor ideology and sentimentalism. Rather, doing good is redressing injustice and promoting human dignity, the kind that enables women to live better and flourishing lives. In this context the goal of a Vatican III would include the full and equal participation of women in theological reflection and decision-making processes founded on the affirmation of human dignity in the likeness of God, who groans with creation at childbirth, while sharing the suffering of women, muffled by injustice and violence.

Joseph Healey, who has devoted a lifetime of research and writing to the emergence, history, and development of small Christian communities (SCCs) in Africa, explores the implications of Francis's invitation to boldness, creativity, generosity, and courage in envisaging new models of evangelization and reforming ecclesial structures. Healey draws on several examples to demonstrate the desirability and feasibility of reform in the governance of the church according to the thinking of Francis. SCCs offer a concrete context for experimenting and practicing reform and renewal in the church. These communities emphasize and live the values of active participation, ownership, and belonging at the grassroots level. Because of their unique position, SCCs play a pivotal role in addressing real and present pastoral challenges, such as "Eucharistic Famine" and "Marriage in Stages." Healey's bold and creative proposals are bound to be controversial. SCCs are not the only pastoral solutions, but they are part of a movement with a promising potential for the world church. The issues that Healey raises bear affinity to pastoral situations in other parts of the world, especially North America and Europe, thus underscoring the importance of conversation as content, method, and process of theology, and mutuality in learning from one another's pastoral experiences.

Nontando Hadebe draws on multiple contemporary sources, events, and research findings to demonstrate that the violence inflicted on women and sexual minorities constitutes a theological crisis that the church cannot avoid. She joins Arabome (in part 1) in constructing a phenomenological narrative of the revolting violence inflicted on women and sexual minorities by poverty, disease, subordination, exclusion, marginalization, and multiple forms of distorted masculinities. Religion and culture collude to aggravate this violence, but the situation is not irredeemable. Hadebe examines the rich tradition of Catholic social teaching to retrieve key resources for generating liberative and transformative practices in church and society. Further, she underlines the present situation as a kairos moment for the church to lament and to act. The act of lamentation and liberation exemplify the fundamental identity and mission of the church as guardian, sustainer, and protector of life.

Drawing on Pope Francis' *Laudato Si'*, Peter Knox addresses a clear and present cosmic danger: the anthropogenic breach of planetary boundaries and the calamitous consequences for human and environmental ecology. He joins a truly global debate on the future of the planet and the moral responsibility to act, as Pope Francis also stresses in his encyclical letter. Knox's account is sobering if not chilling, for the way he categorizes and describes the evil of human and systemic instrumentation that provokes climate change. In this context he advocates a convergence of discourse that combines the best of Christian, African, and scientific understanding of salvation and the practical and moral exigencies for decisive and sustainable individual and collective action. Each of the three approaches that Knox discusses is an embodiment of rich traditions, teachings, and knowledge that are best used in a manner that is complementary and mutually reinforcing. Such an approach places humanity and the global community in a better position to deal with the ecological crisis. In this way, Knox's essay offers a condensed model of a Christian theology of ecology and integrity of creation.

Marguerite Akossi-Mvongo revisits the neuralgic question of access to full ministerial roles for women in the church, which Ngalula avoids, but Healey examines. Following her argument, just as Arabome argues, the manner in which the issue has been dealt with reveals a gaping chasm between stirring rhetoric and inadequate practice. What is striking about her approach is that she bases her position on the result of a numerical sampling of opinion. In this sense, perhaps, her contribution is significant from the point of view of methodology that demonstrates how to do theology and address critical issues in the church in a way that is grounded in reality. Thus she confirms the position of the International Theological Commission that theologians ought to place themselves in "the school of *sensus fidelium*."[5] This approach corrects the assumption and hubris that make theologians think they know what the people want. Her conclusion would surprise those who maintain the erroneous belief that such trenchant argumentation coming from women in the church is illogical, emotional, and biased.

Mercy Amba Oduyoye's inspiring epilogue is a fitting conclusion to this volume and a stimulating overture to the future envisaged by the theological project that gave rise to the essays collected in this volume. This matriarch of theological research and scholarship in Africa casts epilogue and conclusion in a metaphor of a journey, an ongoing quest that thrives on collaboration, conversation, accompaniment, mutuality, inclusion, respect, and account-

---

[5] International Theological Commission, "*Sensus Fidei* in the Life of the Church" (2014), nos. 81–82.

ability. Although she does not use the term, hers is a vivid description of synodality, as understood by Francis. A theological enterprise that successfully integrates these qualities offers hope for a future that will welcome the reforms and transformations of a third Vatican Council.

Some Pointers for Readers

In reading these essays, it is important to keep in mind that they are a selection from a much larger collection. Overall, TCCRSA produced at least sixty essays in three volumes, the third and final of which is in editorial process in preparation for publication. With this information as a backdrop, this volume attempts to introduce elements of current theological scholarship in Africa to a global audience. As I have indicated above, it is hoped that readers will appreciate the richness and diversity of perspectives characteristic of the theological enterprise in Africa and discover connections and convergences across a range of issues and ways in which theological scholarship in various regions of the world could be mutually enriching.

Similarly, the number of scholars who participated in TCCRSA is significant from the point of view of the composition. By many accounts, and as demonstrated in the composition of contributors to this volume, TCCRSA did not follow the familiar and usual format of a theological talk-shop where scholars present erudite, abstract theses, and theories, or ecclesiastics declaim lofty doctrinal propositions, exhortations, and admonitions. Judging by its composition, methodology, and focus, TCCRSA offers a glimpse of the shape of theology in Africa today and the promise it holds for the world church. Over a three-year period, nearly half the participants were women, both lay and religious. This is something new and different. A gathering of theologians where women are not the negligible minority is unprecedented in Africa. At best it would have been customary to allow a token representation of no more than a couple of African women theologians.

TCCRSA consolidates an overdue and growing trend in Africa, namely, the increasing accessibility to theological education by African women. A new generation of African women theologians is in the making across an ecclesial and theological landscape where hitherto they were unrepresented, their voices ignored, and their contributions unacknowledged. As the veil of invisibility and nonrecognition lifts, African women are taking a critical stand on weighty matters in church and society. They speak their own truths as scholars with passion, confidence, and authority rather than being spoken about as passive objects in theological conferences, workshops, and seminars conducted and dominated by male theologians—clerics and ecclesiastics. It is not surprising that the essays in this volume authored by African women, theologically astute African women of the new generation, express understandings of faith and the concomitant ramifications for religious, socioeconomic, and political contexts in Africa that differ radically from traditional positions, and they open new paths toward action-oriented theological initiatives.

As mentioned in the preface, several ecclesial leaders participated actively in TCCRSA, although essays by only a couple of them are included in this volume. They participated in the colloquium as colleagues rather than as keynoters. In this role, the ecclesial leaders contributed to and enriched the conversation by offering candid views and relating moving personal testimonies of their experience of leadership in the church, a fact that is evident in the essays by Dowling and Kambanda. Here, again, something new is emerging across the continent: it is not customary for theologians to dialogue with ecclesial leaders on level ground. The conversational methodology breaks new ground in theological scholarship in Africa.

Throughout this volume the personality and presence of Pope Francis loom large. This is a testimony both to his transformational leadership of the world church and his exemplification of a theological and pastoral style that transcends fascination with facile nostrums and worn platitudes. As several of the contributors point out, his understanding of Christianity as mercy in action and compassion without borders, and his personal witness to a life of faith in the God of compassion, demonstrates how theological research and scholarship summon us to "to begin with the people and their everyday problems."[6] African theologians have been quick to notice and hold up the implications of his exemplary life and leadership qualities for the African church. The lesson is for all Christians without exception.

It is not mere coincidence that several contributors retrieve or evoke the language of kairos as a hermeneutical key for characterizing theology, ethics, and ecclesiology in twenty-first-century Africa. Kairos is an oppor-

---

[6] Address of His Holiness Pope Francis on the 50th Anniversary of the Institution of the Synod of Bishops.

tune time to discern and act. The act of discernment is frequently mentioned by Francis (occurring no fewer than twenty times in *Evangelii Gaudium*) in his vision of ecclesial reform and renewal. Properly construed, discernment is a prelude to action that is inspired and guided by the light, wisdom, and courage of the Spirit. Through discernment, "the Church can also come to see that certain customs not directly connected to the heart of the Gospel, even some which have deep historical roots, are no longer properly understood and appreciated. Some of these customs may be beautiful, but they no longer serve as means of communicating the Gospel. We should not be afraid to re-examine them. At the same time, the Church has rules or precepts which may have been quite effective in their time, but no longer have the same usefulness for directing and shaping people's lives" (*Evangelii Gaudium*, no. 43). In a real sense, the examples of theology, ethics, and ecclesiology in this volume make an important contribution to discernment and action about which Francis speaks by engaging in the task of reexamining tradition and generating new practices that are more closely "connected to the heart of the Gospel." In this way, the authors form part of an initiative to envision a future direction for the mission of the global ecclesial community that is inclusive, focused on prophetic proclamation of the good news, and a fulfillment of its identity as salt, leaven, and light, especially in times of great socioeconomic, religious, and political uncertainty.

Speaking of a future for the church, the TCCRSA participants envisaged the project to be a beginning of a process whose trajectory opens to a variety of outcomes, including the idea of Vatican III. As used in this volume, Vatican III is best understood as a metaphor. As such, it is an attempt to generate thinking beyond the staid and familiar; to imagine with boldness, creativity, generosity, and courage issues that stretch and expand the boundaries of theological thinking in the church. This attempt, it should be said, is anything but chaotic. In this process of envisioning Vatican III, rather than giving free rein to the imagination to run wild, theological ideas are expressed and debated in a respectful process of mutually enriching conversation. This is the principle for the selection of these essays. Where they appear critical, such criticisms need to be situated in the context of conversation which, as Oduyoye figuratively depicts it, occasionally resembles a fight between teeth and tongue.

Thus the adoption of the metaphor of Vatican III points perceptively to the future horizons of the path that opens up for the church. To reiterate Oduyoye's wise counsel in her epilogue, it falls to all theologians to widen, deepen, and extend this path guided by a realistic vision of God's dream for the world church. If in fact Vatican III happens, the church would be well served to consider these initial conversations as a useful catalyst for and preliminary elaboration of the task of theological inquiry and a more incisive understanding of the identity and mission of the church in the twenty-first century.

Part One
The Francis Effect
and the Church in Africa

Bishops as Theologians

Listening, Discerning, and Dialogue

Bishop Kevin Dowling

I would like to begin this essay with some insights from Richard Rohr that I consider thought-provoking:

> Those at the edge of any system and those excluded from any system, ironically and invariably hold the secret for the conversion and wholeness of that very group. They always hold the feared, rejected, and denied parts of the group's soul. You see, therefore, why the church was meant to be that group that constantly went to the edges, to the "least of the brothers and sisters," and even to the enemy. Jesus was not just a theological genius, but he was also a psychological and sociological genius. *When any church defines itself by exclusion, it is always wrong.* It is avoiding its only vocation, which is to be the Christ.
>
> Only as the People of God receive the stranger, the sinner, and the immigrant, those who don't play our game our way, do we discover not only the hidden, feared, and hated parts of our own souls, but the fullness of Jesus himself. We need them for our own conversion.
>
> The Church is always converted when the outcasts are reinvited back into the temple. You see this in Jesus commonly sending marginalized people that he has healed back into the village, back to their family, or back to the temple to "show themselves to the priests." It is not just for their reinclusion and acceptance, but actually for the group itself to be renewed.[1]

---

[1] Richard Rohr, adapted from *Radical Grace: Daily Meditations* (Cincinnati: St. Anthony Messenger Press, 1993), 28, day 2.

These insights caused me to reflect long and deeply about a number of possible interpretations of the role of bishops as theologians. Is the bishop's primary role as a teacher or as a theologian to simply articulate for his people the teachings of the magisterium? And in any difficult situation in terms of faith and morals, is he simply called to consult the professional theologians if, like me, he is not a professional theologian? Must he discern with professional theologians to find what teaching he should give so it can be an authentic interpretation of the magisterium? Or is the bishop called to do what I would term "theologizing" in the context of his people's situations, actual challenges, and even sufferings? Is he called to "do" theology on the front lines, as his experience of his people and situation unfolds?

Listening to the Call of the Poor

As a religious, priest, and bishop, I have always taken my inspiration in my calling and ministry from the founder of my religious community, Saint Alphonsus Liguori, the patron saint of moral theologians. His conversion in his calling and mission came about through a chance encounter as a priest with poor shepherds in an area south of Naples; they were poor people who were completely marginalized in society and the church. In a very real way, he was evangelized by the poor in their context, and that reality shaped his theology as a moral theologian despite the influence of Jansenism; the pastoral context provided the locus for his theology. I will never forget the comment of one of Alphonsus's great followers, Bernard Häring, at the launch of one of his books in Rome: "I have learned all my theology from the poor of the world."

This mirrors the call and challenge of Pope Francis that church leaders should work with the sheep and smell like them. Pope Francis is calling the church and its leadership "to go to those 'at the periphery' and 'at the margins,' especially the poor—as he himself did as bishop and even as cardinal. He compares such an evangelical church to a church that is 'self-referential,' which becomes, in his word, 'sick.' He has even said that it is better to go to the margins and make mistakes than become self-absorbed."[2] But unless we bishops actually leave our offices and chanceries and go into the "mess" of life as it really is and experience it personally, firsthand, we will perhaps risk perpetuating a model of church that focuses inwardly on our

---

[2] *National Catholic Reporter*, July 2, 2013.

"churchy" concerns, which will put us at a further risk of becoming ever more self-referential. And then our theology and our role as bishop-theologians will similarly risk being out of touch with the reality of people's lives and concerns, and consequently our word and teaching may become meaningless and irrelevant for the poor and suffering.

But what about the relationship between professional theologians and the institutional church, specifically, its bishops? A strong focus in the church in past years has been on the so-called new evangelization. At the conclusion of the recent conference of the Catholic Theological Society of America on the theme of conversion, the outgoing president, Susan Ross, said,

> I think it is fair to say that one basic truth emerging from the new evangelization is that both the world and the church are continually in need of conversion.... How can theologians, in cooperation with the institutional church, engage in the new evangelization through imagination, humor, commitment, discernment, and hospitality?[3]

The answer, she believes, lies in dialogue with the institutional church; she was referring to the context of the church in the United States. The question could be asked of theologians in Africa: What is the calling and mission of the theologian in Africa, whether the professional theologian or bishop-theologian? How can the theologian explain and apply with ever greater clarity the teachings of the magisterium to our church situation in Africa without a sensitivity to or a feel for the cultural and socioeconomic contexts in Africa? Should the call and mission of an African theologian per se be to push the boundaries, as it were, in our discernment as church in Africa of the revelation of God? Such discernment needs to be interpreted and reinterpreted in the ever-changing reality of our African society, with its own African worldview and all its needs, including the need to care for God's earth on which we as Africans depend for survival.

Smelling of Sheep

Many years ago, I sat in a steaming hot zinc and wood shack amid hundreds of other shacks in a so-called informal settlement next to one of the shafts of platinum mines in the diocese where I minister as bishop. In

---

[3] *National Catholic Reporter*, June 10, 2013.

front of me sat a seriously ill young mother; next to her lay a dying baby. They were both afflicted with AIDS and the infections that go with the disease. They were among the many thousands of such people who have become central to my life as a bishop since 1992, when I first encountered the horror of AIDS in my diocese. Perspiration poured down her face, but this could not hide the tears streaming down her cheeks or the utter hopelessness in her eyes. She said, "Father, I have no hope. There is no hope for me." Her shoulders slumped as she stared at her dying baby. As she spoke to me, all I could do was hold her in my arms and quietly repeat that my community carers would love her and look after her every day, and if she passed on, they would also care for her baby.

However, this was before the advent of antiretroviral drugs. There was indeed no hope for her. She died a horrible death, as did her baby. The community carers on my AIDS team found her one day on the ground in her shack. She was dead, covered in vomit and excrement.

I went through that experience scores of times over the years as I walked around the shacks with my community carers and nurses, trying also to keep up the spirits of those carers so they could indeed love and care for those little ones of God, whose lives I believed and still believe were and are infinitely precious to our God.

And that is precisely the point: if their lives were and are infinitely precious to God, what was—indeed, what is—my role and calling as bishop and theologian? That woman was dying not because she had had any choice about being infected with HIV; she had been subjected to unspeakable brutality and injustice. She, like hundreds of thousands of rural women in South Africa and countries north of South Africa, had been forced to leave her rural home because of extreme poverty, no work, and nothing on which to survive. She had ended up in this shack settlement next to a mine in the vain hope she could somehow find a job and survive. She found quickly she was in an even worse poverty trap. There were no jobs for anyone like her. Her only way to survive for even just a day was to sell herself for sex with men who had money, the miners, who themselves had left their homes and wives far away for employment at the mine.

I quickly termed her only possibility of putting some bread on the table as "survival sex." She would get paid for sex—all she had—to come up with enough for twenty-four hours, and then she would have to do that again and again and again. What utter, despicable, systemic injustice and degradation. The inevitable results were HIV infection, TB, pneumonia, cancer, other infections, pregnancy, birth of an HIV-positive baby—utter misery, and finally death.

Defining a Bishop-Theologian

What does it mean to do theology in such a situation, to be a theologian, even a bishop-theologian, in the face of such horror? What does it mean to be pro-life in such conditions? How do I as bishop-theologian listen to God speak to me through these "signs of the times" and interpret what God's will and Word means in such degradation? Is the teaching of the magisterium sufficient for me to respond to that situation, or does it perhaps appear to be irrelevant to that situation in terms of being a message of hope to the suffering and poor of our continent? If so, what am I called to as a bishop-theologian?

Our reality in Africa points to the need to positively revive and ground a reflection on the meaning of "collegiality" and of "subsidiarity" as core principles of Catholic social teaching. Subsidiarity in the sociopolitical arena calls for an understanding, namely, that what can be done at the "lower level" of society should not be subsumed, still less done, for the "lower level" by those at the "higher level" of governance in society. The purpose of this should be to ensure the common good of all by promoting a social compact in which everyone in society participates in a spirit of solidarity and collaboration to ensure that all citizens, especially the poorest and most vulnerable, experience growth in their human dignity as human beings made in God's image. In this sense, ensuring that subsidiarity actually works is the way to transform citizens into becoming and being active agents of transformation in their own communities by using their insights and experience to develop policies and practices that will make a real difference in their quality of life.

If we as church are going to challenge political leadership in our countries to promote the common good on the basis of the values and principles of subsidiarity, this calls for a similar commitment on church leadership at all levels to ensure the common good of the church community through promoting subsidiarity as the basis for a living collegiality.

In the first place, the bishop as shepherd and theologian is called to discern with all the people of God in the diocese what the Spirit is saying to that local church with all its particular characteristics, possibilities, needs, and challenges. And I stress the word "discern." To discern in the Spirit does not simply involve discussion about a particular issue, for example, and then making a decision. Rather, it requires a prayerful spirit of listening to what the Spirit is saying through each person's faith, listening to people's personal experiences in life's realities of the presence and call of Jesus to self-sacrifice and service in view of the common good. It requires an honest acceptance of the human failings present in all of us, including our prejudices, likes, and dislikes (especially with regard to others and their opinions). It requires an openness to admitting, as part of sharing and listening, that our attitudes and perhaps first opinions or thoughts about an issue require a change.

I believe the bishop as shepherd and theologian in the local church must take the lead in this by creating a spirit and atmosphere of respect for the other, listening not only to words but also to the spirit and experience behind the words, and above all, "feeling" in the people of God that he, the shepherd, deeply values each person and wants the same spirit to be shared by all.

Despite the inevitable ups and downs due to our human limitations, with good will, this approach could create the conditions for a real discernment in the Spirit and allow the bishop to affirm the *sensus fidelium* and truly speak those faith-filled words at the closure of the discernment: "It seems good to the Spirit and to all of us" at this moment in time that we begin this journey, that we embark on this pastoral plan, that we respond to this need in this way, and so on, but that we remain always open to new insights and inspiration in the faith community.

If this can be done at the local level with sincerity, and despite setbacks and human failures, it needs to be taken to the next level, where the bishops' conference discerns as a college of bishops through reflecting in the same way with local theologians and a national leadership of priests, religious, and lay faithful. The next level, the regional conferences of bishops and the synod of bishops, can follow the same model of discerning with theologians and other key advisers so the synod truly discerns and decides what the "Spirit seems to be saying to us and to the worldwide Church" at this time. The role of the various dicasteries in Rome should take on a different spirit, as it were, to confirm the faith and fidelity of the discernment process of the College of Bishops gathered with the Bishop of Rome and to offer the regional conferences and local conferences of bishops all the practical support the dicasteries can give to implementing the pastoral vision discerned in faith by the College of Bishops united with the Bishop of Rome.

That "spirit" of respect and valuing what can be discerned and done at the level of the local church, that is, subsidiarity, is crucial for the future of African theology and the call and ministry of the African theologian per se and the African bishop as theologian. We in Africa have a very particular sociocultural context affected by economic policies and decisions taken at global levels and by powerful political entities in Africa and elsewhere.

What is the Spirit saying to the African church? What is the Spirit inviting and calling the African church to be and do on our continent and as our particular gift to the worldwide church? That is the question African theologians and African bishops must grapple with, and we should be trusted and given the space to continue this journey of faith and discernment together as a community that "does" theology in our unique context, which is different from other sociocultural contexts, for example, those in Europe, the Americas, and Asia-Oceania.

The task of a theologian is not simply to articulate and reinterpret church teaching as it has come down to us over the centuries or to dictate the way the deposit of faith is to be understood by God's people through ever deeper theological reflection and research as if God's revelation is complete for all time.

God is continuing to reveal God's Word and will in the unfolding circumstances of every moment and age. And so, if we are open and discerning people, God will continue to challenge our theological reflection on the critical issues that affect the quality of life of humankind, the planet, and its resources in Africa and elsewhere.

That is how I view the call and mission of the bishop as theologian. My primary role in relation to the people of God among whom I live and minister in the diocese is not only and not simply to hand on the faith, to empower and instruct my catechists in handing on the faith to children and adults, and faithfully to articulate the teachings of the magisterium. My primary role is to discern what God seems to be saying in all the situations in which God seems absent and in which church maybe *is* absent in terms of its presence and ministry.

The church may be absent in terms of a presence that gives hope where there is only despair and where people cannot make any sense out of life; a presence of healing when there is only hurt and pain and a sense of loss; a presence that allows us to open the door for God to speak and be present to the little ones of the world in a way that enables them to begin again and take the next step through us and because of us as a church community.

The bishop-theologian or teacher needs to respond to the actual lived reality in the spirit and practice of listening deeply, discerning what the Spirit seems to be saying to the churches, and engaging in a dialogical process with the people to promote and build a *sensus fidelium* that will allow God's Word and the mission of Jesus to be incarnated anew in the unfolding reality of people's lives and especially the most vulnerable members of our communities and societies.

The topic of bishops as theologians posits the following questions, among others: How do pastoral experience, pastoral sensitivity, and pastoral reflection affect the church's living theological tradition? Is it possible for pastoral reality to reform or shape church teaching so this can be understood and experienced as relevant and valid for our particular time? Should not pastoral ministry be a most powerful and necessary "source" of theology shaped by our African context with its widespread poverty, disease, wars, millions of refugees, and the struggle many go through to live minimally decent lives? Should a bishop's particular pastoral perspective with his people be a key factor in this dynamic?

In that sense, a bishop is or should be a theologian par excellence and constantly invite professional theologians to respond and commit to renewed partnership with all bishops and pastoral workers, because together we seek to discern God's Word and the meaning of faith and evangelization in the reality in which we live and minister.

THE CHURCH OF POPE FRANCIS

An Ecclesiology of Accountability, Accompaniment, and Action

Stan Chu Ilo

This essay undertakes four important and related tasks. First, as the world is presently enchanted by the freshness of Pope Francis and the Francis effect, I pose a hypothetical question of what kind of pope an African cardinal would have been if one had been elected to the chair of Peter instead of Jorge Bergoglio. Second, I argue that Pope Francis is not ushering in a new ecclesiology; the germs of what Pope Francis is doing are all hidden in the spiritual treasures and teachings of the church, especially in the ecclesiology of Vatican II. Third, I show how the words and deeds of Pope Francis have become an exegesis of the spirit of Vatican II. Fourth, I propose that the pope's teachings and ministry offer a model for the renewal of African Catholicism through a "triple A" ecclesiology—an ecclesiology of Accountability, a pastoral theology of Accompaniment, and a spirituality of Action. I argue that these three A's should be present in the priorities and practices of the church in Africa because they are present in the life of the Trinity as the foundation of the church.

Could Africa Have Produced a Pope Francis?

Although we may not be able to predict how the Holy Spirit would have worked in an African pope, my fear is that if any African cardinal had emerged, he may not have been as courageous or as revolutionary as Pope Francis. An African pope would seek a more centrist approach to church governance and would be cautious about embracing any changes dictated by Western social pressures.

An African pope would wholeheartedly enforce a rigorous interpretation of authority in the church while proposing unquestioning obedience to church authority with a top-down exercise of authority. In addition, an African pope might reject the concerns in the church for an urgent solution to the problems and pains caused in the church by such burning issues as celibacy; the place of women in the church; separated, divorced, and remarried Catholics; unresolved questions about polygamy, especially in Africa; and the questions about the use of condoms in the fight against HIV/AIDS.

An African pope would not be amenable to granting greater autonomy to local churches and confronting the unacceptable and unhelpful prevalence of clericalism in the church. Most of these challenges would be interpreted by an African pope as the results of a spiritual or moral crisis, Western cultural bereavement, cultural relativism, and religious syncretism that arose as a result of an inadequate understanding of the faith.

In response to these challenges, an African pope would call for more spiritual depth, a life of holiness and prayers, faith formation, sacramentalization of the people, and greater spiritual devotions and pious activities. He would also draw a clear line between faithful Catholics and the rest and make a distinction between the true Catholic Church of Rome and other ecclesial communities outside the Catholic Church.

My guess is that an African pope would also emphasize a synchronizing and transcendental ecclesiology rather than embrace a contextual, historically sensitive, and dynamic ecclesiology of communion. Contextual ecclesiology would be seen by him as ecclesiological relativism or tribal Catholicism. An African pope would be wary of African Pentecostalism, Catholic charismatic spirituality, popular piety and devotions, and African initiatives in Christianity because they do not fit into the liturgical norms and rituals of the church or the Catholic canon of orthodoxy. He would also be cautious with regard to ecumenism, interfaith dialogue, and joint actions with other Christians and people of goodwill in faith and nonfaith contexts.

Although an African pope might speak out against poverty, secularism, materialism, neoliberal capitalism, and the rough edges of globalization, I am not sure he would renounce the papal palace and reject most of the trappings of power and authority at the Vatican; he would use those trappings to validate his authority.

African Catholicism as it is today cannot produce a reforming and transforming pope who would courageously challenge the church to move away from self-referential assertions and triumphalist ecclesial claims. An African pope might not desire to change some of the practices and priorities in the church that lead to what Pope Francis calls "a form of leprosy,"[1] and spiritual worldliness.

African Catholicism has not been very successful in producing enduring theological movements, spiritual traditions, and forms of ecclesial action that have become very influential in the shaping of African Catholicism and with an impact on the wider African society. No one should expect African Catholicism to produce a Pope Francis when African Catholicism has few reforming and transforming local priests, nuns, bishops, and cardinals. This is not to deny, however, that some clergy and religious in Africa have incarnated in their lives of faith and pastoral practices the lifestyle of the poor man of Galilee and have sacramentalized the values and virtues of an incarnational ministry and humble service to God's people.

Despite the claims in contemporary discussion on world Christianity that Africa is the new center of gravity for world Catholicism, I am calling for a more sober discernment of African Christianity and Catholicism in particular. This invites African theologians to move away from a merely sociological analysis of the demographics of church expansion in Africa to a theological interpretation and judgment. This requires raising fundamental questions as to the foundation, nature, character, and identity of African Catholicism. What does God say about who we are, where we are, and what is moving forward in the life of faith in our continent? What ecclesiological images and models are discoverable in the pastoral priorities and practices of African Catholicism that reflect the family traits of what one may clearly identify as Catholicism and as originating from the heart of the Trinity?

Though these questions are not easy to answer, doing so is fundamental to understanding why African Catholicism may not be able to produce a Pope Francis at this time. It will also help us ask some serious questions about the nature and shape of African Catholic ecclesiology and

---

[1] See Pope Francis's address to the community of the Pontifical Ecclesiastical Academy, June 6, 2013, in Pope Francis, *The Church of Mercy: A Vision for the Church* (Chicago: Loyola Press, 2014), 115.

offer realistic pastoral proposals for the future of the Christian enterprise
in Africa.

Five factors among many could explain the present state of affairs in
African Catholic ecclesiology. These factors are presented also as challenges
that need to be addressed to bring about the kind of church we want, or
rather, the kind of church God wishes to bring about in Africa. The first is
Catholic education that is truly Catholic and truly African. Catholic education in Africa is very generalized, normative, and very Roman and Western.
In many instances, it lacks historical context and is not open to critical
engagement with history or the forces of social change.

The "banking" approach to education is still prevalent in African seminaries and Catholic schools. The bank, in this context, is the Congregation
of Catholic Education and the Congregation for the Evangelization of
Peoples that approve, control, and supervise the curriculum, syllabus, and
structure of the academic programs of our seminaries and Catholic universities in Africa. They also approve the teachers in African theology faculties
and seminaries. In addition, there is a cargo-based formation that promotes
a generic educational content and delivery without regard to differentiated
learning needs and the uniqueness of each person and the specific socialization and faith formation dictated by cultural contexts.

How can we bridge the gulf between the classicist theological traditions
of Rome that have been replicated in African seminaries and faculties of
theology and the need for empirical and contextual approaches to theology?
How can we make the mission of God central and a guide to discovering the
mission of the church as the faith crosses different cultural and religious fron-
tiers in Africa? The catechetical instruction for African children and young
people is still based on memorizing catechetical formulas and repeating and
assimilating doctrinal claims and creeds without questioning them.

The second factor deals with pastoral formation brewed in an African
pot. The type of pastoral formation African priests and religious receive,
contrary to the teaching of *Ecclesia in Africa* (nos. 11, 57, 62, 63, 79, 94, 95)
and *Africae Munus* (nos. 10, 15, 37, 38, 109, 137) does not prepare them
adequately to meet the personal, professional, pastoral, and contextual challenges of ministry in Africa. Rather, it prepares them to see themselves more
as Roman or Western than as African in their understanding of Catholicism
and in the choice of pastoral priorities and methods in pastoral ministries.
This explains why the rise in Pentecostalism in Africa, for example, and

the exploitation of our poor faithful have not been met with a different Pentecostal/charismatic Catholicism that goes beyond the magical, the immediate, and the pragmatic with regard to problem solving or Christian discipleship in the face of limit situations.

The third factor is lay formation that prepares the African faithful to bear witness to the faith in the Africa of today, the kind of ecclesial life that is being offered to the laity in Africa that makes them spiritual clients and pastoral beneficiaries of the pastoral ministries of the clergy and the hierarchy. It also limits the baptismal rights of Catholic laity as full members of the church and equal stakeholders in shaping the church and in realizing the eschatological fruits of God's kingdom (*Lumen Gentium*, no. 30). Ours is still a highly clericalized and male-dominated church that is top-down in its approach to pastoral life, and elitist, essentialist, and neoscholastic in its theology and pastoral approach.

It is not surprising that the African Catholic laity remains largely a quiescent majority, lacking basic information and deep knowledge of the faith or Catholic social teaching. They are also ill-equipped to hold the clergy accountable and to take an active part in shaping the church in Africa and Africa itself. The basic Christian communities should become a more effective and dynamic instrument for new evangelization rather than new ways of developing channels for fund-raising for church projects.

The fourth factor is concerned with Rome being the center of Catholicism and Africa being on the margins. African Catholicism is still under the "protection" of *Propaganda Fidei* as a mission church. This has wide implications with regard to the degree of autonomy local African churches can exercise in their relationship with Rome and in choosing their pastoral practices, the nature of Catholic education, and the liturgical life of local churches. African Catholic dioceses see themselves as administrative outposts of the Vatican because they are financially dependent on Rome. Most pastoral plans, strategies, and programs for the formation of the clergy, the religious, and the laity are often replications of generic patterns and forms approved by or copied from one office of the Vatican or another. Some of these norms and regulations were received from pre–Vatican II missionaries and have remained unchanged since then.

The inculturation of the church in Africa and the dialogue and reconciliation called for by the two African synods seem to be marginal in the life of African Catholicism. This is because of the sad ecclesial drought of inactivity in the areas of inculturation of the local churches in Africa. In most cases, these local churches are stymied by rules and guidelines from Rome and seem incapable of creativity and innovation in meeting the local challenges and pastoral opportunities of the times.

Creativity and innovation in African Catholicism will require more than seminars, synods, and statements by episcopal conferences. The prophetic witnessing required in meeting the challenging social context in which most Catholics in Africa live will demand more than good homilies, soothing Lenten pastorals, and occasional letters and statements directed against the government. It will also go beyond the uncritical assumption of an African *ubuntu* or of the Africa in which life and family are revered and where community is primary.

Indeed, creative and transformative ecclesiologies in Africa will require a more direct harvesting of the riches of the faith through a living faith in communion with a learning faith for all members of the church that brings about authentic and credible witnessing to the Catholic faith through experiential and contextual faith in action. It will require some measured experimentation led by the Holy Spirit and some courageous steps by local parishes and dioceses in liturgical and pastoral faith formation. It needs fully engaged laity who are respected as adults in the church with significant contributions to make beyond financial contributions or receiving honors and awards. Above all, it will require clearly planned integrative steps for deep faith and spirituality, social transformation, wealth creation, and social engagement. This I believe will produce giant Christians and transformative Catholic churches in Africa that are signposts to other communities of faith and nonfaith of how to live together as salt and light in diverse societies in Africa.

The fifth factor is concerned with the status of Catholic bishops in Africa as vicars of Christ rather than legates of Rome. Contrary to the teachings of Vatican II,[2] most Catholic bishops in Africa see themselves as vicars and legates of the pope instead of the vicars of Christ. Their fidelity to Rome has been elevated to a metaphysics. Doing the will of Rome—whatever that means—or "according to the Holy Father" has become an art and

---

[2] "The individual bishops are the visible source and foundation of unity in their own particular churches, which are constituted after the model of the universal church; it is in these formed out of them that the one and unique Catholic Church exists" (*Lumen Gentium*, no. 23).

sometimes a veneer laid over glaring pastoral failures on the part of many Catholic bishops in Africa to become true shepherds of the local church where the Catholic Church is fully present according to the teaching of *Lumen Gentium.*[3]

What Rome says becomes a convenient excuse offered by many Catholic bishops to legitimate concerns about the use and abuse of ecclesial power and authority and the ongoing concerns about accountability and transparency in the use of the spiritual and temporal treasures of the church (*Africae Munus*, no. 104). African bishops should not shirk their responsibility through appeals to Rome in matters that lie within their competence, especially now that Pope Francis is asking local churches to do more in being creative, faithful, and transformative in meeting local pastoral challenges and opportunities (*Evangelii Gaudium*, nos. 32–33, 129). In the church led by Francis, Rome wants to know what the local/particular church wants for itself and how to support it in doing so. Rome wants to live fully the principle of subsidiarity—one cannot take away from a local church and place in the hand of Rome that which the local church can handle on its own.

How Did Pope Francis Emerge?

Pope Francis did not just drop down from heaven. He exemplifies the kind of local church in which he was socialized. He is the product of the Latin American church, which championed the theology of accompaniment of the poor through the theology of liberation. He emerged from a Latin American church that pioneered grassroots evangelization and an activist faith formation of the people through small Christian communities truly rooted in the living faith experience of the people and popular piety.

The church that gave us Pope Francis has many challenges, as do other churches in many parts of the world. However, it is a church that bears the marks of humility and still carries the wounds of being battle tested through prophetic witnessing and courageous confrontation with the worst forms of dictatorship in Latin America. Such a church immediately marginalized those clerics who kowtowed to the oppressive regimes of the times or who were more interested in the hierarchy of power and authority than they were in embracing with humility the privilege of service.

---

[3] See also *Lumen Gentium*, no. 21.

This is also a church that walked with the poor and is always socially engaged while shunning any form of compromise with the state or being a client to the officers of the state or a beneficiary of the filthy lucre that is often given by corrupt government officials.

Pope Francis is also the product of a church that became the voice of the people not only through the kind of theologies and theologians it produced but also because of the relevance of their theologies to the most pressing questions and challenges confronting the people. Pope Francis is the product of a church whose legitimacy was validated by the credibility of the simple lifestyle of the Catholic hierarchy, clergy, and religious.

We are told that when Pope Francis was a cardinal, he took public transport, cooked his own meals, and so on. One can recall the powerful statements of the Latin American church at Medellín (1968—*The Church in the Present Transformation of Latin America in Light of the Second Vatican Council*), Puebla (the third general conference of the bishops of Latin America and the Caribbean, January 28, 1979) and the Aparecida document (May 29, 2007). Pope Francis refers to this document that he helped draft more than ten times in *Evangelii Gaudium*. I am not aware of documents from SECAM (Symposium of Episcopal Conferences of Africa and Madagascar) that have had such a powerful and lasting impact in the shaping of African Catholicism that their promulgation is celebrated annually. What is the input of African bishops to *Ecclesia in Africa* or *Africae Munus*? Can African Catholicism claim ownership of these documents? How is today's African Catholicism being led by the teachings, principles, and recommendations of these two synods?

My concern here is that the church in Africa would have given the world a pope who would not be like Pope Francis but who would bring the blessings and the limitations of African Catholicism to global Catholicism. How that could have played out is purely academic. However, I argue that the church in Africa has all it needs to begin the journey to becoming the kind of church that will help provide answers to the pressing questions in the hearts of many Africans.

The church in Africa is richly blessed by God to seize the moment of grace in our times toward the realization of the eschatological fruits of God's kingdom in Africa. Indeed, it is possible in our times for the church in Africa to become truly African and truly Catholic through a faithful commitment to the implications and challenges of these dual identities.

The Ecclesiology of Pope Francis as Rooted in *Lumen Gentium*, no. 8, and *Gaudium et Spes*, no. 1

Pope Francis highlighted three key dimensions of Catholic ecclesiology in his words and deeds since becoming the bishop of Rome. One was an understanding of the church as a dynamic and diverse people of God called to communion of the Trinity with each other in the church and with the world and the cosmos. These people of God are led by the Spirit on a pilgrimage toward the realization of God's reign on earth. The beauty of these chosen people is reflected in the diversity of experience and expression of the selfsame faith in multiple ways.

The second dimension was an understanding of service in the church as an act of humility modeled after the example of Christ and the instrumental nature of all service in the church. The third dimension was the image of the church as the church of the poor and guardian of humanity and of creation. This image of the church is grounded in Vatican II's ecclesiology of the church. Pope Francis is not writing a new text for a new ecclesiology; rather, he is giving a practical application and concrete interpretation of the ecclesiology of Vatican II through his pastoral style, priorities, and mission.

Pope Francis's ecclesiology is an exegesis of *Lumen Gentium*, no. 8, and *Gaudium et Spes*, no. 1, because following these important conciliar documents, Pope Francis wants a church that speaks of God and points toward Christ instead of a church that points toward itself. In addition, he wants a church that speaks of mercy and the eternal word of love spoken from the cross rather than a church bogged down by laws and prescriptions. He wants a church that cries out for justice for the poor more than a church that is enslaved by its systems and structures. The identity and mission of this kind of church could be summarized through an interpretation of the ecclesiology presented by the conciliar fathers in *Lumen Gentium*, no. 8:

1. Christ is the one mediator who established and ever sustains the church on earth; this society is structured in a hierarchy of service so that truth and grace may be communicated to all people. Divine communication is central to the mission of the church, and it happens in the diversity of peoples and cultures through a "communion

rooted in the initiating action of the Trinity, in the Eucharist and in anthropology."[4]

2. The church is incarnational and sacramental, a mystery of the people of God in history. Therefore, it bears the marks of the heavenly and the earthly kingdoms. However, there is no dualism between the sacred realities embodied in the church and its earthly life, nor should there be a separation between the sacred and the secular, the good sheep and the bad sheep, the rejected and the beloved, the conservative and the progressive.

   The sacramental nature of the church and the existence of the church in time serve the church as an organ or instrument of salvation, and its structures are alive, not dead, because of the Spirit of Christ that vivifies the church. This instrumental nature of the church calls it and its members to a spirit of humility, mercy, attentive listening to what God is saying through the signs of the times, and a ready openness to God and to one another. This dual reality puts the church at the juncture of both mediating heavenly realities to God's people as well as communicating God's transformative grace to the concrete situations of sin, evil, joys, brokenness, poverty, pains, hopes, and fears of God's people in history, especially those on the margins.

3. The church subsists in the Catholic Church, but the mission of the church is not to determine those who are within the Catholic family but rather to attract many to this fold and to be open to those who may not belong fully to this church. Through washing the feet of a Muslim on Holy Thursday, for instance, Pope Francis was teaching us that we are all brothers and sisters. Above all, he was reminding Catholics that there are elements of sanctification and of truth found outside the visible structures of the church that call us to unity in seeking the things that hold us together rather than the things that divide us. I recall a saying attributed to Saint Augustine: "Many whom God has, the Church does not have; and many whom the Church has, God does not have."[5]

---

[4] Bruno Forte, *The Church Icon of the Trinity: A Brief Study*, trans. Robert Paolucci (Boston: St. Paul Books and Media, 1991), 74.

[5] Quoted in Richard P. McBrien, *The Church: The Evolution of Catholicism* (New York: Harper Collins, 2008), 135.

4. Jesus entered into the chaos of human life in the mystery of redemption in poverty and oppression; for this reason, the church is called to follow the same path so it may authentically communicate the fruits of salvation to people as authentic witness to the risen Lord. The church is not set up for earthly glory; ministries in the church are for service, and all ecclesial actions should be directed to God's kingdom and carried on in a spirit of humility, self-denial, and service.

When Pope Francis speaks of a bruised church, a poor church for the poor, or of a dirty and hurting church in *Evangelii Gaudium* or of the church as a "field hospital," he is not saying anything new but is emphasizing an ancient truth and spirituality we have forgotten in the complex cultural climate of our times.[6] *Lumen Gentium*, no. 8, was unequivocal in this regard in what could be termed the guiding charter of Pope Francis's papacy.

> The Church encompasses with her love all those who are afflicted by human misery and she recognizes in those who are poor and who suffer, the image of her poor and suffering founder. She does all in her power to relieve their need and in them she strives to serve Christ.

This same message is found in *Gaudium et Spes*.

> The joy and the hope, the grief and the anguish of the men of this age, especially of those who are poor or in any way afflicted, these are the joy and hope, the grief and anguish of the followers of Christ. Nothing that is genuinely human fails to raise an echo in their hearts. For theirs is a community composed of men. United in Christ, they are led by the Holy Spirit in their journey to the Kingdom of their Father and they have welcomed the news of salvation

---

[6] The encyclopedic study by Peter Brown, *Through the Eye of a Needle: Wealth, the Fall of Rome, and the Making of Christianity in the West* (Princeton, NJ: Princeton University Press, 2012), 350–550, shows the rise of the church in the West and how the self-understanding of the church as the poor church for the poor and the instrumental understanding of wealth in the church competed for and ultimately triumphed over all other forms of philanthropy in the West

which is meant for every man. That is why this community realizes that it is truly linked with mankind and its history by the *deepest of bonds.*[7]

5. The church's power and treasures are not in structures, institutional privileges, the Vatican bank, or in what Pope Francis calls spiritual worldliness. The last paragraph of article 8 of *Lumen Gentium* is clear that the church is a pilgrim and faces persecutions because it cannot be conformed to the ideals of the world but seeks consolations from God, as Saint Augustine says. The power the church should seek in humility is the one it gains by announcing the cross and death of the Lord and relying on the power of the resurrection for strength.

6. Pope Francis, therefore, is living the total ecclesiology of Vatican II, which was an attempt to locate the center of the church at the very heart of the Trinity, to see our membership in the church as a call to be totally available to God, and to be open to listening to what God says to us about the church rather than what we say about the church. So for Pope Francis, it is not the church we want but rather the church God has given to us through his Son, led by the Holy Spirit. It is an invitation to be open to others and to the world and to find through the heightened attention that comes to the humble of heart the way the Spirit opens to us into the future.

7. The central ecclesial action of such a church is mercy, not judgment.[8] The church is both the object and subject of mercy.[9] The message of mercy has always been at the center of the church's preaching. In his

---

[7] *Gaudium et Spes*, no. 1.

[8] In his address to participants in the plenary of the Pontifical Council for Promoting the New Evangelization (October 14, 2013), Pope Francis taught: "We need Christians who make God's mercy and tenderness for every creature visible to the men of our day. We all know that the crisis of modern man is not superficial but profound. That is why the New Evangelization, while it calls us to have the courage to swim against the tide and to be converted from idols to the true God, cannot but use a language of mercy, which is expressed in gestures and attitudes even before words."

[9] Walter Kasper, *Mercy: The Essence of the Gospel and the Key to Christian Life*, trans. William Madges (New York: Paulist Press, 2014), 157–80. On page 157, Kasper wrote, "The church encounters Christ himself in its own members and in people who are in need of help. The church is supposed to make present the gospel of mercy, which Jesus Christ is in person, through word, sacrament, its whole life in history, and the life of individual Christians. However, the church too is the object of God's mercy."

opening address at the start of Vatican II, Pope John XXIII pointed out that whereas the church would always oppose errors regarding the faith, in the past, it did this

> with greatest severity. Nowadays, however, the spouse of the Christ prefers to make use of the medicine of mercy rather than severity. She considers that she meets the needs of the present day by demonstrating the validity of her teaching rather than by condemnations.

John XXIII said that the church expressed through the council a desire "to show herself to be the loving mother of all, benign, patient, full of mercy and goodness toward children separated from her."[10] This is indeed the church of Pope Francis!

The Renewal of African Ecclesiology in the Spirit of Pope Francis

The renewal of African ecclesiology in the spirit of Pope Francis can be accomplished through many ways. However, I have proposed three ways of being church that should be present in the pastoral priorities and practices of the church in Africa. I have termed this a "triple A" ecclesiology, namely, an ecclesiology of Accountability, a pastoral theology of Accompaniment, and a spirituality of Action.

An Ecclesiology of Accountability

The biblical images for this proposal are from Saint Peter's call (1 Peter 3:15) to Christians to always be ready to give an account of the hope and faith they have embraced, the parable of the steward (Luke 16:2), the parable of the talent (Matthew 25:14–30), the parable of the sower (Matthew 13:1–23), the parable of the lost sheep and the lost coin (Luke 15:1–10), and the good shepherd analogy (John 10). Three things among many in these three passages help guide pastoral action and methods in ministry.

Accountability in scripture begins with recognizing that all good things around us, including the church, are gifts we have received in earthen vessels

---

[10] Quoted in McBrien, *Church,* 159.

(2 Corinthians 4:7). Stewardship of these treasures requires affirming constantly their source and the model we have received from the Lord on how to live faithfully and fully the reality of these gifts. The Lord is the owner of the vineyard, the Lord is in charge, and the Lord is the one whose logos is our being; this logos is our mission and our ultimate destiny.

We are servants, not masters in the vineyard (Luke 16:2, 17:10; Romans 1:1–4). The Lord has given to the church in Africa the gift of faith and has planted in Africa different seeds of the Word. One can think of the rich spiritual, temporal, and cultural gifts of Africa and how we can ground our church life on gratitude, adoration, and praise. Therefore, it is necessary to begin African ecclesiology with fundamental questions: What is the Lord telling us through what is going on in our churches and wider societies in Africa? What does the Lord want us to realize in the church in Africa using the gifts God has given, especially the gift of his Son, who is the concrete norm of life for African Christians, and the gift of the Spirit, who continues to sustain the faith in Africa by giving comfort, strength, courage, and hope to many weather-beaten African faithful? How are we managing these gifts and temporal resources of the church? Are all the priorities and practices in our churches gifts from the Lord? How do we discern in the midst of our churches and the cultural shifts of our times what is of the Lord and what is not of the Lord?

Accountability in scripture also underlies the decisiveness of human agency, human freedom, and human cooperation with God in bringing about in history God's plans for Africa through the enthusiastic and unfailing faith of African Christians. It implies that a dialectic of relationship, partnership, cooperation, participation, and stewardship exists between the human subject and God and with creation. God's plan is not a magical irruption of the kingdom upon unwilling and disobedient children. On the contrary, it is the gradual emergence in history of God's kingdom through men and women who respond to God's initiative with full obedience and who work with God freely in realizing the divine purposes.

Thus, if we are singing today of the exponential growth in the church in Africa in terms of numbers, institutions, personnel, and so on, the question should also be asked about how the African church is harvesting the rich gifts of faith in our land through these channels. How have we used the talents of our laity, our priests, hierarchy, men and women religious, and our strong African women of faith who flock to our churches, chanceries, and rectories? What account do we give to the Lord of the rich cultural traditions of Africa and the rich history of our continent and its rich resources? In many instances, most of these gifts have not been well used to bring about human and cosmic flourishing and the eschatological fruits of God's kingdom.

Accountability as presented in scripture also speaks of the sad reality of division, loss, and despair. In the parable of the good shepherd and the lost coin, we see the grief of the master when he took stock of his treasures and his flock, and the grief of the woman, when she realized her loss. Here, one sees a link between this biblical insight and our ecclesial reality in Africa. I refer to the experience of those who are inside and those who are outside: those who are accounted for because they are in the house and those who are lost; those who are saved and those who are damned; those who are on their way to the Promised Land and those who are lost in the desert; those who are right and those who are wrong; those who are beloved and those who are rebels; those who are poor, voiceless, and powerless, and those who are rich and powerful.

An accountable church in Africa would also be concerned about what Africa is losing to global capitalism, of the wealth, resources, and talents of this continent that are being drained from Africa, and the thousands of refugee Africans who are dying and drowning as they flee across the Sahara or the Mediterranean.

This also brings to the fore the divisions in our churches and the needed reconciliation in the church in Africa. When the Second African Synod (2009) called for reconciliation, it was inviting African Christians to heal the wounds of division in our churches and wider society and to bring everyone home. This will require that all Christians are transformed into disciples of reconciliation while churches create through their pastoral plans and priorities a church of communion and of the Eucharist, where everyone can eat at the same table.

There should no longer be any Lazarus left at the gates of divine mercy and God's love in the church of the family of God. We must give account of the many Abels who are being slaughtered in violence, hatred, wars, terrorist attacks, and crimes; of the many Rachels whose children are dying of diseases or starving to death because of hunger, famine, and dislocation in refugee camps. We must give account to the Lord and to the poor in Africa of the many donations and grants that church officials ask for or receive in the name of the poor but that in some cases are diverted or misused.

We must also give account to the Lord not only of those who are with us in every sense of the word but also of those who are not with us—divorced and separated Catholics, Catholics who are denied communion because of their marriage situations, our brothers and sisters from other denominations and from other faiths, those who have left our churches, the married priests and nuns, the abused and violated, those searching for their sexual or ethnic identities, and so on, and all those who are far from the home of the family of God.

The church in Africa must be a sign, symbol, and agency for hope for those who are outside, the minority ethnic groups, the marginal groups, and those who are condemned to die due to poverty, starvation, Ebola, HIV/AIDS, or neglect.

Pope Francis is teaching us that everyone counts and that we should not count anyone out whom God counts as belonging to God. It is no longer the kind of membership but the degree of belongingness to the church that should be decisive in an African ecclesiology grounded in Vatican II and the Trinitarian origin of the church.

A Pastoral Theology of Accompaniment

Pope Francis wrote in *Evangelii Gaudium*, no. 169, of "the art of accompaniment" as the pastoral approach that would bring us closer to each other in solidarity; heal divisions, ethnocentrism, and nepotism; and cure the ailments of negative ecclesial spirit of rank segregation. This way of living would make the church a center of love and intersubjective connection, participation in the life of all, and communion with God, especially commitment to those who are poor and on the margins.

Bruno Forte argued that the Catholicity of the gospel message referred to the total ecclesiology that touched all the dimensions of the life of the Christian called to love and embrace the Word, the grace of God, and the gift of the church. According to him, every local church

> must be *a travelling companion* [my emphasis] of the people to whom it proclaims the Word of God, so that the Gospel may be interlaced with the daily deeds of fraternity, where love becomes concrete and credible in the sharing of day-to-day life and in the choices taken on the side of the poor and the little ones of the earth.[11]

---

[11] Forte, *Church Icon of the Trinity*, 76.

Among other practices, Pope Francis recommends that we remove our sandals before others because when we come into the presence of another—no matter how weak or vulnerable—we must remember we are standing on holy ground. This accompaniment requires humility, listening to the other person, honest communication, conversion, openness of heart, and genuine spiritual encounter.

At the heart of this pastoral presence is the incarnational principle of totally identifying with other people, especially those in need, to experience what they are experiencing by a pastoral attitude of vulnerability. This is what Pope Francis highlighted in a speech to newly appointed bishops on September 19, 2013, when he taught that the art of accompaniment requires pastoral presence that has the following characteristics:

(1) becoming pastors who have the smell of the sheep because the priests and bishops are in the midst of the people as Jesus was with his disciples;

(2) walking together in love, knowing that ministry in the church is a service or office of love (*amoris officium*) as Saint Augustine pointed out. In this light, the priests and bishops who serve the people of God are not above the people of God:

> The bishop journeys with and among his flock. This means setting out with one's faithful and with all those who turn to you, sharing in their joys and hopes, their difficulties and sufferings, as brothers and as friends, but especially as fathers who can listen, understand, help, and guide.[12]

(3) Pope Francis also teaches that it is only through pastoral accompaniment that the leaders in the church can discern the *sensus fidei, sensus fidelium,* and *consensus fidei* of the people of God.[13]

(4) *Walking together* also challenges pastoral workers to *work together* in helping one another, asking and receiving forgiveness, acknowledging

---

[12] Pope Francis, *Church of Mercy*, 86. He elaborates further on this in the same speech when he wrote, "A pastoral presence means walking with the People of God, walking in front of them, showing them the way, showing them the path; walking in their midst, to strengthen them in unity; walking behind them, to make sure no gets left behind, but especially, never to lose the scent of the People of God in order to find roads." (See also *Evangelii Gaudium*, no. 31.)

[13] Pope Francis, *Church of Mercy*, 76.

one's mistakes and limitations, and building flexible and open structures
of accountability to one another and unity and love in the local churches.

(5) The pastoral theology of accompaniment is the invitation to enter
into the life of the poor, to move from providing social services, social
activism, and social empowerment to psychosocial encounters that lead
to social transformation. This way, the church in Africa can become an
instrument for building on the spiritual and material assets of the poor
rather than attending only to their needs, and the church can strengthen
the poor to take ownership of their lives and future. This requires being
present to the poor as they are present to us.

Many gulfs separate people in Africa, including the lack of physical, social,
and spiritual proximity between the churches and the poor in many of Africa's
cities. Accompaniment is being at home with the poor and making a home
for them in our churches and homes. It is the mutual indwelling of hospitality
between two people who see God's presence in each other no matter how
diverse their social status or economic or spiritual circumstances are.

Accompaniment also reflects the African sense of community and
interconnectedness of all things through a vital union of participation.
This reflects the inner harmony that comes about when we walk together
for justice to reign on earth so all creation can enjoy the abundant life and
peace in Christ (John 10:10). To borrow a phrase from US theologian James
Keenan, when we enter "into the chaos of another's life" through a vulnerable mission, heaven floods our souls and God's kingdom begins to emerge
in a renewal of creation. Roberto Goizueta wrote,

> As a society, we are happy to help and serve the poor, as long as we
> don't have to walk with them where they walk, that is, as long as we
> can minister to them from our safe enclosures. The poor can then
> remain passive objects of our actions, rather than friends, *companeros*
> and *companeras* with whom we interact. As long as we can be sure
> that we will not have to live with them, and thus have inter-personal
> relationships with them, we will try to help "the poor"—but, again,
> only from a controllable, geographical distance.[14]

---

[14] Quoted in Michael Griffin and Jennie Weiss Block, eds., *In the Company of the Poor: Conversations with Dr. Paul Farmer and Fr. Gustavo Gutierrez* (Maryknoll, NY: Orbis Books, 2013), 128.

A Spirituality of Action

A spirituality of action requires the church in Africa to move from words to deeds, from ecclesial claims to ecclesial witnessing. It also challenges the church in Africa to conversion from glorying in the growth of Christianity in Africa or the majesty and splendor of our Catholicism and the solidity of our institutional prerogatives as the true apostolic church to showing through authentic and credible ecclesial being and deeds that we are living in the light of Christ. It involves performance, praxis, testimony, witnessing, martyrdom, and sacramentalizing what we profess.

African Catholic ecclesiology should be grounded in theological aesthetics that embrace the church and creation as gifts that we have received by seeing reality as filled with the splendor and love of God as revealed in Christ through the Holy Spirit, and theodrama, that is, seeing things as they have been saved and transformed in Christ through the Paschal mystery that is continued in the mission and ministry of the church in history. It should also be grounded in a transformative spirituality of action or deeds to change reality through an ecclesial mission modeled and renewed constantly through the priorities and practices of Christ to bring abundant life to God's creation and thus realize the will of God.

As Hans Urs von Balthasar proposed,

Following Christ, which has become possible through his self-surrender, will not consist in doing some right thing but in fundamentally surrendering everything, and surrendering it to the God who has totally emptied himself so that he can use (that right thing) for the world according to his own purposes.[15]

Living like Christ is the goal of all ecclesiology, and invariably, it is not our words and our claims that change people but our credible living out of the gospel.

This essay holds an intrinsic tension, in that I have considered African Catholic ecclesiology instead of African ecclesiology. I am not a prophet, but I believe the reality facing Africa today is a new realization that the

---

[15] Quoted in Roberto S. Goizueta, "Theo-Drama as Liberative Praxis," *Cross Currents* 63, no. 1 (March 2013), 69.

denominational boundaries and exclusions we inherited in Africa from the West will need to collapse as we walk together to the future.

Maybe in the years to come, Africa will be a model of the new church of Christ in which there will be no more Catholics and Anglicans, no more Charismatic and non-Charismatic Catholics, and no more walls separating the traditional orthodox churches from African initiatives in Christianity. It may seem like a long journey in coming, but the convergence of meaning and the greater impulse and influence of cultural grammar in the shaping of Christian consciousness in Africa will lead to the realization of the common spiritual heritage and religious values that point toward a greater discovery of common grounds among all African Christians.

When I watched Pope Francis embracing a rabbi and an imam in front of the Wailing Wall, something told me that living in such a way was possible not simply as an external gesture but as the full realization of the Trinitarian origin of the church. I have tried to demonstrate how we can show the face of this God to Africa through an ecclesiology of accountability, a pastoral theology of accompaniment, and a spirituality of action following the examples of Pope Francis.

Milestones in Achieving a More Incisive Feminine Presence in the Church of Pope Francis

Josée Ngalula

The apostolic exhortation of Pope Francis' *Evangelii Gaudium* includes several assertions that have generated much joy and hope in the Catholic Church. One is:

> But we need to create still broader opportunities for a more incisive female presence in the Church. . . . The presence of women must also be guaranteed in the workplace and in the various other settings where important decisions are made, both in the Church and in social structures. (no. 103)

What can this mean in Christian communities today, especially in Africa? In my experience, I found that this expansion of opportunities must take urgent priority in the minds, attitudes, and hearts of males and females alike in our Christian communities. This happens at least at three levels: in relation to cultural prejudices, the relationship within the meaning of *fidelium,* and in relationship to the wounded hearts in the church.

Making Progress by Not Projecting Cultural Biases into the Biblical and Magisterial Texts

The texts affirming the equal dignity of men and women in the church are not rare but many.[1] But in pastoral practice, things happen as if these

---

[1] At least ten theological documents of the Catholic Church affirm the dignity of the woman, including Pope Paul VI's *The Place of Women in Society Today* (1975),

texts did not exist, either because they are little known or because they are interpreted in the light of cultural patterns. There is a lack of women in positions in the church where, in theory, they are actually supposed to be. This is primarily attributable to a certain illiteracy.

I often find myself in theological milieus and have been teaching theology to future priests for the past twenty years. I have found that in Catholic circles, a fairly large number of men and women are ignorant of the major biblical and magisterial texts that affirm the dignity of women. By contrast, they have internalized the texts of some of the fathers and doctors of the church who have instilled into Western religious culture ideas that imply that women by nature are "inferior," "deficient," and "tempting" and therefore dangerous to men. Those who are theologically illiterate about this and in positions of responsibility do not imagine women can do anything other than be sacristans, make flower bouquets, take on household jobs, and be receptionists.

As soon as women theologians[2] speak of the dignity of women and assert that women can occupy other positions in the church apart from these, we automatically tag them as feminists. But when Pope John Paul II wrote an encyclical on the dignity of women, nobody considered his action an act of feminism. When *Christifideles Laici*, no. 51, and *Evangelii Gaudium*, no. 103, speak of making more room for women in the decision-making bodies in the church, nobody mentions feminism.

When the major texts of Pope John Paul II and of some synods on the dignity of women and the higher places they could occupy in the church are put before some members of the church, they are likely to blurt out, "The fact that women cannot be priests in the Catholic Church says a lot about the difference between men and women in the mind of Christ, who chose only men as apostles."

The Status of Women (1977), and *The Call to Women* (1977). From Pope John Paul II: *Familiaris Consortio* (1981, in some passages); *Mulieris Dignitatem* (1988); *Christifideles Laici* (1988 in certain passages); *Ordinatio Sacerdotalis* (1994 in certain passages); *Letter to Women* (1995); *The Importance of Women in the Life of the Priest* (1995). Of the Sacred Congregation for the Doctrine of the Faith: *Letter to the Bishops of the Catholic Church on the Collaboration of Man and Woman in the Church and in the World* (2004).

  [2] See, for example, Clement of Alexandria, for whom the woman must feel "shame" in thinking about her nature of being a woman (*Paedagogus* II, 33.2); Thomas Aquinas, for whom the nature of the woman is the second purpose of nature, in the same way as putrefaction, deformity, and decrepitude (*Summa Theologiae* q 52a 1 ad 2), etc.

Beyond this apparent theological illiteracy is a serious but hidden attempt to interpret and understand the biblical and magisterial texts not according to their internal logic but under the guidance of certain cultural biases. A classic example is the case of some fathers and doctors of the church who dared to declare the woman as a "deformed man"[3] by reading Genesis 2–3, Sirach 25:24, 1 Corinthians 11:7–11, and Ephesians 5:22 in the light of the philosophical bias permeating Western culture according to which the woman is "an underdeveloped man." A good number of African pastoral agents (men and women) advise women never to argue with their husbands because "Eve was drawn from the side of Adam." Is this a transmission of biblical anthropology or rather the projection of a certain African traditional mentality into the biblical texts?

In a recent debate in an assembly of theologians on the question of girl altar servers, some referred to Old Testament texts and argued that in the Catholic Church, due to the impurity of menstruation, a woman cannot receive the sacrament of Holy Orders. Is this Catholic doctrine or the projection of certain cultural beliefs into the Catholic doctrine (in Africa as well as elsewhere) relating to menstruation? Fortunately,[4] this is not Catholic doctrine; no magisterial document giving the reasons for this restriction evokes the issue of menstruation.[5]

If these fathers or doctors of the church and these current pastoral agents had interpreted these Bible verses in the light of God's love for all of

---

[3] See especially Albert the Great (*Quaestiones super de animalibus* XV, q11), where the woman is less qualified compared to the man in terms of moral rights and is a "defective man" because she has a defective and imperfect nature.

[4] On the contrary, the liturgical norms in force in the Catholic Church encourage the presence of women readers, proclaimers of the Word, and extraordinary ministers of communion; similarly, "Girls or women may be admitted to this service of the altar, in the judgment of the diocesan Bishop; in this case, we must follow the standards established in this respect" (*Redemptionis Sacramentum*, no. 47).

[5] The reasons advanced officially in the texts of the magisterium for the nonordination of women are not anthropological but rather ecclesiological and christological. The point here is not the woman, who would be unworthy in herself, but rather Christ and his free choice. In effect, from the behavior of Jesus, the magisterium has retained that he chose only men by free option and not at all due to contempt for women: "By only calling men to be his Apostles, Christ acted in a totally free and sovereign manner. Christ did this, in the same freedom with which he valued the dignity and vocation of women by all his behavior, without complying with the usages, which prevailed, or the traditions that sanctioned the legislation of his time" (*Mulieris Dignitatem*, no. 26).

God's creation and in the light of the behavior of Jesus Christ, they certainly would have arrived at the same general conclusions that John Paul II's encyclical *Mulieris Dignitatem* arrived at or the *Compendium of the Social Doctrine of the Church*'s great affirmation:

> The woman is the complement of man, as man is the complement of woman.... The woman is "a helper" for the man, just as the man is "a helper" for the woman! In the encounter of man and woman a unitary conception of the human person is brought about, based not on the logic of self-centeredness and self-affirmation, but on that of love and solidarity.[6]

Those who are not conscious of this and are marked by cultural beliefs that look down on women would not neglect the practical implementation of this passage from *Christifideles Laici*:

> The revised Code of Canon Law contains many provisions on the participation of women in the life and mission of the Church: An example comes to mind in the participation of women on diocesan and parochial Pastoral Councils as well as Diocesan Synods and particular Councils. In this regard the Synod Fathers have written: "Without discrimination women should be participants in the life of the Church, and also in consultation and the process of coming to decisions" (no. 51).

Thus there is an illiteracy of ecclesial provisions that stipulate the active presence and participation of women in the life of the church.

These examples show the urgency that exists to ensure two preconditions for the realization of the wishes for a more incisive female presence in the church, as expressed in *Evangelii Gaudium*, no. 103. The first concerns "theological illiteracy," which affects the majority of the Catholic faithful, including clerics. There is an urgent need to make provisions for the major texts of the Catholic Church on the dignity of women (which were inspired by the biblical texts) to be made available and internalized.

---

[6] *Compendium of the Social Doctrine of the Church*, no. 147.

The second prerequisite concerns the relationship with the ambient or traditional culture: it is urgent that we teach the Catholic faithful, laity and clerics alike, to interact with their cultural prejudices on the topic of gender relations in the new light of the gospel instead of subjecting this new Christianity to these cultural prejudices.

In what ways can this approach help African and other continents' women concerned daily about survival? Adequate knowledge of the main affirmations of the Catholic Church on the dignity of women (which come from the Bible) will liberate them from the manipulations of NGOs and some international forums that lead women to believe the United Nations is the first institution to be concerned about women and their dignity. It is even more liberating to come to know that, long before the United Nations and the NGOs, at heart, God has always regarded women with respect and dignity, as biblical texts attest.

It is also liberating to come to an awareness that well before the Beijing or Mexico City conferences, which gave an impetus to the struggle of women for their dignity, Christian women were treated without sexual discrimination in the list of martyrs and saints and that there are even some women who are doctors of the church. Each time I go out into the poor parishes and say this to illiterate women, I often hear them say, "Therefore we are important, not inferior! I can also give my point of view!" This makes them value themselves, which is an important asset for harmony in society and in the church. There is nothing worse than inferiority or superiority complexes.

Making Progress by Listening to the *Sensus Fidelium*

People's deep-rooted habits and structures can inhibit or even prevent the evolution of a more incisive presence of women in the church. Consider the automatic response, "This is how it has always been done!" However, ancient and recent church history is rich in facts establishing that by the power of the Holy Spirit the people of God can easily shift from one behavior to another, inspired by what they have discerned to be the fruit of the Holy Spirit. Here are two interesting facts about a more prominent presence of women in some ecclesial milieus.

First, there was a time during Eucharistic celebrations when women were grouped on one side of the church while the men were on the other, thus physically separating couples and families at the heart of the Eucharistic celebration. Such separation continued sometimes at other public events. For centuries, this was considered normal. With time, at least in urban areas, this separation changed spontaneously without involving a lot of theory or theology and without any decrees or encyclicals from the magisterium: this is what *sensus fidelium* has experimented and found to be good and beautiful. Today, the old separation between genders appears bizarre, at least in the urban Africa.

Second, for centuries, the Catholic Church has experienced celebrations in which all those who played major liturgical roles were men: lectors, acolytes, boys' choir, priests, choristers, and so on. In other words, the question of the separation of the sexes in the ecclesial space existed not at the level of the assembly in prayer but rather at the level of those playing major roles in leading the rest in prayer. When any authority was at stake, one of the two sexes was absent. Yet today, in the majority of the dioceses in Africa, both in the liturgy and in other areas of ecclesial life, we find a mixture of the sexes when any authority is at stake. At least in urban areas, we find women in the Eucharistic celebrations side by side with or alternating with men and leading others in prayer. This suggests the existence of more and more women as choristers, leaders of choirs, lectors, extraordinary ministers of communion, in charge of protocol and of girls' choirs (in some dioceses), and so on. This will be extended to other areas of ecclesial life as shown by the greater presence of women in parish councils, leading small Christian communities, and, on rare occasions, in the financial advisory commissions of some parishes or dioceses.

Here again, the experience has begun, and the *sensus fidelium* found it to be good and beautiful: it is for this reason that the experience is spreading from one parish to another, from one diocese to another without being prompted or mandated by decrees or encyclicals. The point is that the skill, not the sex, is what counts.

From this experience I draw the lesson, first, that the *sensus fidelium* has positively sanctioned a way of distributing the sexes in the ecclesial space that breaks neither family communion nor fraternal communion.

The *sensus fidelium* has also placed emphasis on competence regardless of sex. Falling back on relying on a person's sex as the basis of our actions and refusing to take account of his or her skills or ability to acquire those skills is a step back for the current generations of Catholic faithful and will leave them with a bitter taste.

The second lesson is more important. To see women acting with authority where they had been absent through the centuries changes the traditionally rooted anthropology in the unconscious of the majority of Catholics. I will relate two stories about what happened with the introduction of women as extraordinary ministers of the Eucharist and of girls as choristers in the parishes of the Kinshasa Archdiocese.

Concerning women as extraordinary ministers of the Eucharist, I still remember my discussions with some priests when, after the synod on the Eucharist, a parish priest was forming men and women for the distribution of communion. Some asked, "How dare he allow a woman to touch the communion?" and others asked, "What's the problem?" The first group said, "We know women. They're cowards who won't make it through the formation process."

However, the first women extraordinary ministers of the Eucharist in Kinshasa have become so skilled in their roles that the experience has spread like wildfire to several parishes. These women are competent because they had been trained. And then, all of a sudden, the people realized that men were not competent because of their sex but because of their training.

The same is true with girl choristers. A few years ago, a first pastor of a parish in Kinshasa decided that on one particular day, all the children of the choir would be girls; he trained them and had rehearsals with them exactly in the same way as he had done with the boys. After the celebration, the people acclaimed, "This is beautiful!" When the cardinal celebrated Mass at the parish, he was the only man up there; he was surrounded by women lectors, the girls' choir, and so on. At the end, the cardinal exclaimed, "It is beautiful, isn't it?" Something clicked in people's minds; the priests in other parishes invited girls into their choirs.

The spectacle of this complementarity was so beautiful that one day, an old woman asked me, "All this while, why have we separated what God has joined together?" Here again, this competence is the result of the investment of the Catholic Church in training women to handle different tasks.

These facts have changed the traditional clichés about women. Certainly, all women in the parishes are not intended to exercise these liturgical functions because there is a diversity of functions and tasks in the church. But seeing men and women side by side at liturgical services has emboldened and encouraged many women, rich and poor, who had internalized the idea that women were inferior to men. Some poor women who dared not publicly voice their opinions gained the courage to express themselves just because the liturgical symbol was for them a strong sign of their equal value.

One finds the same phenomenon of changing attitudes toward the presence of women in the context of pastoral ministry and theology. Experience or Christian praxis is certainly one of the major areas in which we must theologize on the question of a more incisive presence of women in the ecclesial space. They are already present in several places, and this works because of the investments made in their training. Their competence and the need for evangelization make it possible to say that this is beautiful and good for the church, the witness of Christ.

Making Further Progress by Maternally Soothing the Church's Wounded Hearts

The opportunities for the presence of women and men in the church are numerous and diverse, and within that diversity, the Catholic faithful can respond to the call of God in complementarity with the others. This diversity and complementarity are patterns of joy and apostolic fruitfulness. However, in the Catholic Church, there is a place relating to a more incisive presence in the church that causes tensions and even suffering in the hearts of a small group—Holy Orders. This has already been decided by the Catholic magisterium, so I will not be questioning its decision here. In addition, the majority of Catholic women in the world are not concerned at all with the question of the ordination of women because they have other concerns. *Evangelii Gaudium,* no. 46, notes that the church is

> a Church whose doors are open. Going out to others in order to reach the fringes of humanity does not mean rushing out aimlessly into the world. Often it is better simply to slow down, to put aside our eagerness in order to see and listen to others, to stop rushing from one thing to another and to remain with someone who has faltered along the way. At times we have to be like the father of the prodigal son, who always keeps his door open so that when the son returns, he can readily pass through it.

The media shows North American religious regularly going to Rome to seek audiences with the pope to give voice to their suffering by all kinds of strategies. *Evangelii Gaudium* insisted on the "fringes"; are we not here in the presence of theological "fringes" in the sense of a sustained dialogue until fears and anxieties are allayed? Their situation is close to

> the baptized whose lives do not reflect the demands of Baptism, who lack a meaningful relationship to the Church and no longer experience the consolation born of faith. The Church, in her maternal concern, tries to help them experience a conversion which will restore the joy of faith to their hearts and inspire a commitment to the Gospel. (*Evangelii Gaudium*, no. 15)

I recap briefly a few theological places where the meeting with "fringes" is expected by those who suffer hideously to the point of going regularly to Rome to seek audiences. First, there is the Christological question: if the nuances between the concepts of "particularity" and "singularity" when applied to Jesus Christ are reworked in depth, a calm dialogue could perhaps take place. In fact, the singularity of Christ is that he is absolutely unique as the Son of God incarnate, for example, the effect of being both divine and human or even the fact of the resurrection as the inauguration of a new world, or even the virginal birth, and so on. By contrast, the particularity is linked to the circumstances or specific details identified, which means we are not simply generalizing here. For example, every human being has a specific sex, height, eye color, hair, voice, and other distinct attributes. What is particular to one can be found in another, but it is the whole of the particular aspects of an individual linked to his or her historical journey that makes that person unique. Concerning Christ, the following components are part of his particularity: his being Jewish and male, his height, sandal size, and so on.

It is therefore important that the exegetes and the dogmaticians help us clarify this: Did the Word of God become human or male? The question deserves a definitive answer. Does the fact that he chose to be male bind masculinity to God and his church forever? Historians can help us understand the options of the apostles in the primitive church: If the apostles had decided they should not make absolute the particularity of circumcision, the symbol of Judaism, for the church of Christ, why does the particularity of masculinity play any role at all?

We see here that we must come to an understanding of the incarnation in depth. The liturgists and the dogmaticians can help assess the consequences for the symbolic representation of Christ in the liturgy: If the priest represents Christ, is it at the level of his singularity or his particularity? If it is at the level of his particularity, in the name of what theological principle do we choose some aspects and not others? Why stop at the particularity of masculinity and put aside all the other characteristics that are in Judaism, such as circumcision and the Eucharistic species, which were peculiar to his time.

Some people derive implications from this to link the twelve apostles with the sacrament of Holy Orders: they were twelve, all male, all Jews, all Galileans, some single, and others married. If we must take any of this seriously, in theory, the church was supposed to include twelve Jewish, Galilean, circumcised men, some married and others not. If the historians could help discover the theological basis for particularizing being male but ignoring the other characteristics, this could put our minds at rest. Today it is important to help the people who are suffering and will regularly seek audience in St. Peter's Square to clarify these issues if we want to take the drama out of the debates on the symbolic representation of Christ in the liturgy.

Then there is the symbolic realm. The liturgists and dogmaticians can help answer the following common questions. Are priests powerful in the Eucharistic celebration because they are male or because they have been trained by the church for the task? Do they make sense symbolically because of their sex or because they have been assigned the role of bearing references to Christ? Clarifying and specifying the response to these may placate the spirits of the people on the fringes because of theological misunderstandings related to this aspect of the problem of Holy Orders.

Finally, digging into the symbolism used by Christ himself could broaden prospects for dialogue. To speak of the mystery of his passion, death, and resurrection, Christ took symbols of the gift of life from male and female, including the Good Shepherd who gave his life for his sheep (John 10:11) and the woman in the pain of childbirth (John 16:21). The shepherd and the woman were saying, "I give you my body." Taking into consideration the symbolism Christ used can clarify the debate and broaden perspectives.

Evangelii Gaudium no. 103 expresses a desire for a more incisive female presence in the church to be accomplished; magisterial decisions alone will not suffice. The people of God must interiorize the biblical and magisterial texts relating to the dignity of women to the point of evangelizing the ambient negative cultural prejudices. Also, the people of God must be in dialogue with God and welcome the Holy Spirit, which is in accordance with the harmony desired by God. All misunderstandings must be clarified. It is interesting to note in *Christifideles Laici*, no. 52:

> The fundamental reason that requires and explains the presence and the collaboration of both men and women. . . . It is, rather, the original plan of the Creator who from the "beginning" willed the human being to be a "unity of the two," and willed man and woman to be the prime community of persons, source of every other community, and, at the same time, to be a "sign" of that interpersonal communion of love which constitutes the mystical, intimate life of God, One in Three.

And when the community of the faithful feels this "unity of the two," the community is at ease in the Holy Spirit, and the changes that should take place in favor of this opening up can occur with much ease.

Translated from the French by Andrew Setsoafia, SJ

Reviving a Church of the Poor and for the Poor, and Reclaiming Faith Doing Justice and Seeking Liberation

Convergence between Pope Francis and Jean-Marc Ela

Bienvenu Mayemba

This essay is about two major contemporary theological and pastoral figures. One is from Argentina, Pope Francis; the other from Cameroon, Jean-Marc Ela, a humble peasant priest who has already passed from the city of the earth to the city of heaven. Their sociopolitical commitments and their theological and ecclesiological visions reflect the prophetic dimension of not only our Christian faith but also of the Roman Catholic Church as it understood and defined itself during Vatican II, especially through *Gaudium et Spes* and *Lumen Gentium*.

My objective is to bring out the convergence or the commonality between these two theological and pastoral thinkers even though they come from different contexts, backgrounds, and ecclesial settings. I adopt a comparative approach that focuses on what these two theologians and pastors have in common in terms of theological vision and ecclesiological understanding and perception. So there will not be a section about contrasting these two men of God and of the church.

My essay has four points:

1. The impact of Pope Francis's and Jean-Marc Ela's sociopolitical and ecclesio-cultural contexts on their anthropo-ecclesio-theological vision.
2. Love and mercy make our faith visible and our church credible: Pope Francis's cry for a church of and for the poor.

3. From revelation to salvation as liberation: Jean-Marc Ela's preferential option for the poor and for a prophetic church.
4. The church as the Good Samaritan and the prophet: An ecclesio-theological convergence between Pope Francis and Jean-Marc Ela.

Pope Francis's and Jean-Marc Ela's Sociopolitical and Ecclesio-Cultural Contexts

Jorge Mario Bergoglio, who is now Pope Francis, was born in Buenos Aires, the capital of Argentina, in 1936, the same year that Jean-Marc Ela was born.[1] Because Bergoglio spent most of his life in his country, he knew it as a child, an adult layperson who was a nightclub bouncer and a chemical technician before becoming a Jesuit scholastic, and as a priest, bishop, archbishop, cardinal, and pope.

---

[1] Here is an extract from the Vatican biography of Francis (w2.vatican.va):

He was born in Buenos Aires on 17 December 1936, the son of Italian immigrants. His father Mario was an accountant employed by the railways and his mother Regina Sivori was a committed wife dedicated to raising their five children. He graduated as a chemical technician and then chose the path of the priesthood, entering the Diocesan Seminary of Villa Devoto. On 11 March 1958 he entered the novitiate of the Society of Jesus. He completed his studies of the humanities in Chile and returned to Argentina in 1963 to graduate with a degree in philosophy from the Colegio de San José in San Miguel. From 1964 to 1965 he taught literature and psychology at Immaculate Conception College in Santa Fé and in 1966 he taught the same subject at the Colegio del Salvatore in Buenos Aires. From 1967 to 1970 he studied theology and obtained a degree from the Colegio of San José.

On 13 December 1969 he was ordained a priest by Archbishop Ramón José Castellano. He continued his training between 1970 and 1971 at the University of Alcalá de Henares, Spain, and on 22 April 1973 made his final profession with the Jesuits. Back in Argentina, he was novice master at Villa Barilari, San Miguel; professor at the Faculty of Theology of San Miguel; consultor to the Province of the Society of Jesus and also Rector of the Colegio Máximo of the Faculty of Philosophy and Theology.

On 31 July 1973 he was appointed Provincial of the Jesuits in Argentina, an office he held for six years. He then resumed his work in the university sector and from 1980 to 1986 served once again as Rector of the Colegio de San José, as well as parish priest, again in San Miguel. In March 1986 he went to Germany to finish his doctoral thesis; his superiors then sent him to the Colegio del Salvador in Buenos Aires and next to the Jesuit Church in the city of Córdoba as spiritual director and confessor.

Argentina went through many tumultuous periods marked by political instability and insecurity, social chaos, and economic crisis. Argentineans have suffered under repressive political regimes with no respect for democratic institutions and human rights and dignity. There were violent conflicts between pro-government and pro-opposition citizens. Some opponents formed guerrilla groups that fought the government. Innocent people were unjustly intimidated, silenced, abused, abducted, arrested, tortured, and executed. It was a reign of arbitrary terror.[2]

Bergoglio was aware of this sociopolitical context and atmosphere that instilled in the country's citizens fear, despair, and defeat, and was sensitive to what his fellow citizens were going through. He knew that politicians told lies and made promises they didn't always fulfill. As did his fellow Argentineans, he longed for peace, justice, security, stability, freedom, and democracy. But he was conscious of his powerlessness and experienced his people's powerlessness; he suffered with them and shared their pains and joys.

"My people are poor and I am one of them," he said more than once, explaining his decision to live in an apartment and cook his own supper.[3] He knew that many people were poor, jobless, homeless, and hopeless, and he knew change was necessary for the promotion of the common good and social justice as a major component of distributive justice.

Jean-Marc Ela was born in the village of Ngoazip, in Ebolowa, a city in southern Cameroon in 1936, the same year as Pope Francis. He was also invested in different phases of his country's struggle for identity, independence, freedom, democracy, and political pluralism.[4]

Ela experienced racism and discrimination while studying for a master's degree in philosophy, for a doctorate in systematic theology at the University of Strasbourg, and for a doctorate in sociology at the University of Sorbonne. He was inspired by Frantz Fanon's anticolonialism and antiracism, by Aimé Césaire's discourse on colonialism, and by Martin Luther

---

[2] Bienvenu Mayemba, "Le drame des sociétes sans dialogue: Violence, arbitraire et terreur," *Promotio Iustitiae* 78, no. 2 (2003): 1–6; "Violence, arbitraire, terreur . . . Le drame des sociétés sans dialogue," *Foi et Développement*, Bulletin of Centre L.-J. Lebret, Paris, no. 303 (May 2002): 1–4; "La terreur de l'arbitraire. Le drame d'une société sans sens du dialogue," *Congo-Afrique*, no. 360 (December 2001): 595–606.

[3] "Biography of the Holy Father Pope Francis," w2.vatican.va/.

[4] Yao Assogba, *Jean-Marc Ela, Le sociologue et théologien en boubou* (Paris: L'Harmattan, 1999), 107.

King Jr.'s struggle for civil rights for African Americans. He copied and kept with him his "I have a dream" speech.

When he returned to his country, Ela spent fourteen years in the far north of Cameroon, living in the village of Tokombéré and ministering to the Kirdi people.[5] He moved to Yaoundé as a professor at the University of Yaoundé and a pastor at Saint Paul de Ndzong Melen parish, residing in a rented apartment in the working-class neighborhood of Melen. The misery, poverty, oppression, discrimination, intimidation, and exploitation by the political authorities of the Kirdi people[6] called him to commit himself to the struggle for social justice and to rethink his pastoral ministry and theological thought.

This sociopolitical commitment led him to develop his sociology of development[7] and his African theology of liberation articulated through his books, such as *Repenser la théologie africaine,*[8] *L'irruption des pauvres,*[9]

---

[5] *Structures sociales traditionnelles et changements économiques chez les montagnards du Nord Cameroun. L' exemple de Tokombéré;* thèse de doctorat en sociologie (Paris V-Sorbonne, Réné Descartes, 1978).

[6] Cf. *Quand l'Etat pénètre en brousse . . . Les ripostes paysannes à la crise* (Paris: Karthala, 1990); *L'Afrique des villages* (Paris: Karthala, 1982); *La ville en Afrique noire* (Paris: Karthala, 1983);_*Restituer l'histoire aux sociétés africaines: Pour la promotion des sciences sociales en Afrique* (Paris: L'Harmattan, 1994); *Innovations sociales et renaissance de l'Afrique noire: Les défis du "monde d'en-bas"* (Montreal/Paris: L'Harmattan, 1998).

[7] *Quand l'Etat pénètre en brousse; . . . Les ripostes paysannes à la crise* (Paris: Karthala, 1990); *Restituer l'histoire aux sociétés africaines: Pour la promotion des sciences sociales en Afrique* (Paris: L'Harmattan, 1994); *Innovations sociales et renaissance de l'Afrique noire: Les défis du "monde d'en-bas"* (Montreal/Paris: L'Harmattan, 1998); *Travail et entreprise en Afrique: Les fondements sociaux de la réussite économique* (Paris: Karthala, 2006), 318.

[8] Jean-Marc Ela, *Repenser la théologie africaine: Le Dieu qui libère* (Paris: Karthala, 2003).

[9] Ibid., 53–89; Jean-Marc Ela, *L'Afrique a l'ère du savoir: Science, société et pouvoir* (Paris: L'Harmattan, 2006); *Transcendance de Dieu et existence humaine selon Luther: Essai d'introduction à la logique d'une théologie,* thèse de doctorat en théologie (Strasbourg, 1969). *La plume et la Pioche: Réflexion sur l'enseignement et la société dans le développement de l'Afrique Noire* (Yaoundé: C.L.E, 1971); *Le Cri de l'homme africain* (Paris: L'Harmattan, 1980); *Voici le temps des Héritiers: Eglises d'Afrique et voies nouvelles,* in collaboration with René Luneau (Paris: Karthala, 1981); *De l'assistance à la liberation: Les tâches actuelles de l'Eglise en milieu africain* (Paris: Centre Lebret, 1981); *L'Afrique des villages* (Paris: Karthala, 1982); *La ville en Afrique noire* (Paris: Karthala, 1983); *Ma foi d'Africain* (Paris: Karthala, 1985); *Cheik Anta Diop ou l'honneur de penser* (Paris: L'Harmattan, 1989); _*Quand l'Etat pénètre en brousse . . . Les ripostes paysannes à*

Le cri de l'homme Africain, and *Ma foi d'Africain*.[10]

Ela became involved in challenging and denouncing the Cameroonian government,[11] and so he was forced into exile in Canada, where he died alone and away from his country on December 26, 2008.[12] A prophet is never accepted in his own country.

Pope Francis's and Jean-Marc Ela's Theological and Ecclesiological Contexts

In addition to their sociopolitical and cultural contexts, the pope and Ela were influenced by the religious and theological context of their respective countries and continents. When they were both twenty-nine, Vatican II brought a new wind of change to the church. Its dogmatic constitution, *Lumen Gentium*, showed how the church renewed its understanding and definition of itself as the people of God and as the sacrament of God's kingdom, bearing in its bosom both righteous and sinners and being open to constant renewal and purification.

Vatican II's pastoral constitution *Gaudium et Spes* reflects how the church renewed its perception of the world and its mission in that world seen as a "divine milieu,"[13] as the historical locus where we encounter God, where revelation takes place, where we experience God's epiphany,

---

la crise (Paris: Karthala, 1990); *Le message de Jean Baptiste: De la conversion à la réforme dans les églises africaines* (Yaoundé: CLE, 1992); *Guide pédagogique de formation à la recherche pour le développement en Afrique* (Paris: L'Harmattan, 2001); *Afrique, l'irruption des pauvres: Société contre Ingérence, Pouvoir et Argent* (Paris: L'Harmattan, 1994); *Recherche scientifique et crise de la rationalité* (Paris: L'Harmattan, 2007); *Les cultures africaines dans le champ de la rationalité scientifique* (Paris: L'Harmattan, 2007); *La recherche africaine face au défi de l'excellence scientifique* (Paris: L'Harmattan, 2007); *Fécondité et migrations africaines—Les nouveaux enjeux* (Paris: L'Harmattan, 2006).

[10] Jean-Marc Ela, *Le cri de l'homme africain: Questions aux chrétiens et aux églises d'Afrique* (Paris: L'Harmattan, 1980; 2nd ed., 1993); Ela and Luneau, *Voici le temps des Héritiers.*

[11] *Le cri de l'homme africain* (1980); *Ma foi d'Africain* (Paris: Karthala, 1985); *Quand l'Etat pénètre en brousse . . . Les ripostes paysannes à la crise* (Paris: Karthala, 1990); *L'Afrique des villages* (Paris: Karthala, 1982).

[12] Achille Mbembe, Celestin Monga, and Yao Assogba, "Ela prit l'exil forcé," in www.politique-africaine.com; Achille Mbembe, "Le veilleur s'en est allé," in http://cjf. qc.ca.

[13] Cf. Teilhard de Chardin, *The Divine Milieu* (New York: Harper & Row, 1968).

and where we walk and journey with Jesus as did the disciples of Emmaus.

Taking up the theological and the ecclesiological renewal promoted by Vatican II, the Latin American bishops' conference held influential meetings, including one in 1968 in Medellín, Colombia, officially embracing the project of "basic ecclesial communities" and the theology of liberation later articulated by Gustavo Gutiérrez, Bishop Oscar Romero, Cardinal Dom Hélder Câmara, Jon Sobrino, Leonardo Boff, and many other theologians.[14]

In the 1979 Puebla, Mexico, conference on evangelization in Latin America, they defined the concept of a "preferential option for the poor." Then in 2007, in Aparecida (a town in the city of São Paulo, Brazil), they spoke of the new challenges facing the evangelization under the theme "Disciples and Missionaries of Jesus Christ" so our people may have life in him. "I am the way, the truth, and the life." In a similar manner, the Jesuits' thirty-second general congregation in 1975 spoke of the preferential option for the poor in decree no. 4, "Our Mission Today: The Service of Faith and the Promotion of Justice."

These meetings and documents reminded Bergoglio that change would not come from the powerful and the wealthy and that the church had to commit to the social, political, and theological transformation of Argentina and Latin America to contribute to the liberation of the country and its poor. Indeed, "He became a reference point because of the strong stances he took during the dramatic financial crisis that overwhelmed the country in 2001."[15] He believed that the church had to find new ways of evangelizing and of being in solidarity with the "crucified people"[16] in the name of the "crucified God."[17] He has always advised his priests to show mercy and apostolic courage and to keep their doors open to everyone. He has said on various occasions that the worst thing that

---

[14] Cf. Gustavo Gutiérrez, *A Theology of Liberation: History, Politics and Salvation* (Maryknoll, NY: Orbis Books, 1973); Jon Sobrino, *Jesus the Liberator: A Historical-Theological Reading of Jesus of Nazareth* (Maryknoll, NY: Orbis Books, 1994); *Christ the Liberator: A View from the Victims* (Maryknoll, NY: Orbis Books, 2001); Leonardo Boff, *Trinity and Society* (Maryknoll, NY: Orbis Books, 1988).

[15] "Biography of the Holy Father Pope Francis," w2.vatican.va.

[16] Cf. Ignacio Ellacuría, "Crucified People," in Ignacio Ellacuría and Jon Sobrino, *Mysterium Liberationis: Fundamental Concepts of Liberation Theology* (Maryknoll, NY: Orbis Books, 1999), 251–88.

[17] Jürgen Moltmann, *The Crucified God: The Cross of Christ as the Foundation and Criticism of Christian Theology* (Augsburg, MN: Fortress Publishers, 1993), 326.

could happen to the church "is what de Lubac called spiritual worldliness," which means, "being self-centered." And when he speaks of social justice, he calls people first of all to pick up the catechism and to rediscover the Ten Commandments and the Beatitudes. His project is simple: if you follow Christ, you understand that "trampling upon a person's dignity is a serious sin."[18]

On the African side, Vatican II's recognition of the value of multiculturalism and theological pluralism came to confirm the desire of most of African Christians to promote an African theological discourse[19] and to develop an African liturgical celebration of the Mass.[20] This rediscovery of the value of cultural and theological pluralism and of African personality, identity, and authenticity[21] was revived by Paul VI's discourses such as "Discourse to African Bishops in Kampala," letters such as *Africae Terrarum*, and exhortations such as *Evangelii Nuntiandi*,[22] and by the Ecumenical Association of African Theologians.

---

[18] "Biography of the Holy Father Pope Francis," w2.vatican.va.

[19] Cf. *Des prêtres noirs s'interrogent* (Paris: Présence Africaine, 1956); Meinard Hebga, ed., *Personnalité africaine et catholicisme* (Paris: Présence Africaine, 1963), 59–81; the debate between Tshibangu and Vanneste: Kita Nsoki, "Genèse de l'expression '*théologie africaine*,'" *Telema*, no. 4 (1979): 43–57; Alphonse Ngindu-Mushete, "L'histoire de la théologie en Afrique: De la polémique à l'irénisme critique," in *Libération ou adaptation? La théologie africain s'interroge,* Actes du Colloque des Théologiens du Tiers-Monde, Accra, December 17–23, 1977 (Paris: L'Harmattan, 1979), 30–48.

[20] Cf. Cardinal Malula, François Kabasele, Simon-Pierre Boka, etc.

[21] Fabien Eboussi Boulaga, "*La Bantou problématique,*" *Présence Africaine*, no. 66 (1968): 4–40; *La crise du Muntu: Authenticité africaine et philosophie* (Paris: Présence Africaine, 1977); Kä Mana, *Afrique-va-t-elle mourir: Essai d'éthique politique* (Paris: Karthala, 1993); Meinrad Hebga, *Emancipation d'Eglises sous-tutelle: essai sur l'ère post-missionnaire* (Paris: Présence africaine, 1976); "Eloge de l'ethnophilosophie," *Présence Africaine*, no. 123 (1982); Engelbert Mveng, *L'Afrique dans l'Eglise: Paroles d'un croyant* (Paris: L'Harmattan, 1985); Engelbert Mveng, "Essai d'anthropologie négro-africaine: La personnalité humaine . . . ," *Cahier des Religions Africaines*, no. 12 (1978): 85–96; "Structures de la prière négro-africaine," in *Personnalité africaine et catholicisime*, ed. Meinrad Hebga (Paris: Présence Africaine, 1963), 153–200.

[22] Paul VI, *Africae Terrarum*, in *Documentation Catholique,* no. 1505 (1967), col. 1937–56; *Acta Apostolicae Sedis* (October 29, 1967): 1076–77; "Allocution au Symposium des Conférences Episcopales d'Afrique et du Madagascar (SCEAM) à Kampala." *Documentation Catholique*, no. 1546 (1969), 763–65; *Acta Apostolica Sedis*, no. 61 (1969); *Evangelii Nuntiandi: Sur l'évangélisation dans le monde moderne* (December 8, 1975).

It was also revived by the promotion of African Christianity and the emergence of the African theology of inculturation[23] and African theologians such as Vincent Mulago, Meinrad Hebga, Engelbert Mveng, Cardinal Malula, Charles Nyamiti, John Mbiti, Bolaji Idowu, Albert Nolan, Simon-Pierre Boka, Fabien Eboussi-Boulaga, Oscar Bimwenyi-Kweshi, Alphonse Ngin-du-Mushete, and others. All these theologians and these phases and aspects of African theology had an impact on Ela, who opted for a theology of liberation that took seriously not only the sociopolitical experience, as do Latin American theologians, but also the cultural and anthropological experience.[24]

In fact, Ela was involved in the quest for Vatican II to take seriously African peoples and African voices and experiences. For this reason, in 1962, right before the start of the council, he joined Meinrad Hebga, Léopold S. Senghor, and other African priests to hold a colloquium on *Personnalité africaine et catholicisme*, edited and published in 1963, by Meinrad Hebga; Alioune Diop traveled to Rome to distribute copies of it to council participants.

Ela's contribution, his first official theological article, drew praise from Léopold S. Senghor among others, and it drew criticism from some Catholic missionaries because of his denunciation of the church and of the ambiguity of mission in Africa[25] and his hermeneutical embrace of Frantz Fanon. It was titled *L'Eglise, le monde noir et le concile.*[26] This first text on liberation theology was written in 1962, even before the council and before Latin American theology of liberation.

Pope Francis's Cry for a Church of the Poor and for the Poor

Two concepts characterize Pope Francis's theology: love and mercy. His vision of the church was one of a church of the poor and for the poor.

---

[23] Vincent Mulago, Cardinal Malula, Meinrad Hebga, Alexis Kagame, Charles Nyamiti, Anselme Sanon, Bimwenyi Kweshi, Simon-Pierre Boka, Theoneste Nkeramihigo, François Kabasélé, Cécé Kolié, etc.

[24] Jean-Marc Ela, *African Cry* (Eugene, OR: Wipf & Stock, 2005); *My Faith as an African* (Eugene, OR: Wipf & Stock, 2009); *Repenser la théologie africaine: Le Dieu qui libère* (Paris: Karthala, 2003).

[25] Jean-Marc Ela, "Les ambiguïtés de la mission: Le cas africain," in Jean-Marc Ela, *Le cri de l'homme africain: Questions aux chrétiens et aux Eglises d'Afrique* (Paris: L'Harmattan, 1980), 18–39.

[26] Jean-Marc Ela, "L'Eglise, le monde noir et le concile," in *Personnalité africaine et catholicisme*, ed. Meinrad Hebga (Paris: Présence Africaine, 1963), 59–81.

The preferential option for the poor is what is driving the Holy Father, who works for the inclusion of the poor in today's society (*Evangelii Gaudium* [*EG*], nos. 186–216).

For him, love and mercy make our faith visible and our church credible. He cries for a church that is close to the people, a church that hears the plea of the poor crying out for justice like the blood of Abel, a church in which shepherds carry the smell of the sheep. A church of mercy and of proximity. A church that is engaged in mission. A church that constantly goes forth, willing and ready to take the first step, to be involved and supportive, to bear fruit and to rejoice (*EG*, nos. 20–24). A church that is like a mother with an open heart (*EG*, nos. 46–49). A church that takes seriously the social dimension of evangelization and combines confession of faith and commitment to society (*EG*, nos. 78–79).

Pope Francis would like the church to recognize the special place of the poor in the midst of God's people and kingdom (*EG*, nos. 197–201), to develop a greater care and concern for the vulnerable (*EG*, nos. 209–16), and to promote social justice as an aspect of distributive justice that includes the just redistribution of goods, resources, and income (*EG*, nos. 202–08). For him, if the church wants to stay credible or become more credible, it should face the challenges of today's world (*EG*, nos. 52–75) and say no to what is bad, wrong, and evil and say yes to what is good, benevolent, and right. The church should say no to an economy of exclusion (*EG*, nos. 53–54), to the new idolatry of money (*EG*, nos. 55–56), and to a financial system that rules rather than serves (*EG*, nos. 57–58). It should say no to inequality that spawns violence (*EG*, nos. 59–60), to selfishness and spiritual sloth (*EG*, nos. 81–83), to sterile pessimism (*EG*, nos. 84–86), to spiritual worldliness (*EG*, nos. 93–97), and to warring among ourselves (*EG*, nos. 98–101).

On the contrary, it should say yes to the challenge of a missionary spirituality (*EG*, nos. 78–80), to the new relationships brought by Christ (*EG*, nos. 87–92), and to inculturating the faith (*EG*, nos. 68–70). Pope Francis is the pope of divine mercy as a theological category.[27]

---

[27] "The Coat of Arms of Pope Francis," w2.vatican.va. The motto of Pope Francis is taken from a passage from the venerable Bede, Homily 21 (CCL 122, 149–51), on the Feast of Matthew, which reads: "Jesus therefore sees the tax collector, and since he sees by having mercy and by choosing, he says to him, 'follow me.'" This homily is a tribute to divine mercy and is read during the Liturgy of the Hours on the Feast of

Jean-Marc Ela's Preferential Option for the
Poor and for a Prophetic Church

Three concepts are important in the theology of Ela: revelation, salvation, and liberation. For Ela, there can be no revelation without salvation and liberation, no salvation without revelation and liberation, and no liberation without revelation and salvation.[28] They are interconnected aspects of his liberation theology.

God reveals God's self as the one who saves through the process of revelation as presented in Exodus. Ela's understanding of revelation does not focus, as did Karl Barth's or Karl Rahner's, on the self-communication of God. In effect, Barth in his *Dogmatics*[29] and Rahner in his *Foundations of Christian Faith*,[30] in which he basically followed Barth, developed a theology of revelation centered on God and on God's self-communication. For them, revelation tells us about the "lordness of God" or *la seigneurie de Dieu*, about the height and the depth of God's mystery, and about God's proximity to human beings through Jesus Christ, the plenitude of hypostatic union, the universal Savior.

Ela's understanding of revelation embraced the theology of revelation as articulated by René Latourelle[31] and Wolfhart Pannenberg[32] with their insistence on the link between revelation and history, but it goes beyond that by naming the components of that history and giving priority to the poor, the marginalized, and the crucified. In that sense, his theology of revelation is

---

Matthew. This has particular significance in the life and spirituality of the pope. In fact, on the Feast of Matthew in 1953, the young Jorge Bergoglio experienced, at age seventeen, in a very special way, the loving presence of God in his life. Following confession, he felt his heart touched, and he sensed the descent of the mercy of God, who with a gaze of tender love, called him to religious life, following the example of Saint Ignatius of Loyola. Once he had been ordained a bishop, Monsignor Bergoglio, in memory of this event that signified the beginning of his total consecration to God in his church, chose, as his motto and as his program of life the words of Saint Bede: "Miserando atque eligendo" (roughly, "shown mercy and chosen"). This he has chosen to keep in his papal coat of arms.

[28] Ela, *Repenser la théologie africaine: Le Dieu qui libère; Ma foi d'africain.*

[29] Karl Barth, *Dogmatique: La doctrine de la parole Dieu. Prolégomènes à la dogmatique*, vol. 1 (Geneva: Labor et Fides, 1953).

[30] Karl Rahner, *Traité fondamental de la foi* (Paris: Cerf, 2011).

[31] René Latourelle, *Théologie de la révélation* (Paris: DDB, 1963).

[32] Wolfhart Pannenberg, *Revelation as History* (New York: Macmillan-Collier, 1968); *Théologie systématique* (Paris: Cerf, 2008).

close to the theology of revelation of Gustavo Gutiérrez, Leonardo Boff, Jon Sobrino, Ignacio Ellacuría, and Pope Francis.

Ela's theology of revelation is also close to the theology of faith in history and society as developed by Johann Baptist Metz[33] but with more sociopolitical involvement, narratives, and impact. He took the cross seriously as did James Cone[34] and Jürgen Moltmann.[35] In *My Faith as an African*, Ela makes clear that "God is not neutral," that God takes stands and takes sides; God supports and protects the weak, the vulnerable, and the poor.[36]

The Church as the Good Samaritan and the Prophet: Ecclesio-Theological Convergence

Ela and Francis agree that the church should exemplify the qualities of a prophet and a Good Samaritan.[37] It has to share and proclaim *Evangelii Gaudium*, the joy of the gospel. It also has to challenge, question, and denounce what it opposes. It should be involved socially by works of mercy and charity. Its ministry should cultivate the sense of charity and of solidarity that reminds people of the Good Samaritan. Ela and Francis share an understanding of the church that embraces the poor, the migrants,[38] the prisoners, the jobless, the homeless, the starving,[39] the marginalized, and the uneducated. They understand the importance of respecting difference[40] and the "dignity of difference."[41]

---

[33] Johann Baptist Metz, *Faith in History and Society: Toward a Practical Fundamental Theology* (London: Burns & Oates, 1980).

[34] James Cone, *God of the Oppressed* (New York: Seabury Press, 1975); *A Black Theology of Liberation* (Maryknoll, NY: Orbis Books,1990).

[35] Moltmann, *Crucified God*.

[36] Jean-Marc Ela, *Ma foi d'africain* (Paris: Karthala, 1985).

[37] Speaking of the interaction between the prophet and the Good Samaritan means combining faith and justice, that is, faith that does justice. Cf. Elias O. Opongo and Agbonkhianmeghe E. Orobator, *Faith Doing Justice. A Manual for Social Analysis, Catholic Social Teaching and Social Justice* (Nairobi: Paulines, 2007).

[38] Pope Francis visited Lampedousa; Jean-Marc Ela, *Fécondité et migrations africaines: Les nouveaux enjeux* (Paris: L'Harmattan, 2006).

[39] *Evangelii Gaudium*, no. 89.

[40] Jean-Marc Ela, "Le droit à la différence ou l'enjeu actuel des églises locales en Arique noire," in *Civilisation noire et Eglise catholique*, Actes du Colloque d'Abidjan, (Paris-Abidjan-Dakar: Présence Africaine-Les Nouvelles Editions Africaines, 1978), 204–17.

[41] Jonathan Sacks, *The Dignity of Difference: How to Avoid the Clash of Civilizations* (London: Continuum, 2002).

While Ela speaks of cultural difference and identities, Francis speaks more of dialogue between Christian churches[42] and between religions, especially between Roman Christianity and Judaism. Seeing the pope praying and embracing a rabbi and an imam is very inspiring. In the future, this dialogue should include not only Islam, Judaism, Hinduism, and Buddhism but also African traditional religions.[43]

Pope Francis and Jean-Marc Ela are both men of God, of the church, of their countries, and of the poor. They both believe in the power of compassion and the power of love. They both believe in the interaction between love and faith, between faith and compassion, between community and solidarity, and faith and justice.[44] Their lives, theologies, and their ecclesiologies are committed to reviving a church of and for the poor and to reclaiming faith doing justice and seeking liberation. For them, theology is not only faith seeking understanding or faith concerned with its intelligibility in a rational sense. Theology is an active quest for and concrete practice of love and mercy, faith and compassion, and liberation and justice.

---

[42] *Evangelii Gaudium*, nos. 242–43, 250–54.

[43] Cf. John Mbiti, *African Religions and Philosophy*, 2nd ed. (Oxford: Heinemann, 1990); Laurenti Magesa, *African Religion: Moral Traditions of Abundant Life* (Maryknoll, NY: Orbis Books, 1997); Vincent Mulago, "Vital Participation: The Cohesive Principle of the Bantu Community," ed. Kwesi A. Dickson and Paul Ellingworth, *Biblical Revelation and African Beliefs* (Maryknoll, NY: Orbis Books, 1969), 137–58.

[44] *Evangelii Gaudium*, no. 87.

WHEN A SLEEPING WOMAN WAKES...

A Conversation with Pope Francis in Evangelii Gaudium *about the Feminization of Poverty*

Anne Arabome

On November 27, 2015, during his inaugural visit to Africa, Pope Francis addressed a crowd of people gathered in a neighborhood parish in one of the slums of Nairobi, Kenya, with the following words:

> I am here because I want you to know that your joys and hopes, your troubles and your sorrows, are not indifferent to me. I realize the difficulties which you experience daily! How can I not denounce the injustices which you suffer?[1]

Francis was personalizing the famous opening lines of Vatican II's pastoral constitution on the church in the modern world (*Gaudium et Spes*). A focus on the joys and hopes, pain and anguish of the poor has become a hallmark of Francis's papacy. A considerable portion of his recent apostolic exhortation *Evangelii Gaudium* and encyclical *Laudato Si'* explore the challenges and experience of the poor and the implications for the self-understanding and evangelizing mission of the church.

Francis's concern for the poor stems from a simple hermeneutical principle that underlies his reading of the gospel. As he told the poor in Nairobi, "The path of Jesus began on the peripheries; it goes from the poor and with the poor, towards others."[2] This hermeneutics contain ecclesiological implications. For Francis, it would seem, over and above the familiar doctrinal "marks of the church," ecclesial capacity to enter into solidarity with the

---

[1] Pope Francis, address in Nairobi, November 27, 2015, http://www.news.va.
[2] Ibid.

poor and undertake a mission of transformation and liberation from the shackles of poverty, is the defining mark of the Christian community.

In light of how the "Francis effect" is changing the face of the church and creating a not-so-silent reform, my focus in this essay is to examine what effect, if any, the pope's reforms would have on the women of Africa. This may seem an impossible task and overly generalizing. Yet on reflection one discovers that in Africa what Francis has repeatedly designated as the "church of the poor" is mostly composed of women who carry significant burdens of family and social life. In other words, the poor of Africa do not constitute an undifferentiated mass. There are distinguishing factors that allow us to recognize them in the social, economic, political, and cultural contexts of the continent. Thus we could speak of categories of the poor such as migrants, refugees, and people living with HIV/AIDS. In a particular way, the majority of the poor in Africa are women.

The Joys and Hopes of Women?

Arguably, the joys and hopes that are celebrated in *Gaudium et Spes* continue to be overshadowed by the pain and anguish of women who are marginalized and impoverished in a variety of ways too numerous to be listed. Pope Francis would agree with this assessment. For as he sees it in *Evangelii Gaudium (EG)*, "The joy of living frequently fades, lack of respect for others and violence are on the rise, and inequality is increasingly evident. It is a struggle to live and, often, to live with precious little dignity."[3] As mentioned, in this essay, I have chosen to engage with Francis's document *Evangelii Gaudium* in order to raise pertinent questions, identify significant implications, and explore appropriate meanings.

In the context of theological pedagogy and ethical discourse we run the risk of adopting a narrow lens and projecting an illusion of the "joys and hopes" of the world while glossing over the pain and anguish of women who are marginalized and impoverished in a variety of ways. Judging by historical accounts and contemporary experiences of economic degradation, poverty is not a disembodied, disincarnate reality. The ethical implications of poverty cannot be debated or addressed based solely on a consideration of economic criteria. It is imperative to pay attention to the narratives of those most

---

[3] *Evangelii Gaudium*, no. 52.

affected by poverty, which call into question the moral and ethical responsibility to women by church and society. Presently, there are no narratives of poverty in the theater of deprivation more harrowing than those visited upon women's lives and bodies. As Charlayne Hunter-Gault has observed, "The open secret about poverty in Africa is that it has a woman's face."[4]

In light of this pressing and disturbing correlation of poverty and femininity, I pose these questions: How does the Francis effect translate in Africa? What are the contours and images of a Francis church in Africa? More radical queries underlie those: Does the Francis effect translate positively in the lives of African women? What difference does it make in the lives of African women?

The life of an African woman is filled with struggles and challenges. She faces subordination, hard work, family care, limited economic resources and opportunities; her joys and hopes are very dim, as she has to depend most often solely on men. Poverty does not necessarily equate material deprivation; perhaps even worse is the "social exclusion and human degradation" that poverty generates on account of the gender of a particular segment of the population.[5] According to a UN report, "Human poverty is more than income poverty. It is the denial of choices and opportunities for living a tolerable life."[6] Along the same line, Pope Francis notes,

> Human beings are themselves considered consumer goods to be used and then discarded. We have created a "disposable" culture which is now spreading. It is no longer simply about exploitation and oppression, but something new. Exclusion ultimately has to do with what it means to be a part of the society in which we live; those excluded are no longer society's underside or its fringes or its disenfranchised—they are no longer even a part of it. The excluded are not the "exploited" but the outcast, the "leftovers." (*EG*, no. 53)

---

[4] Charlayne Hunter-Gault, "African Women and the Struggle against Poverty," http://www.npr.org.

[5] Barbara Bailey, "Feminization of Poverty across Pan-African Societies: The Church's Response—Alleviative or Emancipatory?" in *Religion and Poverty: Pan-African Perspectives*, ed. Peter J. Paris (Durham, NC: Duke University Press, 2009), 39.

[6] United Nations Development Programme, *Human Development Report 1997* (New York: Oxford University Press, 1997), 2.

While I agree with Francis, I would add that the victims of this "disposable culture" are not just human beings in general; in so many instances, women in particular are the consumer goods that are being used and then discarded. In this context, a certain "globalization of indifference" develops: "Almost without being aware of it, we end up being incapable of feeling compassion at the outcry of the poor, weeping for other people's pain, and feeling a need to help them, as though all this were someone else's responsibility and not our own" (*EG*, no. 54).

There is objective and empirical evidence confirming the wretched status and condition of many women. According to a UN report, "Women are disproportionately poor and too often disempowered and burdened by the strains of productive work, the birth and care of children and other household and community responsibilities."[7] In addition, in many places, women cannot own property. They have few assets or collateral that could provide a base for doing business.

Another harsh reality faces the feminine half of the human race in the sub-Saharan regions of Africa: "In 2013, 74 per cent of new HIV infections among African adolescents were among adolescent girls. . . . Young women and adolescent girls acquire HIV on average five to seven years earlier than young men, and in some countries in the region, HIV prevalence among this population can be as much as seven times that of their male counterparts."[8]

As the UN report further observed poignantly, "It is in the deprivation of the lives people lead that poverty manifests itself. Poverty can mean more than a lack of what is necessary for material well-being. It can also mean the denial of opportunities and choices most basic to human development to lead a long, healthy, creative life and to enjoy a decent standard of living, freedom, dignity, self-esteem and the respect of others."[9]

Insights from *Evangelii Gaudium* for Transformation

In *Evangelii Gaudium*, Francis states several categorical "nos"—no to an economy of exclusion, no to the new idolatry of money, no to a financial system that rules rather than serves, and no to the inequality that spawns

---

[7] Ibid., 3.

[8] "Women and Girls in Africa 'Being Left Behind' in Fight against HIV/AIDS—UN Report." http://www.un.org.

[9] United Nations Development Programme, *Human Development Report 1997*, 3.

violence (*EG*, nos. 53–60). It is striking that in all of Francis's comments, there seems to be little or no recognition of women as playing the role of subordinate human beings. The subordination, abuse, and exploitation of women in church and society all warrant a bigger no. To his credit, Francis recognizes that "doubly poor are those women who endure situations of exclusion, mistreatment and violence, since they are frequently less able to defend their rights. Even so, we constantly witness among them impressive examples of daily heroism in defending and protecting their vulnerable families" (*EG*, no. 212). However, these few statements do not seem sufficient for convincing any woman that the church is finally at a point where genuine human equality for women is a recognized as an indisputable fact.

In reality, African women have no choice but to be heroic in the face of many inequalities. Consistently, women are the caregivers and the bearers of the children and victims of the world's inequality. Francis is correct when he states that women are "doubly poor." But the truer reality, I would argue, is that the nonrecognition of women in the church contributes to this poverty. Secular society does not have a monopoly on social exclusion that leads to human degradation. The second-class status imposed on women in Africa by the nonrecognition and nonreception of their gifts in ministry, leadership, and governance amounts to a degrading form of exclusion. It is a situation that still awaits a remedy in the community called church.

Without a doubt, Francis is an incredible presence in the church. He is a breath of fresh air with a profoundly positive global impact not only on the church but also on the entire world. Nevertheless, in this one area concerning women, the pope seems incapable of fully recognizing the burden of prejudice and discrimination against women in the church. He makes a genuine claim to want a church in which the shepherds "smell of the sheep" (*EG*, no. 24). For the church in Africa to smell of the sheep, there must be a change in how women are viewed by the hierarchical church and, indeed, treated by this same church. Can a patently patriarchal and androcentric church take on the smell of ewes? Presuming a genuine desire on the part of Francis, it is to him that we must turn for guidance and direction.

Francis concedes with candor that "demands that the legitimate rights of women be respected, based on the firm conviction that men and women are equal in dignity, present the Church with profound and challenging questions which cannot be lightly evaded" (*EG*, no. 104). Strikingly, adducing a rationale based on Mariological considerations, the pope tilts the bar of equality in favor of women. For him, "Indeed, a woman, Mary, is more important than the bishops" (*EG*, no. 104). Whatever we chose to extrapolate from this assertion, a possible implication is that women are to be compared to Mary and men are to be compared to Christ. Such a dualistic and unequal comparison would only intensify the degrading exclusion of women in the church. A more balanced and favorable interpretation is that women, too, are bearers of the *imago Dei* and, indeed, through baptism, are "other Christs." It would be disappointing if the pope's intention was to promote a dualistic comparison that would compare women exclusively to Mary and not to Jesus Christ, even though she is the mother of Jesus Christ.

Another pivotal issue that needs to be addressed concerns maternity and motherhood. Oftentimes, official church documents and teachings pile encomiums effusively on women as mothers, but pay little attention to the sad reality that maternity and motherhood often form a deadly combination for women in developing countries. As theologian Tina Beattie—herself a mother and a grandmother—has stated, "Maternal mortality is often a direct consequence of poverty. Of an estimated 280,000 maternal deaths a year, 99 percent occur in the world's poorest countries—mostly in sub-Saharan Africa and south Asia."[10] Clearly, it is dangerous to be a mother in Africa! Sadly, official magisterium continues to view women through the narrow lens of maternity and motherhood to deny them their proper place as equals in the exercise of ministry and authority in the church.

Another important insight from Francis with relevance for the status of women is his conception and understanding of the function of power in the church. Hierarchical function "is not power understood as domination, but the power to administer the sacrament of the Eucharist" (*EG*, no. 104). Authority is an act of humble service conferred in trust. Clearly, regardless of the interpretation, experience amply demonstrates that hierarchy does, in fact, arrogate an aura of domination. In this context, the pope's statement that "the Church [is faced] with profound and challenging questions which cannot be lightly evaded" retains its poignancy. It bears asking: Just what are those "challenging questions" regarding women that cannot be evaded? Certainly, it is not possible for us to know what might be in the pontiff's mind when he makes this statement. However, returning to the issue of the

---

[10] Tina Beattie, "Pope Francis Has Done Little to Improve Women's Lives." http://www.theguardian.com.

Francis effect on Africa, we are emboldened to pose more profound and challenging questions that reach to the heart of women's marginal status in the church. I list these questions in no particular order of priority.

- Are women present in the decision-making process of the African church? It is important to recall that three women were allowed to speak at the second African synod in 2009, each for five minutes on behalf of all women in Africa!
- Why were African women largely absent in the preparation for the Synod on the Family? Are they included in conversations regarding family and the role of women in the church?
- Where is the teaching church in regard to issues of rape and domestic violence?
- What is the church teaching regarding female genital mutilation, early childhood marriage, and polygamous marriages?
- Where are the conversations with women about the use of prophylactics to protect them against death at the hands of a partner who brings home HIV/AIDS?
- In what way will the "Francis effect" actually have an impact on men in the hierarchy, leaders in parish communities, and husbands in families, and transform them to become more compassionate and humble learners?

These are just some of the questions that "ewes" are raising. African women continue to wait to be asked to share their opinions and, indeed, be deeply regarded and listened to so that the Spirit of God might make this voice heard. Short of episodic tokenism, African women have not been given the opportunities to fully express themselves and their desire for fullness of life as God-given gifts. I contend that to listen to the voice of women is to heed the *sensus fidelium.*

Francis's understanding of *sensus fidelium* opens a path toward dialogue with women in Africa and in the world church. In Francis's perspective, "As part of his mysterious love for humanity, God furnishes the totality of the faithful with an instinct of faith—*sensus fidei*—which helps them to discern what is truly of God. The presence of the Spirit gives Christians a certain connaturality with divine realities, and a wisdom which enables them to grasp those realities intuitively, even when they lack the wherewithal to give them precise expression" (*EG*, no. 119). Being the other half of the human race, women are ready to bring their chairs to the table of conversation and dialogue, and to express their opinions. In the interest of acknowledging the fullness of the *sensus fidelium*, it is time for the "fathers" in the church to listen to their mothers, to their daughters, and to their grandmothers. This act of humble listening is imperative if the voice of the Spirit is to be heard in its fullness. Listening is not an act of charity. As Elochukwu Uzukwu has demonstrated beyond doubt, listening is constitutive of a church that is constantly attuned and open to receiving what the Spirit says to the church. Listening with compassion, mercy, and humility is an indispensable mark of the church.

As a practical suggestion for listening to the voice of women, I would recommend to the pope to initiate hearings on issues that matter wherein women's voices could be heard without fear of reprisals—a synod of women, for women, and by women, where women speak from the depths of their experiences and voice their dreams and aspirations for a church that recognizes, honors, and receives their gifts for the edification of the body of Christ. Such forums might contribute to some fundamental attitudinal change. It is fair to hope that the Francis effect will lead to change for African women. A necessary prerequisite would be the elimination of entrenched patriarchal attitudes and mind-sets. Only the Spirit of God can effect this change.

On listening as a mark of the church, Francis intuitively knows what he—and the church—must do. In his own words, "We need to practice the art of listening, which is more than simply hearing. Listening, in communication, is an openness of heart which makes possible that closeness without which genuine spiritual encounter cannot occur. Listening helps us to find the right gesture and word which shows that we are more than simply bystanders" (*EG*, no. 171). Only a church that is awake can engage in listening with an open heart.

An African proverb says: "When a sleeping woman wakes, mountains move." As Francis declared in his speech at a Nairobi slum: "I also appreciate the struggles of those women who fight heroically to protect their sons and daughters from these dangers. I ask God that that the authorities may embark, together with you, upon the path of social inclusion, education, sport, community action, and the protection of families, for this is the only guarantee of a peace that is just, authentic and enduring."[11] African women do not accept poverty as their lot. Across the continent, African women are rising from their slumber, and the church ought to take heed. African women are ready to move mountains, the church included!

---

[11] Hunter-Gault, "African Women and the Struggle against Poverty."

"If You Want Cows, You Must Sleep Like a Cow"

The Bishop in the Church of Pope Francis

Bishop Antoine Kambanda

In the effort to evangelize Africa today, theologians and pastors have to take into consideration the life and the culture of the people in a world that is changing rapidly and becoming more and more complex.

Africa was first evangelized by missionaries from Europe, and for a long time the theology of evangelization was (and still is) heavily influenced by Western culture. But the crisis of faith—a challenge to evangelization—is even stronger in Western society, in which the traditional approach can hardly address the mind-set of the people today. For this reason, the church has to find new ways and means for an adequate evangelization, as the society today does not easily accept the message of the gospel of salvation. The challenge of evangelizing our society today is not an African problem only but a concern for the whole church.

In Africa, we are called to see if in our cultural resources we can find the wisdom that will enable us to touch the hearts of the people to evangelize them. We need to make the gospel feel at home in Africa so Christianity will no longer be considered a foreign religion. African theologians are called to bring forward the African cultural values and life experiences that can contribute to an adequate communication of the message on the continent. Pastoral experiences and best practices from African Christian communities, in their efforts to live the gospel in different and challenging situations, can be shared and be useful even to the universal church.

In these efforts for evangelization today, we are not alone because the Spirit of the Lord is with us. Jesus Christ said, "Go, therefore, make disciples of all nations; baptize them in the name of the Father and of the Son and of the Holy Spirit, and teach them to observe all the commands I gave you. And look, I am with you always; yes, to the end of time" (Matthew 28:19–20 NAB). The church is guided by the Holy Spirit, and this can be seen in the history of the church when it survived difficult periods and resolved crises inside and outside the divine institution.

Sometimes, from the human point of view, one would think the church would not survive such crises, but the Spirit has guided it through the storms of history and enabled it to continue its mission in the world until today. However, it requires a theological reading of the history of the church to see the hand of God in the guidance of the church. This is the foundation of our optimism that always confirms us in faith and gives us hope to continue courageously despite the tribulations and contradictions the church has met and will continue to meet.

The Situation of the Church Today

Recent church history has been characterized by a general decline in the number of practicing Catholics and of vocations, especially in the old Christian countries. Churches, seminaries, and convents are closing. Even in the young Christian countries, where there is thirst for God and spiritual enthusiasm, the increasing number of sects and new, different religious confessions pose some challenges. The sects attract many Catholics, especially the youth, who thus abandon the Catholic Church. Some Christians are becoming indifferent to the practice of faith and are preoccupied with business or other interests. Others engage in some degree of syncretism; they practice the Christian faith but continue their traditional religions. This occurs particularly when they face problems such as sickness or other dangers that drive them to seek security in traditional practices.

Political instability that generates violent conflicts and as a consequence poverty and misery in many African countries is a serious challenge to the good news of salvation. Africa is like that man in the gospel who, on his way from Jericho to Jerusalem, fell into the hands of the brigands who left him half-dead on the road.[1] The gospel must be presented in a way that responds to the needs of peace, justice, reconciliation, and development so it can propose a relevant salvation in these situations. Above all, it requires the credibility of the agents of evangelization.[2]

---

[1] Pope Benedict XVI, *Africae Munus*, no. 9.
[2] Pope John Paul II, *Ecclesia in Africa*, no. 21.

In the last few years, the church has faced a difficult period due particularly to scandals some clerics were involved in. The media clearly amplified them in an attempt to damage the image and credibility of the church. It seems there was an interest in undermining the moral authority of the church, which often contradicts the moral disorder in our society today that goes as far as justifying, legitimating, and even legalizing morally contentious practices such as abortion, euthanasia, divorce, homosexuality, and so on. The scandals in the church, widely disseminated in the media, were a shock and a humiliation for the priests and the faithful alike. They caused serious harm and damage to people who put their trust in the church and its pastoral personnel. This also intensified serious critics of some of the church's activities, traditions, and values.

It was during this time that Pope Benedict XVI surprised people by resigning, something no pope has done for the last 450 years. So many speculations followed. Some thought the church's situation was so critical that the pope had to resign. Many Catholics, especially in Africa, were perplexed and did not know what to say, while some sects were commenting that it was the end of the church because the pope had resigned. Today we see that it was the providential guidance of the Holy Spirit in the church that brought Pope Francis to the leadership of the church.

A New Spirit in the Church with Pope Francis

The Holy Spirit, who guides the church, had a good surprise for us in the person of Pope Francis, who came in at the right time. Pope Benedict, taking into consideration the situation that required the renewal of church life, prepared a synod for the new evangelization. The Spirit of the Lord had prepared Pope Francis to come in when the situation was ripe and start the new evangelization. Many expected a young pope who spoke many languages. This was not the case with Pope Francis. But from the time he started his pontificate, he brought a new spirit to the church. Less than a year after he became pope, St. Peter's Square was too small for the ever-growing crowd of Christians and even non-Christians who came to see him and listen to his teaching.

The pessimistic spirit in the church shortly before his election gave way to a new era of enthusiasm and hope. This does not mean he has solved all the problems of the church; it still faces problems, but he drew people out of consideration of particular problems and widened their horizons. He comes from a Third World country with its own problems, but this does not take away Christians' joy and hope in Christ. Pope Francis insists we should not close in on ourselves but should always come out of ourselves, out of our problems, structures, and bureaucracies. He recommends that we "go out to others, seek those who have fallen away, stand at the crossroads, and welcome the outcast."[3]

But has Pope Francis really brought a fundamental change in the practice of authority and leadership in the church, or is this mere rhetoric? In the efforts for the new evangelization, how is the role of the bishop changing in the church led by Francis? This is the question I want to answer. The responsibility of the bishop today is quite challenging. So first of all Pope Francis reminded bishops and all evangelizers to listen—to listen to and allow the Holy Spirit to guide their creative efforts and initiatives. He said:

> How I long to find the right words to stir up enthusiasm for a new chapter of evangelization full of fervor, joy, generosity, courage, boundless love and attraction! Yet I realize that no words of encouragement will be enough unless the fire of the Holy Spirit burns in our hearts. A spirit-filled evangelization is one guided by the Holy Spirit, for he is the soul of the Church called to proclaim the Gospel. Before offering some spiritual motivations and suggestions, I once more invoke the Holy Spirit. I implore him to come and renew the Church, to stir and impel her to go forth boldly to evangelize all peoples.[4]

Bishops have to be attentive to what the Spirit tells them and at the same time listen and observe the work of the Spirit in members of the church—theologians, priests, religious, and faithful alike—so they can lead the community of the faithful in fulfilling the will of God. *Episcopos* in Greek means "overseer" or "surveyor," one who keeps watch over the flock so the proclamation of the Word of God might go on effectively. The bishop must lead the way. In a speech to the congregation of the bishops, Pope Francis spoke of the leadership the people of God need:

---

[3] Pope Francis, *Evangelii Gaudium*, no. 24.
[4] Ibid., no. 261.

The holy People of God continues to speak: we need one who will watch over us from above; we need one who will see us with the fullness of God's heart; we do not need a manager, a chief executive officer of a company, nor one who remains at the level of our pettiness and little pretensions. We need someone who knows how to raise himself to the heights of God's gaze over us in order to lead us to him. Our future lies in God's gaze.[5]

There is no doubt Pope Francis brought a new spirit to the church. Particularly, he is renewing the concept and the exercise of leadership of a bishop in the church today. In a short time, Pope Francis has revealed so many qualities of a pastor that cannot be exhausted in a chapter, so I will limit myself to writing about three of his pastoral qualities: his compassion, his particular love and concern for the poor, and his pastoral work for the people.

Compassion

Today, the church needs pastors with compassionate hearts, and this is what Pope Francis is showing us in his pastoral ministry; it has enabled him to touch the hearts of so many Christians and even non-Christians. When he sees a handicapped person in a wheelchair in St. Peter's Square, he leaves the popemobile and bends down to bless the person. In 2013, on Holy Thursday, he washed and kissed the feet of twelve young prisoners in Casal del Marmo prison in Rome.[6] Later that year, when a boat of immigrants drowned off the coast of Lampedusa, he visited the island and threw a wreath of flowers in the sea as a sign of his mourning and compassion for the poor people who had lost their lives while seeking a better life in Europe.[7] That is the spirit of compassion the church today needs.

Pope Francis observed that there is a kind of insensibility and indifference to the suffering of the people today. He said:

Almost without being aware of it, we end up being incapable of feeling compassion at the outcry of the poor.[8] We need to practice

---

[5] Pope Francis, "Address to the Congregation of Bishops," February 27, 2014.

[6] *Catholic Herald*, March 28, 2013.

[7] *The Guardian*, July 8, 2013.

[8] Pope Francis, *Evangelii Gaudium*, no. 54.

the art of listening . . . to find the right gesture and word which shows that we are more than simply bystanders. Only through such respectful and compassionate listening can we enter on the paths of true growth and awaken a yearning for the Christian ideal: the desire to respond fully to God's love and to bring to fruition what he has sown in our lives.[9]

In Rwanda, after the genocide perpetrated against the Tutsi, we faced a very difficult situation. The genocide was committed by Rwandans against fellow Rwandans; they were people they grew up with, neighbors, schoolmates, teachers who taught them, catechists who prepared them for the sacraments, priests and religious who evangelized them, and even in-laws, cousins, and uncles in ethnically mixed marriages.

After the genocide, the survivors and the families of the perpetrators had to live together side by side as they could not do otherwise. It was a very complex and tense situation. We had to forge a new way of doing pastoral work in these communities to find the way for reconciliation and forgiveness that is a prerequisite for any community life.

This complex pastoral work coincided with the jubilee of 2,000 years of Christianity and 100 years of the evangelization of Rwanda. In the context in which the church in Rwanda was, we could not just celebrate the jubilee as others were doing after a genocide in which more than a million people were killed and a great number of the people who committed these crimes were baptized Christians who had killed fellow Christians. We thought of a way of living this important historical event of the universal church that could bear pastoral fruit in our particular context. The church in Rwanda decided to mark the jubilee with a synod on ethnic division and conflict in our society to make an examination of conscience and an assessment of the centenary of evangelization.

People in small Christian communities could sit down and share stories of their suffering. Everyone was suffering—victims and perpetrators alike. By listening to the suffering of others without judging, you come to understand their suffering; you put yourself in the place of the suffering and suffer with them; you suffer for them. In this way, you are moved to compassion, and this facilitates forgiveness and reconciliation. As a matter of fact, in

---

[9] Ibid., no. 171.

the Kinyarwanda language, the word for forgiveness is *kubabarira*[10] which means to suffer because of the suffering of another. It is taking upon oneself others' suffering, empathizing with them, and having mercy on them.

In a way, we see this experience of the relationship between compassion and conversion in the gospel. The reaction of the second criminal on the cross showed that the man had compassion for the suffering of Jesus, who was innocent and had been unjustly condemned to die on the cross. This compassion was the basis for his miraculous salvation in the last moment of his life. He put aside his own suffering and empathized with Jesus on the cross; he said to his fellow criminal,

> "Have you no fear of God, for you are subject to the same condemnation? And indeed, we have been condemned justly, for the sentence we received corresponds to our crimes, but this man has done nothing criminal." Then he said, "Jesus, remember me when you come into your kingdom." He replied to him, "Amen, I say to you, today you will be with me in Paradise." (Luke 23:40–43 NAB)

Compassionate listening has helped the Christian community avoid the spiral of violence and develop a degree of forgiveness and reconciliation. It also facilitated justice, because the Christians, who repented for their crimes in their communities, were encouraged to confess in the courts.[11] These courts, inspired by the Rwandan traditional system of justice, aimed not only at justice but also at reconciliation. So this pastoral work of the church in Rwanda has contributed a lot to the reconstruction of the country in the last twenty years.

In the new spirit of the pontificate of Pope Francis, a bishop should take time to listen with compassion to his people. When those who suffer feel their voices are heard, they experience healing and will be well disposed to

---

[10] *Kubabarira*, "to forgive," comes from the verb *kubabara*, which means "to suffer," and *ubabarira* literally means "to suffer for another person who suffers" or "to take upon oneself the suffering of the other."

[11] After the genocide in Rwanda, there were more than 120,000 prisoners waiting for justice, and it was calculated that it would take more than 110 years for ordinary, classic courts to judge these cases, yet there were still others suspected of the same crimes. This means that many would die without having justice, so the government organized these traditional community courts, *Gacaca* courts, to solve the problem.

receive the Word of God. Such a heart becomes fertile ground for the seed of the Word of God to take root and bear abundant fruits in the life of those people and the community.

Love and Concern for the Poor

The second pastoral quality that characterizes the pontificate of Pope Francis is his emphasis on the privileged place of the poor in the church. A pastor should identify, meet, love, and serve Christ in the poor.

> God's heart has a special place for the poor, so much so that he himself "became poor" (2 Cor 8:9). The entire history of our redemption is marked by the presence of the poor. . . . The Savior was born in a manger, in the midst of animals, like children of poor families. . . . When he began to preach the Kingdom, crowds of the dispossessed followed him, illustrating his words: "The Spirit of the Lord is upon me, because he has anointed me to preach good news to the poor" (Lk 4:18). He assured those burdened by sorrow and crushed by poverty that God has a special place for them in his heart: "Blessed are you poor, yours is the kingdom of God" (Lk 6:20); he made himself one of them: "I was hungry and you gave me food to eat," and he taught them that mercy towards all of these is the key to heaven (cf. Mt 25:5ff.).[12]

Our faith as well as its expression in pastoral work is essentially related to the way we welcome the poor in the church because "there is an insep-arable bond between our faith and the poor."[13] If people are leaving the Catholic Church for other faith communities today, it is often because of "lack of pastoral care among the poor, the failure of our institutions to be welcoming, and our difficulty in restoring a mystical adherence to the faith in a pluralistic religious landscape."[14] The commitment to the care of the poor purifies our church of a worldly mentality and corruption. When we are with the poor, we are sure of an authentic pastoral life because we are continuously in touch with Christ, who suffers with the poor. For this

---

[12] Pope Francis, *Evangelii Gaudium*, no. 197.
[13] Ibid., no. 48.
[14] Ibid., no. 70.

reason, the church has a preferential option for the poor. Pope Francis said, "This option—as Benedict has taught—'is implicit in our Christian faith in a God who became poor for us, so as to enrich us with his poverty.' This is why I want a Church which is poor and for the poor."[15]

In the search for a new way of evangelizing our society today, we can learn much from the poor. Because of their closeness to Christ, the poor have a share in Christ's suffering; they are members of the body of Christ who suffer and call for our love and service.

> The new evangelization is an invitation to acknowledge the saving power at work in their lives and to put them at the centre of the Church's pilgrim way. We are called to find Christ in them, to lend our voice to their causes, but also to be their friends, to listen to them, to speak for them and to embrace the mysterious wisdom which God wishes to share with us through them.[16]

Our care and concern for the poor make the gospel today credible and show its relevance to salvation. We need to esteem and value the poor in their dignity as a special image of Christ and particular friends of God. They should be made to feel at home in our Christian communities; we should ensure for them the necessary religious services and spiritual care in our pastoral work. They are usually people with hearts open to God, and we can enrich their faith lives. Pope Francis affirmed,

> Without the preferential option for the poor, the proclamation of the Gospel, which is itself the prime form of charity, risks being misunderstood or submerged by the ocean of words which daily engulfs us in today's society of mass communications.[17]

Given the central place of the poor in the church, nobody is exempt from the responsibility to give special attention and pastoral care to the poor.[18]

---

[15] Ibid., no. 198. "Address at the Inaugural Session of the Fifth General Conference of the Latin American and Caribbean Bishops" (May 13, 2007) 3, *AAS* (*Acta Apostolicae Sedis*): 99 (2007): 450.

[16] Pope Francis, *Evangelii Gaudium*, no. 198.

[17] Ibid., no. 199; Pope John Paul II, *Novo Millennio Ineunte*, no. 303.

[18] Pope Francis, *Evangelii Gaudium*, no. 201.

Among the poor, women are particularly vulnerable. They need our attention and care in the church.[19] Women are not only victims of poverty and misery; they are also often exposed to exploitation and violence. During wars and violent conflicts, they are exposed to tragic abuse and humiliation. In many parts of Africa, particularly in Rwanda and the Great Lakes Region, women suffered the torture of rape and bearing children due to this torment. They still have to bring them up with motherly love and care, which can be a very serious trial, a cross to bear. Bringing to such people the good news of salvation is very challenging pastoral work that requires creativity, compassion, and expertise.

In these troubled areas, many women are widows or have husbands in prison, so they take on full responsibility for their families.[20] We must not forget that women are the majority of the dedicated servants of the church. In the book Cardinal Francis Arinze wrote on the office of the bishop, he made a collection of the expectations of the people for their bishop when a new bishop was appointed to a diocese. Concerning women, one of the messages read,

> I ask the bishop to realize that most of the workers in this parish are women, and we work very diligently and care very much for our church. But we ask one question of him: we ask him to consider us as part of the church and move to overcome the sin of sexism.[21]

Pastoral Work Close to the People

The third pastoral quality that Pope Francis displays for the new era of evangelization is that of a bishop who goes out and reaches the people. The pastor must be close to the sheep and even "take on the smell of the sheep."[22] Then the sheep will identify themselves with him and listen to him willingly. As a Rwandan proverb puts it, "If you want cows, you must sleep like a cow." A good pastor must be close to his sheep and lead their life such that where they sleep, he can also sleep. This traditional wisdom helps us understand

---

[19] Ibid., no. 212.

[20] This is particularly the case in Rwanda. The genocide perpetrated against the Tutsi in 1994, during which more than a million people were killed, created a situation of many widows and orphans and thousands of prisoners condemned for the killings.

[21] Francis Arinze, *Our Bishop, Reflections on the Office of the Bishop in the Church* (Nairobi: Paulines Publication Africa, 2012), 24.

[22] Pope Francis, *Evangelii Gaudium*, no. 24.

and explain the logic of the theology of incarnation. Jesus came so close, to to the point of sharing our lives and history, to bring us salvation.

This pastoral work, which draws one close to the people, was expressed in the first special assembly of the Synod of Bishops for Africa. The synod, in the spirit of inculturation, opted for the image of "the church as God's family" as its guiding idea for the evangelization of Africa.[23] The church as a family of God, whereby the bishop in a particular church is a father representing the paternity of God, suits well the African culture and responds to the needs of close pastoral work.

To put into practice this pastoral option, the church in Africa adopted the pastoral work of small or basic Christian communities and tried to develop them in the spirit of a family. As Joseph Healey shows in his essay in this volume, through the pastoral work of basic Christian communities, the church comes close to the people. Basic Christian communities live a closely related life. In Rwanda, after the genocide, there were so many orphans and children without any family. Basic Christian communities made new families in which new family relations were created. This also helped in the integration of foreigners and others, who are far from their families, to feel at home in the new communities of faith. The Kinyarwanda word for basic Christian communities is *umuryangoremezor,* literally, "a basic family"; in other words, the family of believers and the spirit of the family are emphasized and enriched.

The real work of reconciliation takes place in these basic Christian communities. It is here that the stories of the suffering of the people are shared, and this promotes forgiveness and reconciliation. Close, pastoral work is conducted in these communities, and they call for the active participation of every member.

Different ministries and responsibilities are shared by members of the community as a family. There is the ministry of leadership, evangelization, catechism, and promotion of vocations. There is the ministry of the liturgical celebrations and prayers. There is the ministry of care of the sick, the poor, and the needy inside and outside the community. There is the ministry for justice, peace, management of conflicts, and reconciliation. Then there is the ministry for development of the community and providing the means for pastoral services. All these services are conducted in a family spirit, and

---

[23] Pope John Paul II, *Ecclesia in Africa*, no. 63.

the more this spirit grows, the more the community becomes stronger in faith and efficient and effective in evangelization.

The image of the shepherd who "takes on the smell of the sheep" sums up the fundamental change Pope Francis brought to the concept of the bishops' leadership. A bishop should be a shepherd who walks ahead of his sheep to show them the way. But he should also walk in the midst of his sheep to become one with them. As Saint Augustine wrote, "To you I am a Bishop, but with you I am a Christian. The first is an office, the second a grace; the first a danger, the second, salvation."[24]

The bishop walks behind his sheep as well to protect them and make sure the weak are not left behind.

> Often it is better simply to slow down, to put aside our eagerness in order to see and listen to others, to stop rushing from one thing to another and to remain with someone who has faltered along the way.[25]

In his address to the participants in a course for new bishops, Pope Francis said,

> Be welcoming Pastors . . . journeying with your people, with affection, with mercy, with sweetness of expression and paternal firmness, with humility and discretion, being able to see your own limitations, and with a good sense of humor . . . and remain with your flock![26]

This is the new spirit of Pope Francis that should guide bishops to renew the concept and the exercise of leadership in the church.

---

[24] Saint Augustine, *Sermo* 340, 1: *PL* 38, 1438.
[25] Pope Francis, *Evangelii Gaudium*, no. 46.
[26] *L'Osservatore Romano*, September 19, 2013.

Part Two
Critique of Theological Methodology and Ecclesial Practice

Truly African, Fully Christian?

In Search of a New African Christian Spirituality

Laurenti Magesa

The American theologian David Tracy describes the time we live in as "an age that cannot name itself." Traditionalists, modernists, and postmodernists, he says, all have different interpretations of the present moment in history as well as different expectations of and from it: "These three conflicting namings of the present situation are at the heart of the conflict of interpretations [of the current era]." They affect perceptions of both culture and Christian theology.[1] While Tracy notes he is describing the situation in the Western world, I contend that the condition of uncertainty is global and that its symptoms and impact on the African continent and church are inescapable.

Indeed, one of, if not the most striking feature of, the various dimensions of existence in Africa today is complexity brought about by a sense of overriding self-doubt induced by the experience of rapid change. Current developments belie former unequivocal perceptions of life aspirations. Multiple visions and interpretations of reality manifestly characterize contemporary African life, often bringing about contradictory value-goals. These opposing expectations and goals are immediately present to many as real choices thanks to modern information and communication technology (ICT). ICT has made the phenomenon we call globalization a fact of African life as well.

Emerging worldwide in a new way since the last several decades of the last century, the globalization movement has bred a state of uncertainty that deeply affects the ways people view themselves and the world and everything in it. Empirically, globalization involves an inevitable but generally desta-

---

[1] David Tracy, *On Naming the Present: God, Hermeneutics, and Church* (Maryknoll, NY: Orbis Books, 1994), 3.

bilizing, rapid, and relatively unrestrained social, economic, political, and cultural exchange. It facilitates easy mobility "of people, products, plants, animals, technologies and ideas,"[2] including negative environmental conditions around the globe. On account of this, on the social and theological levels, old claims to certain clearly defined identities are now radically challenged so that in Africa the puzzle of whether we are "truly African" at the same time as we are "fully Christian" has increasingly taken on new urgency no longer as a theoretical conjecture but as a disturbing reality. And "in the process of trying to be both Christian and African, where do we put other religions," specifically Islam?[3]

Amid the multiple social and religious identities that confront us and claim our allegiance in this politically and economically multipolar and polycentric but nonetheless intimately interconnected universe, who we "really" are is a question whose answer is by no means straightforward.

In Africa, there are few if any who in one way or another do not feel overwhelmed by it. Globalization has taken our "innocence" away, so to speak, and like everyone else, Africa stands naked to the world. Our old and neat but now clearly simplistic assertions of exclusivity in relation to our African or Christian identities are confounded. Concerning these, a new quest is under way.

Theological Issues at Stake

Pope Paul VI openly and directly encouraged the quest for a new identity in the Catholic Church in Africa in the 1960s. On July 31, 1969, during a visit to Uganda, he declared to the bishops of Africa assembled in Kampala, "You [Africans] may, and you must, have an African Christianity." About ten years later, on May 3, 1980, Pope John Paul II affirmed the same to Africa through the bishops of the Democratic Republic of Congo (DRC, then Zaire): "You desire to be at the same time fully Christian and fully African,"[4] he insisted.

---

[2] See Wayne Ellwood, *The No-Nonsense Guide to Globalization* (London: New Internationalist, 2001).

[3] This question was raised by African feminist theologian Mercy Amba Oduyoye as a rejoinder to this presentation on August 16, 2013, at the Hekima Institute of Peace Studies and International Relations (HIPSIR), Nairobi, Kenya.

[4] For a collection of extracts of some of the major papal pronouncements on this issue, see http://afrikaworld.net.

Since then, there have been numerous similar public calls by different actors in the church, including African and Africanist theologians. Underlying the issue is the quest for identity. One might say that this quest perhaps encapsulates the deepest aspirations of the entire African church. But what does "African Christianity" mean in practice? Is it merely a new version of African traditional religion?[5]

Furthermore, after so many years of pastoral guidance and theological reflection, one wonders if the "road map" to Christian self-identity in Africa is sufficiently clear. The story of Africa's encounter with Western Christianity, especially since the end of the nineteenth century, still makes this an extremely complex question, the noted attempts to address it notwithstanding. Thus, progress in the process often theologically referred to as inculturation or incarnation—the effort to transform the content and implications of the Christian faith to become comprehensively the "culture" of African Christians—is, in the opinion of some, agonizingly slow. For whatever historical, sociological, and psychological reasons, there may be a basic and general reluctance in the church in Africa to become culturally both Christian and African. This process calls for some painful but necessary concrete steps to reach the goal of authentic self-identity in the church.

Bluntly put, they consist in the demand to deconstruct or break down many historically established mental, social, theological, and attitudinal notions and structures that control life, including Christian life, in Africa to reconstruct them anew in what will be a different form but one intrinsically and radically faithful to the original. Although this may appear at first to be paradoxical or even self-contradictory as a proposal for a way forward, it is in essence the only way to realize the theological and pastoral aspiration of inculturation as a requirement for an authentically African church.

Deconstruction and reconstruction constitute the current vocation of the church in Africa: it is a process that leads to a new way of being truly African and fully Christian. In a real sense the church in Africa must be "no longer truly African, not fully Christian" in the old way to become "at the same time fully Christian and fully African." The process requires an act of the almost sacrilegious destruction of certain time-honored conceptions of

---

[5] A query by one of the participants in the colloquium in which this presentation was given, on August 16, 2013, at HIPSIR.

both Africanness on the one hand and Christianity on the other to regain them anew in a more appropriate contextual manner.

The radical counsel of the Lord on true discipleship is pertinent here as a biblical metaphor for this process: "Whoever wants to save his life will lose it; but whoever loses his life for me will find it" (Matthew 16:25; John 12:24, 3:3, NIV). The loss and gain of life that Jesus is depicted as talking about here is exactly the kind symbolized and realized by his death and resurrection. The fundamental theological point these christological events make is that Jesus' death was not a total destruction, an absolute break with, or complete dissociation from his earthly life. Nor did his bodily resurrection imply the reception of a totally different body than his historical one. Jesus rose from death with a new body in the sense that the same body had been transformed. This is to say that despite, or even because of, the apparent destruction of his earthly body, there remained an essential link and continuity between it and his glorified body in heaven.

As with Jesus, so will it be with us humans; the newness of our resurrected bodies will be, indeed, the fundamental mark of our new way of being with God in heaven. But this is a qualitative rather than a fictitious newness, one constructed as though from nothing. God never destroys, but "saves" or transforms what God has created (see Romans 8:19–22).[6] The "new earth" we await at the end of time is this very earth transformed. In terms of inculturation and Christian self-identity, therefore, the new Christianity emerges from an intricate process of synthesis between the centuries-old Christian understandings (or traditions) of the liberating work of Jesus Christ and the African people's equally time-honored, God-given cultural ways of being. The new Christianity refers to the life of faith of the selfsame African Christian transformed and renewed to become not merely a Christian *in* Africa but truly a Christian *of* Africa, an African Christian.[7]

---

[6] In a homily preached at Hekima Jesuit School of Theology, Nairobi, Kenya, on Sunday, April 28, 2013, Deacon Ablam Atsikin, referring to Revelation 21:1, distinguished between the biblical usage of the terms *kainos* and *neos* to imply qualitative newness and newness as though ex nihilo respectively. According to Atsikin, the seer's vision of "a new heaven and a new earth" means that "despite the discontinuities, the new cosmos will be an identifiable counterpart . . . [of] the old cosmos and a renewal of it, just as the body will be raised without losing its former identity. . . . But renewal does not mean that there will be no literal destruction of the old cosmos, just as the renewed resurrection-body does not exclude a similar destruction of the old."

[7] For this fundamental distinction in Christian identity, see (with reference to

This is no easy task. It is one marked by uncertainty, but uncertainty is in this case not necessarily a liability but an act of hope, as the American missiologist John C. Sivalon describes it. Potentially, it bears a chain of blessings: faith, contemplation, discernment, imagination, and creativity. According to Sivalon, "The gift of uncertainty generates the gift of change and growth. And, most important, the gift of uncertainty grounds our mission within the Mission of God."[8] Thus, the process of finding ourselves as truly African and fully Christian may be founded on the blessing of uncertainty, one that calls for imagination and creativity and grateful, graceful acceptance of growth-inducing change. Above all, uncertainty might help anchor the process of inculturation or authentic African Christian identity in the mystery of the incarnation of Jesus Christ who, as God become human, is the image of true human identity.

The mystery of the incarnation at its core involves death that leads to life, or seeming defeat that brings about solid triumph in the resurrection. The incarnation as the prototype of true identity is a matter of "breaking boundaries."

Since human understandings and interpretations of the gospel are necessarily bounded by forms of situatedness that inform and limit human experience, a fuller appreciation of infinite divine revelation demands the exercise of a dynamic, spiral-like hermeneutics, one that continually tries to transcend local circumscriptions and circumspections. This requires openness, the sort that is the hallmark of true religion or true gospel Christianity. Current understandings of the gospel should never be considered absolute, and neither should cultural categories in which the gospel is and must be understood.

When given expressions of the gospel in their limitations and possibilities encounter specific local realities with their own limitations and possibilities, both must be allowed to expand and break at the seams. Otherwise, Christian identity will be warped, artificially restricted, and fossilized.

Handled with confident faith in God's Spirit working in and through the church and in the world in general, the current crisis of uncertainty is a

---

Asia) Aloysius Pieris, "The New Quest for Asian Christian Identity: Guidelines from the Pioneers of the Past," *Third Millennium: Indian Journal of Evangelization* 12, no. 3 (July–September 2009): 9–28.

[8] John C. Sivalon, *God's Mission and Postmodern Culture: The Gift of Uncertainty* (Maryknoll, NY: Orbis Books, 2012), 17.

seedbed for potentially fabulous human growth. Through the opaqueness of the experience of the death of the old African and Christian identities, a new, expansive African Christian spirituality will emerge. Indeed, a new African spirituality and religious synthesis are beacons on the horizon; the search for them is the real and present task.

The Guest

The narrative of the incarnation, death, and resurrection of Jesus on which the Christian faith is anchored shows that the quest will not be easy or its exact contours predictable. There was no such certainty in the pilgrimage of Jesus on earth. At some times, the map as a whole will be fuzzy; at other times, the paths on the map will be crooked, rendering the search for a true African Christian identity messy and even agonizing, familiar as many of us are with the comfort of the seeming theological clarity of yesteryear. But in the inscrutable functioning of the Holy Spirit, this may be the only authentic path in search of ultimate truth. The goal is eschatological, just as Jesus' own was.

While the ambiguities we face should alert us to the possible and even probable pitfalls along our pilgrim road to authentic African Christian identity, they point also to immense opportunities that can be accessed only through the messy process of "discerning the spirits" (see 1 Corinthians 12). Is it not true, after all, that almost all the doctrines we hold as unquestionable went through a similar route of risk through the untidy dynamics of deconstruction and reconstruction?

At any rate, there is no reason to believe uncertainty is about to be eliminated as the way by which the growth of the church occurs. With increasing globalization, the opposite appears to be the case. The question for true and authentic African Christian identity (or inculturation) is not whether to travel the path of risk but how to handle the risks involved in the journey of how to find one's innate, God-given self-cognition and recognition as an African Christian. The obligation involves how to make present Christ's message of liberation in Africa without violence and damage to African culture and rationality.

Although globalization as a movement has many defects, it also serves to reveal, perhaps in a clearer way than ever, the rich, God-given diversity and beauty of the universe in which we find ourselves and in which we must learn to live. Human beings must try to be at home in the world as citizens of specific places even as they are simultaneously citizens of the diverse world. This is obviously not easy on account of the often contradictory demands of each; so, the danger is real that one will be neither local nor global.

However, here is where the responsibility of finding oneself lies. It is only by trailblazing through these apparent contradictions that one can be authentically local as well as global and so avoid a dangerous state of existential dichotomy such as has recently led to much violence and suffering in the world through what is popularly referred to as the clash of civilizations.

Only through deconstruction can we reconstruct who we are and what and how we want to be as African children of God and believers in Christ. Noted American theologian Robert J. Schreiter speaks of this as "the new Catholicity," a child of theological reciprocity "between the global and the local."[9] It is a Catholicity that avoids homogenizing tendencies based on a unipolar or unicentric set of experiences that are insufficiently sensitive to different local conditions and needs. This situation is challenged by the theology of liberating inculturation and the pastoral need for self-identity. Both theology and pastoral planning must be situated in a local context. If the universal can obviously not be rejected without detriment to the local, it must judiciously be incorporated into the local without running roughshod over it so that as a result, both become new.

The skill lies in the manner of integrating the local and the global for the creation of new horizons. Syncretism, which is fundamental to the process, should not necessarily be perceived as a theological and pastoral deviation. Syncretism is negative only when cultural meanings and values are not integrated and internally expanded but merely superimposed upon one another without inner coherence; it is the forced assimilation of contradictory spiritual and theological cosmologies without any attempt at fundamentally synthesizing their underlying understandings and meanings, or, on the other hand, refusing to recognize the impossibility of doing so.

However, an approach to evangelization disregarding the necessary synthesis of Christian and African cultural values and meanings will, in the long run, be hugely damaging to both Africanness and Christianity in the search for an African Christian identity. As Jesus in Matthew's gospel put

---

[9]   See Robert J. Schreiter, *The New Catholicity: Theology between the Global and the Local* (Maryknoll, NY: Orbis Books, 1997).

it, "Every scribe who has been trained for the kingdom of heaven is like a master of a house, who brings out of his treasure what is new and what is old" (Matthew 13:52).

Attention to the old and new or the global and the local is what Schreiter describes as "glocalization."[10] It demands a different way of proceeding (i.e., deconstruction) for the emergence (i.e., reconstruction) of a new, more humanizing culture. In terms of evangelization, the result is a new Catholicity, the outcome of a creative tension between the two. It is a result of mutual centripetal movements of values and meanings, processes of mutual fertilization between and among different cultures, understandings, and practices of natural revelation in Africa and special revelation through the gospel of Christ.[11]

The process involves various elements and paths. I have space to sketch only two among them, namely, language and ritual.

Beyond Information to Communication

An enlightening article by George A. De Napoli makes the fundamental point that culture is not a "reified" object existing by itself, "something that can be seen, touched, and manipulated"; rather, culture exists only in people. It is the foundation of understandings, meanings, and values whence human behaviors flow. Culture is thus primarily "in the mind and hearts of people."[12] Strictly speaking, understood as such, this should be the target of evangelization or inculturation toward transformation or conversion. The most important carrier of culture in this sense is language in its larger sense as "art, literature, music, artifacts, rituals, etc."[13]

Human beings identify themselves culturally because they employ language in these forms to communicate. Thus, people distinguish them-

---

[10] See Schreiter, *New Catholicity*, 12.

[11] Some light has been shed from the East on this. See Michael Amaladoss, "Attaining Harmony as a Hindu Christian," in *In Search of the Whole: Twelve Essays on Faith and Academic Life*, ed. John C. Haughey (Washington, DC: Georgetown University Press, 2011), 99–110, and Peter C. Phan, *Being Religious Interreligiously: Asian Perspectives on Interfaith Dialogue* (Maryknoll, NY: Orbis Books, 2008).

[12] George A. De Napoli, "Inculturation as Communication," in *Inculturation: Working Papers on Living Faith and Cultures*, ed. Arij A. Roest Crollius (Rome: Centre "Cultures and Religions"—Pontifical Gregorian University, 1987), 74.

[13] See ibid., 73–75.

selves from one another as individuals or groups specifically by the kinds of stories they tell and, in terms of cultural identity, what meanings their stories carry for a kindred group. Here the groups' foundational narratives, which may include any or all combination of the above-mentioned dimensions of language, take pride of place. Such narratives represent and shape the groups' identities and spiritualities and their relationship to one another and to God. Shifts in these stories/narratives, particularly also in how they are told, induce change in social and spiritual behavior. An indicator of the labor pains of the new spiritual creation we seek lies, therefore, in the linguistic dimension of human existence. How and for what purpose we use theological language are, therefore, questions we must pose. How do we tell God's story and, of course, as Christians, the story of Jesus in relation to our location?

Religious discourse in sub-Saharan Africa has for a long time remained unrelated to African experiential story. This accounts for the malaise of the dichotomy between Africanness and Christianity. Theological language in Africa that is incapable of following to its internal conclusion the logic and spirituality of witchcraft, polygamy, divination, traditional healing practices, and so on, except to condemn these beliefs and practices, fails miserably to engage with the African person holistically. It addresses culture as a theoretical object outside the person. But the Bible should indicate the way: the Bible is the language of "evil spirits," "demons," "angels," and "dreams," of "sons of God and daughters of men," and so on (see Genesis 6:1–4). A literal application of a Bultmannian "demythologization" principle might not serve us well.

The verbal and other symbols classically employed to explain and give meaning and direction to Africans' life aspirations inspired by the above-mentioned realities are unable to communicate, even though they may inform. Current Christian theological language abstracts itself from fundamental African experience, which is marked by a loathing of extremes that are antithetical to harmony. In particular, even as it proposes to explain it, Christian religious and theological discourse in Africa appears to pay scant attention to the breadth and depth, the complexity, of the African person's attempt to relate to the divine self-revelation in an African context. Instead of being elastic, as surely befits the complexity of God speech because it addresses an ultimately incomprehensible infinite reality, theological discourse in Africa has for the most part remained rigid and inflexible, seeing as its main purpose the streamlining, *ad extra*, of African divine-human encounters into certain predetermined categories of thought and structures of ritual called dogma. On account of this, theological discourse and the life it seeks to influence and shape have lost much of their African aesthetic character.[14]

But theology that is instrumental for holistic growth must be a form of aesthetics, one that shapes people's lives from within toward that beauty we call God. Therefore, not only logic and dogma are to be cultivated and accorded theological dignity but also art, music, religious artifacts, rituals, meditation, and contemplation. Walter J. Hollenweger alerts us to this imperative when he writes that "conceptual language" and logical "theological arguments" are not the exclusive means of communication, nor are dogmatic "definitions" or "hermeneutical analysis." Important also in Africa are "stories," "testimonies," "participatory dance," "songs," and rituals such as deliverance and "healing."[15] These are the approaches to God, expressed supremely in ritual, that most endure. Ritual is the "speechless speech" that evokes wonder and awe before what Rudolf Otto characterized as the *mysterium tremendum et fascinans*, the awe-inspiring but fascinating mystery that is God.

Scriptural language should serve as a paradigm. The Bible is predominantly a portrait, a picture of hope and laughter or disappointment and tears because this is the experience of all humanity. The story or narrative is the preferred method of theological communication there. The Bible contains simple, straightforward stories of redemption and betrayal, of faithfulness and faithlessness. It contains no mechanistic, how-to prescriptions or directives but a chain of songs of invitation to fidelity, of emotions of disappointment, and of bursts of frustration and anger.

The Bible is unique not because it is particular but because the feelings it evokes are of universal recognition and application; its narratives intimately touch the core of every man and woman—the need for liberation, healing, and other favors humans long for. One is impressed by the magnitude and

---

[14] Who could blame the Shilluk people of Sudan, therefore, for running away from missionaries who went around wearing a figure of a man fixed on a tree, a sign to the Shilluk of ultimate cruelty? See R. G. Lienhardt, "The Dinka and Catholicism," in *Religious Organization and Religious Experience*. AMA Monograph 21, ed. J. Davis (London: Academic Press, 1982).

[15] Walter J. Hollenweger, Foreword to *African Initiatives in Christianity*, by John S. Pobee and Gabriel Ositelu II (Geneva: WWC, 1998), ix.

gratuitousness of divine love just as one is equally disgusted with the human ingratitude and betrayal one encounters there. The Bible addresses the heart of everyone's elementary sense of common humanity in a very accessible manner. Biblical language is a language of Pentecost, recognizable by the most disparate of individuals and communities: "Each of us hears them in our native language!" (see Acts 2:7–11 NIV).

For the purpose of achieving an authentic African Christian spirituality, revelational and dialogical models of theology do not stand as opposites or competitors but as complementary approaches. As Hollenweger puts it, the dimensions of contemplation, participation, and compassionate solidarity "constitute a pastoral triage as old as the Acts of the Apostles but as fresh as any alert Christian community today." These constitute the essence of spiritual growth: "Where [these are] alive and well, there is hope for faith in spite of the complexity of the culture. . . . [and] we are well on the way to re-creating a living [African] Christian culture for our time."[16]

Sacred "Games" We Play

Contemplation, participation, and compassionate solidarity are acted out in ritual and worship. Ritual constitutes the sacred games (or relationships of affection) people play for the creator or other invisible forces with power over humanity. Their importance as symbols for African people and societies cannot be overemphasized. Ignatius Pambe notes:

> Members of an African society feel their unity and perceive their common interests in symbols, and it is their attachment to those symbols which, more than anything else, gives their society cohesion and persistence.[17]

Here, rituals play a special role as part of life-giving sacred language.

The African worldview of the omnipresence of forces and interrelationship between them and humanity necessitates ritual as the essence of harmony in existence. Life can be sustained only by maintaining internal harmony among the various elements of visible and invisible powers of existence

---

[16] Ibid., 139–45.

[17] Ignatius M. Pambe, "Religious Symbols, Inter Culture Communication and Change in Africa," *Service* 5&6 (1980): 20.

through ritual performance. There are rituals to revere good powers, to appease evil or angry ones, and always to try to preserve universal harmony. Still prevalent in Africa are

> rituals that celebrate the cosmic cycle of birth, death and new life; the unity of the visible with the invisible world; the sacredness of the earth; and healing rituals form part not only of indigenous people's worship but of popular religiosity.[18]

To be effective, rituals have to exude or communicate meaning in the present for the people concerned. Thus, as Ignatius Pambe cautions, "To try to formulate a symbol or ritual meaningful to all people, at all times, in all places is a form of pride that anyone interested in communication cannot afford."[19]

Rituals are theology *in* or *as* action. As the venerable Latin axiom has it, *Lex credendi lex orandi lex vivendi* (As we believe so we worship, so we live). It shortchanges African spirituality when ritual is relegated only to predetermined official settings and times, such as in a church on Sunday or even to just liturgical occasions and functions, thus separating them from their place and role as the daily bedrock of the possibility of human and universal existence, unity, and harmony. In health care, for example,

> the African does not believe in unconsecrated "medicine," wherever and however dispensed. So, an object [medicine] which lacks the "official" and "trusted" manipulator is reduced to a secular state and the sacred symbol is pushed to oblivion.[20]

The rituals accompanying quotidian human callings, such as family care, work, salutations, socialization, and so on, which African spirituality perceives as fundamentally sacred, must not be trivialized. If the home is not

---

[18] Margaret Shanthi, "Worship/Rituals," in *Dictionary of Third World Theologies,* ed. Virginia Fabella and R. S. Sugirtharajah (Maryknoll, NY: Orbis Books, 2000), 238.

[19] Pambe, "Religious Symbols," 36. He adds, "The tendency to static formulations [in the Catholic Church] by drawing symbols from medieval Christianity of Europe will be redundant antiquarianism which would not serve effective culture communication in relation to African religion and symbols."

[20] Ibid., 26.

the primary temple where human communion is forged through everyday cognition that life is lived under divine and ancestral power, no other temple will succeed in conveying the message. From the African worldview, these activities not only connect human persons with one another to construct the greater humanity, *ubuntu*; they also underline the sacred vocation of the human person to connect with the entire universe and God.

Renowned African theologian Elochukwu E. Uzukwu makes an important point drawn from the experience of some African initiated churches (AICs) of West Africa: "In times of need, [African] Christians do not ask the theoretical question about the identity of the health-generating *spirit*."[21] With gratitude, they accept healing wherever they can get it. AICs act upon this and thus expand and deepen the function of African healers in the Christian belief in the power of God the Holy Spirit by "successfully [replicating and] integrat[ing] the ministry of diviner-healers into the structures of the church."[22] In this reconstructive approach, the action of the Holy Spirit is allowed its true biblical freedom while the putative autonomous or autochthonous power of spirits in African cosmology is reined in and placed under the overarching power of the Holy Spirit. A form of Christianity, simultaneously true to Africa and to the inspiration of the gospel, is thereby born.

According to Michael Paul Gallagher, "Christian spirituality has to do with building daily bridges between the gift of God in Christ and the limited realities of each one's life-situation." That is why, as he puts it, "spirituality is the essential link between faith and culture. . . . It is the zone where . . . [Christians] opt to give attention or not to the calls of the Spirit, where they shape the quality of their Christian journey, where they protect the freedom of their hearts, and where they learn to discern wisely amid the pressures of the culture."[23] As such, spirituality is "a practical human art, for a more than human adventure [and goal]."[24] In the adventure, both culture and dogma must not be allowed to "remain 'trapped at the surface level,' alienated from

---

[21] Elochukwu Eugene Uzukwu, *God, Spirit, and Human Wholeness: Appropriating Faith and Culture in West African Style* (Eugene, OR: Pickwick, 2012), 177.

[22] Ibid., 177–78.

[23] Michael Paul Gallagher, *Clashing Symbols: An Introduction to Faith and Culture* (New York: Paulist Press, 1998), 138.

[24] Ibid.

the deepest languages of our humanity." The quest toward authentic African Christian identity calls, rather, for balance to be struck between "excessive fear" of the limitations of culture and "excessive innocence" or the uncritical trust in the accuracy of human linguistic formulations of faith in God. It calls for a "new cultural-religious synthesis."

BECOMING THE CHURCH OF THE NEW TESTAMENT

Teresa Okure

The quest for the church we want is in service to the ecclesia in Africa, which can be understood in two ways: the church in Africa as an entity, or the postsynodal apostolic exhortation of the first African synod, *Ecclesia in Africa* (*EIA*). The two are closely related; *EIA* is in service to the mission of the church in Africa; so too is *Africae Munus* (*AM*), the postapostolic exhortation of the Second African Synod. Both deal with the mission of the church in Africa, each using a New Testament (NT) text as the mantra of its theme.[1] Nonetheless, this chapter focuses on the church in Africa as an entity and examines the NT in reference to it.

The issues that define the focus of this chapter can be formulated in the following terms. The controversy about the foundation of the church appears already settled, but the debate continues around key elements of ecclesiology, in particular authority, ministry, ethics, and morality. To what extent can theology draw on the New Testament to settle some of these controversies? Does the NT offer useful solutions or is it too contextualized to be of any relevance in shaping an ecclesiology for the twenty-first century?

The foundation of the church may not be in question, but what is the church? The NT authors grappled with issues of authority, ministry, ethics, and morality in their own contexts. Are their solutions still relevant for us today, or must we discard them since this is the twenty-first century, not 70 CE, the year of the controversial official separation of the church from Judaism? If we do, how today do we address these and other controversial issues in the church?

---

[1] The First African Synod (1994), "The Church in Africa and Her Evangelizing Mission toward the Year 2000: 'You shall be my witnesses' (Acts 1:8)"; the Second (2009), "The Church in Service to Reconciliation, Justice and Peace: 'You are the salt of the earth. . . . You are the light of the world' (Matthew 5:14, 14)."

The task of this chapter is to speak to the church we want in Africa from the perspective of the NT. The assumption is that we are not yet an NT church but want to become one. The present continuous tense in the topic, "becoming," suggests this. What do we understand by the New Testament in this context? To what extent do the many African voices that have spoken on the "church we want" take into foundational consideration the core meaning of "new testament"?[2]

These are some questions for this chapter to address. Given the constraints of space, I focus my exploration not so much on how to become a New Testament church, but on the nature and character of this church and of the NT itself. This approach will hopefully shed light on our questions about the relevance or otherwise of the NT for today[3] and about the church we want to be.

What Is Church?

The central element in our discourse is church, be it the African church or the NT church. Vatican II's pivotal document on the church, *Lumen Gentium* (*LG*), described the church as the people of God: Christians, non-Christians, and atheists; it is God's gathering of alienated or sinful humanity to the divine self through Jesus Christ (no. 2). This view of the church is rooted in the NT. God reconciled to the divine self "things in heaven and things on earth, making peace," bestowing wholeness by Christ's blood on the cross (Colossians 1:20; cf. John 11:52; 12:32).[4]

---

[2] Select examples are Elochukwu Eugene Uzukwu, *A Listening Church* (Maryknoll, NY: Orbis Books, 1996); George Ehusani, *A Prophetic Church* (Ede: Provincial Pastoral Institute, 1996); Musimbi R. A. Kanyoro and Nyambura J Njoroge, eds., *Groaning in Faith: African Women in the Household of God* (Nairobi: Acton, 1996); A. E. Orobator, *The Church as Family of God: African Ecclesiology in Its Social Context* (Nairobi: Paulines, 2000); T. Okure, "The Church in the World: A Dialogue in Ecclesiology," in *Theology and Conversation: Towards a Relational Theology*, ed. J. Haers and P. De Mey, BETL CLXXII (Leuven: Leuven University Press, 2003), 393–437. Nathanael Y. Soede and Ignace Ndongala, eds., *L'Eglise en Afrique 50 ans après les Independence: Actes du Colloque de l'ATA, Nairobi, du 8–12 Nov. 2010* (Abidjan: Editions ATA, 2012); Mgr. Tharcise T. Tshibangu, *Le Concile Vatican II et l'Eglise africane: Mise en ouvre du Concile dans l'Eglise d'Afrique (1960–2012)* (Kinshasa: L'Epiphanie, 2012).

[3] In this chapter, "new testament" in lower case signifies the new covenant; in upper case, it signifies the books of the second part of the Bible, henceforth referred to as NT.

[4] All translations are by the author unless otherwise indicated.

Not only was "God in Christ reconciling the world to the divine self, not counting human sins or transgressions against them"; God also entrusted to Christ's followers "the ministry of reconciliation" (2 Corinthians 5:18–19). Today, with passion, compassion, and zeal, Pope Francis (*Evangelii Gaudium, EG*) has called all Christians back to this truth, citing his predecessors.

Other chapters of *Lumen Gentium* treat the diverse roles played by members of the church—authority, ministry, and so forth. Roles and their functionaries change; the church by nature and character remains because it is essentially God's work born of pure love (2 Corinthians 5:14, 18). Could this be why "the controversy" about "the foundation of the Church" can be considered as settled?[5]

The First African Synod adopted the NT and Vatican II's all-inclusive definition of church as God's people by choosing the family as the model for what it means to be church in Africa. African theologians and theological institutions elaborated copiously on the suitability of family as a paradigm for being church in Africa. The family in Africa is negatively known to be heavily patriarchal and androcentric, with the husband as head and boss and the wife and the children as submissive dependents. Positively (and this is where the synod put its theological and inculturation energy), family in Africa embraces all members on equal terms regardless of personal, social, religious, and other affiliations since one ancestral blood flows in all members and bonds them inseparably. The synod took

> the *Church* as *God's Family* as its guiding idea for the evangelization
> of Africa (99). The Synod Fathers acknowledged it as an expression
> of the Church's nature particularly appropriate for Africa. For this
> image emphasizes care for others, solidarity, warmth in human rela-
> tionships, acceptance, dialogue and trust. (100)[6]

---

[5] Pope Francis (*Evangelii Gaudium*, no. 12), underscores the divine nature of mission and church. For Internet resources on the biblical foundation, nature and dating of the NT church see, for instance, "The Biblical Basis of the *New Testament Church*—Bible Truth" (www.bible-truth.org); "Identifying the *Church* of the *New Testament*—Christian," (www.christiancourier.com); "What Is a *New Testament Church*? | Bible.org; "When & Where Did the *New Testament Church* Begin?" (www.bible.ca).

[6] John Paul II, *Ecclesia in Africa* (*EIA*). no. 63. The figures 99 and 100 in the citation refer to the propositions of the synod (italics original). See further Benedict XVI, *Africae Munus*, nos. 8, 15 (citing *EIA*) and 42–46.

What Is the New Testament?

What come first to mind when we think of the NT are its twenty-seven books. I see the NT as essentially a covenant, the canonical record of how the early Christians received and lived the covenant, a reality bigger than them not exhausted by their receptions, though theirs is of primary importance.

African and other scholars generally approach the NT church discourse primarily from the perspective of the book, pointing out its challenges and relevance for our times. Issues covered include concern for the poor, Christology, church structure, inculturation, youth and women empowerment, gender equality and ministry, cultural pluralism, diversity, and challenges of mission for the church in Africa.[7]

The abundant literature on it is evidence that African scholars consider the NT as still relevant for today's theological and social questions, though not much is written on moral and ethical issues. Morality is the authoritative teaching of a given body such as the church or traditional communities.[8] Ethics deals with one's personal decisions based on one's membership in a group or profession, for instance, medical ethics. Can we equally speak of Christian ethics and the Roman Catholic Church ethics in the discourse on becoming the NT church?

Our concern is with the "new testament" as a concept. A testament is a covenant, a legal deed or contract involving two parties. The Bible contains two covenants, the old and the new. Some nonfaith-based scholars want the words *old* and *new* to be dropped because they consider it as undermining

---

[7] The literature on the relevance of the NT to Africa is too numerous to be cited here. One may refer to the comprehensive bibliography of Grant LeMarquand, "Bibliography of the Bible in Africa," in *The Bible in Africa: Transactions, Trajectories and Trends*, ed. Gerald O. West and Musa W. Dube (Leiden: Brill, 2000), 631–800, available online at www.tsm.edu, with updates covering 2000–2012.

[8] Church teachings on morality that readily come to mind are Paul VI, *Humanae Vitae* (1968), and John Paul II, *Veritatis Splendor* (1993), in *The Encyclicals of John Paul II*, edited with introductions by J. Michael Miller, CSB (Huntington, IN: Our Sunday Visitor, 1996), 651–771; Pontifical Biblical Commission, *The Bible and Morality: Biblical Roots of Christian Conduct* (2008); the International Theological Commission, *In Search of a Universal Ethics: A New Look at the Natural Law* (2009); Dennis J. Murphy, MSC, ed., *The Church and the Bible: Official Documents of the Catholic Church* (Bangalore: Theological Publications in India, 2001). For African morality, see Laurenti Magesa, *African Religion: The Moral Traditions of Abundant Life* (Maryknoll, NY: Orbis Books, 1997).

the Jewish scriptures. Undergirding it is the concern of Western scholars to cope with the guilt of the Holocaust.

The Bible is essentially a Christian book, different from the Jewish scriptures. The words *old* and *new* do not exist in Jewish scriptures, an entity in itself. The church compiled the Bible by incorporating the Jewish scriptures alongside its own writings; it uses the words *old* and *new* to define and differentiate between the two parts of the book compiled for its own use, highlighting "the new" in what God has done through Jesus while seeing both covenants as God's work to be studied as a unity, with Jesus as their ultimate meaning (John 5:3).[9] To blur this point is to negate the unique significance of the new covenant. The Jewish scriptures themselves predicted the coming of a new covenant different from the old (cf. Jeremiah 31:31).

The Bible embodies an old testament or covenant and a new one. The old covenant was made on Mount Sinai (Exodus 19–24) and ratified by the blood of bullocks as communion sacrifices (Exodus 24:5–8). Its continuous reception by successive generations gave birth to the Jewish scriptures and their extra-scriptural works. The new covenant on the other hand is made and ratified in the body and blood of Jesus. Jesus himself, not the early Christians, described it as "the new covenant in my blood" (Luke 22:20). It carries with it other concepts of newness: "a new creation" (2 Corinthians 5:17) and "a new humanity" (Ephesians 2:15), both growing toward fulfillment in the new heaven and new earth (Revelation 21:1).

Our task in wanting to become a New Testament church is to identify the nature and requirements of this church as a covenanted people gathered by God to the divine self, constituted to be this new covenant church in every age, and entrusted with the mission of spreading it among all nations to the ends of the earth and till the end of time on God's terms (Matthew 28:16–20).

The receptions of this covenant by the NT authors serve as our primary resources for this undertaking. But their receptions are not a blueprint for ours, especially when we are confronted with life situations different from theirs. The gospel, Jesus of Nazareth, constitutes the ultimate and abiding yardstick for being a new testament church.

In sum, the new testament is primarily the covenant Jesus cut in his body and blood, ratified with the gift of himself as Eucharist, food, and drink unto the new and eternal life for humanity. He accomplished this once and for

---

[9] *Dei Verbum,* nos. 39–41.

all (John 19:30) by his paschal mystery, passion, death, and resurrection and entrusted to his followers of every age to keep alive among them and proclaim as good news to all humanity. He empowered them to be and do what he did by giving them the Holy Spirit.

In my view, this awareness of the new testament holds the core answer to the questions raised at the beginning and to other questions about being an NT church. It is clear at this point that I am proposing our becoming a new testament church using the New Testament as the unique resource. As the written record of receptions of the new covenant by Jesus' first disciples, the NT has a foundational character for all times. Our knowledge of Jesus and his new covenant derives from it. We learn from the sustained conscious efforts how to become a new covenant church. Though their receptions were inevitably time- and culture-bound, their responses nonetheless challenge us to make Jesus, God's gospel that transcends time and culture, the basic ingredient for becoming a new covenant church. Given its foundational and canonical nature, the NT can never become remote, old, or irrelevant for Christians of any age.

NT Church as "New Testament" Church

Jesus' first disciples were Jews; they carried their Jewish sociocultural and religious mind-set into being Christians. The Sinaitic covenant was the organizing principle and pivot of everything in Judaism. Though their efforts often fell short of the demands of the covenant, the covenant nonetheless constituted their constant reference point in life. Sirach (24:4) and Baruch (4:1) equate wisdom with the Torah. The allegorical, philosophical exegete Philo and the historian Josephus saw their works as responses to the Torah. Jesus' Jewish disciples, with their covenant-conscious background, saw the new testament as a program to be lived, not an idea to discuss, just as the Jews considered the law a rule of life.

The *shema* Israel was the pivot of the old covenant on which Israel based all its activities: "Hear, O Israel: The Lord is our God, the Lord alone. You shall love the Lord your God with all your heart, and with all your soul, and with all your might" (Deuteronomy 6:4–5 NRSV). The rabbis held that to teach the entire Torah standing on one leg, one needed only to recite this *shema*, adding that the rest was interpretation. When asked what "the greatest commandment of the Law" was (Matthew 22:37), Jesus cited this *shema* and added a second: love of neighbor as oneself.

Today, if Christians are asked about the greatest commandment, they will cite this deuteronomic provision. Jesus was asked and replied in the context of the old covenant. When he constituted the new covenant in his blood, he gave it his own new covenant law: "A new commandment I give you, that you love one another as I have loved you," adding that this love was to be the identity mark and sign of his followers (John 13:34–35). In a crucial difference, believers were to love one another, not just the neighbor (a fellow Jew), and as he and God loved us (not "as yourself"?), a love that expresses itself unsurpassably in laying down "one's life for one's friends" (John 15:13).

Just as the old covenant made Israel God's people, so the new covenant makes Jesus' followers God's children; this is the pivot of the new covenant. NT authors proclaimed in different ways this divine begetting by God. The most memorable is 1 John 1:1–3: "Think with what love God has loved us that we should be called God's children. Not only called. That is what we really are."

John's gospel proclaims that God gave all believers the enabling power to become God's children, born of God through a birth that is as real as, though different from, natural birth (John 1:12–13, 3:3–8). Because believers are God's children, they call God *Abba*, daddy, and are God's "heirs" and "coheirs with Christ" (cf. Romans 8:14–17; Galatians 4:4–6). This insight invites us to appreciate better the numerous NT references to Christians as God's children, even the new Israel, just as the Old Testament projects the Jewish people as God's chosen people.

How did NT Christians make their new covenant a program of life? The canonical gospels are testimonies of different receptions and proclamations of the life and mission of Jesus governed by the needs of the audience addressed. They helped the audience, removed as we are from the events in Jesus' lifetime, to get to know Jesus as closely as possible, love, and follow him (1 Peter 1:8–9).

Scholars have long described the Sermon on the Mount as the great charter of the kingdom comparable to the Mosaic Law. What is lacking in the scholarship are efforts to systematically identify how NT Christians made this new law a constant reference point in life as the Israelites had made theirs up to Jesus' lifetime. Jesus' Jewish contemporaries, leaders and people alike, constantly cited the law as the criterion for evaluating his messianic claims and ministry. He was finally crucified because his claim to be God's Son was a serious breach of the law punishable by death (John 19:7).

Similarly, the Christians urged and challenged one another to live according to the Christ they received (Colossians 2:6–7), making their own "the mind of Christ Jesus" (Philippians 2:5). The epistles, Acts of the Apostles, and Revelation are essentially hortatory, exhorting believers to break with sin and live the new life in Christ. Some epistles specifically mention "the new life in Christ."[10] Ephesians sums it up: "Therefore be imitators of God, as beloved children, and live in love, as Christ loved us, and gave himself up for us as a fragrant offering and sacrifice to God" (Ephesians 5:1–2 NRSV).

Living as God's children had its challenges. The greatest challenge for Jewish Christians was to surrender to the gospel and demolish their age-old, ingrained election theology, the very foundation of their Jewish covenant, and rebuild them into Christ. This required socializing with Gentile Christians as members of God's one family "built on the foundations of apostles and prophets with Christ Jesus as the cornerstone" (Ephesians 2:11–22). It is difficult for us today to appreciate what it cost the first disciples (Jew and Gentile alike) to overcome this obstacle given their inbred superiority and inferiority complexes (for example, Peter in the house of Cornelius, in Acts 10:25, 28).

Each had to accept that as God's children by God's grace given on equal terms (God's gift of the Holy Spirit, Acts 11:15–17), they were siblings of Christ and of one another. Having to share table fellowship in life, not just at the Lord's table (Galatians 2:11–14; Acts 11:3; 1 Corinthians 11:17–22) constituted their greatest social challenge.

Ordinary Christians made the transfer faster than did their leaders, for example, the nameless disciples who first preached the gospel to Gentiles in Antioch (Acts 11:19–21) and the community that formed Paul and Barnabas for their worldwide Gentile mission. A core group, the Judaizers, kept insisting on the indispensability of circumcision, the rite of initiation into the Jewish covenant (Genesis 17:9–14). Theoretically, the Council of Jerusalem settled the matter (Acts 15); in reality, it lingered on, as the activities of the Judaizers ("those of the circumcision party") who dogged Paul wherever he went, testify. (Even today, racism, ethnocentrism, sexism, and all forms of cliques continue to thrive in the church.)

---

[10] The references are many. The epistles generally include or conclude with the demands of "the new life in Christ"; see, e.g., Philippians 1:27; Ephesians 4:17–20; 2 Thessalonians 3:7; 1 Peter 1:13–3:17.

The sociocultural pressure was so great that even Peter succumbed before the circumcision party in Antioch after God showed him the light in the house of Cornelius and taught him to call nobody "unclean" (Acts 10:28, 11:3–17). Paul was forced to challenge him for failing to live according to "the truth of the Gospel" (Galatians 2:14).

To make real their theology of God's children and oneness in Christ, they replaced circumcision as the rite of initiation with baptism. Circumcision excluded women, thus making them nonlegal persons. Circumcision was so important that its exact observance superseded that of the Sabbath and Yom Kippur.[11] Yet they were courageous enough to replace it with baptism, evolving theofilial theology, social, and ministerial practices to consolidate the new rite. In place of pejorative socioreligious labels (circumcised/uncircumcised; Greeks/barbarians/Scythians [Colossians 3:11]; clean/unclean, and even dogs), they called one another brothers and sisters, followers of the Way, and Christians (Acts 11:26), in the effort to put to death the anthropological discriminations of racism, classism, and sexism believed to be transcended in Christ, in whom they formed one person through baptism (Galatians 3:25–29).

Though the old sociocultural mind-sets and worldview lingered, they consistently called one another to fix their eyes on Jesus, the author and model of their new covenant. Paul, apostle of the Gentiles, was the flag bearer of this new covenant theology, a theology he personally lived before he inculcated it in others (Philippians 3:3–13). He accepted women and Gentiles as his coworkers; his conversion to working with Gentile women first happened in the church at Philippi by a directive of the Holy Spirit (Acts 16:9–15). There, Lydia, the first convert of Europe, challenged him to live his theology of baptism; he responded positively. As a result, members of the church in Philippi became his uniquely cherished collaborators in the mission.[12]

---

[11] Philip Birnbaum, *Encyclopedia of Jewish Concepts* (New York: Hebrew Publishing, 1995), 102.

[12] See Teresa Okure, "Christ the End of the Law (Romans 10:4): Index to Paul's Conversion Experience," in *Paul Embodiment of the Old and New Testaments*; Acts of CABAN, vol. 2, ed. Luke Ijezie, Teresa Okure, and Camillus Umoh (Port Harcourt: CABAN, 2013), 26–48. See also her "Women in the Church," a paper given at the SECAM Colloquium in honor of Saints John XXIII and John Paul II, Pontifical Urbaniana University, Rome, April 24–26, 2014; available at the SECAM website.

With inclusiveness of persons went diversity of ministries born of the awareness that God was the builder of the church: "It is all God's work" (2 Corinthians 5:18); believers themselves are "God's work of art" (Ephesians 2:10); "God's building" (1 Corinthians 3:9). These ministries were charisms, gifts given by God's Spirit to different members regardless of race, class, or gender; they were not conferred by training or appointment as obtains in today's church, with all the politicking, ethnicism, and character assassination often entailed, especially when it comes to episcopal appointments.

All gifts (apostles; prophets, among whom were the seven daughters of Philip; teachers; evangelists; administrators; helpers; and so on) were in service to the community to build up the church, the body of Christ, not for self-aggrandizement (1 Corinthians 12:4–11, 28–30, 14; Romans 12:6–8; 1 Peter). Being gifts of the Spirit, every ministry was important and was to be exercised in love (Romans 12:9–13), the new covenant law, and the greatest of charisms (1 Corinthians 13).[13] Today, Pope Francis enthusiastically proclaims this foundational truth.[14]

The early church struggled with diverse temptations: the temptation to convert stewardship to ownership, countered by telling the parables of unfaithful stewards of the kingdom; they proscribed individualism and hoarding by sharing all things in common (Acts 2:42–47, 4:32–37), collecting for the needy churches, especially the church in Jerusalem (2 Corinthians 8:1–9:15); and invited one another to remember the enriching poverty of Christ for them. They discountenanced contempt for the poor (the letter of James, the parables of Lazarus and the rich fool) and warned against the temptation to return to traditional, antigospel ways of life or be misguided by seemingly pious but in reality self-demeaning spiritualities that robbed them of their new, God-given dignity and status in Christ.

Christ sufficed for all their needs since they had been incorporated into him (in whom the fullness of divinity dwells bodily) and thus exalted with him at God's right hand. Therefore, to resubject themselves for whatever reason to practices they once discarded was to pursue "mere shadows" (*kenēs apatēs,* Colossians 2:8) in place of "the substance, Christ" (Colossians 2:6–3:4).

---

[13] Rob Weber ("The Church Christ wanted") gives a diagrammatic portrayal of these gifts of the Holy Spirit, eleven, not seven; accessible online.

[14] Pope Francis, *Evangelii Gaudium,* no. 12.

In tackling these and other problems, the NT Christians made Jesus, author of the new covenant, not the church (cf. *EG*, no. 31), their yardstick. Deviations and contradictions rooted in unevangelized cultures notwithstanding (example, the anti-women sections of the Pauline letters), they nonetheless strove to focus on Christ and live by the new covenant as God's children.

The author of Ephesians considered it "a great mystery" hidden since the world's foundation but then made manifest that Jews and Gentiles were God's children by God's free gift in Christ (Ephesians 3:3–6). They challenged and prayed constantly for one another to live by this "truth of the gospel." Their new status as a new testament church carried with it a new way of life and morality in their relation with God, with one another, unbelievers, and all creation.

What Church Do We Want?

How can African theologians reposition their theologizing so that it promotes the church we want? It will be by highlighting the core meaning of the new testament and key ways the NT church sought to live this covenant. This chapter has indicated the gospel path we need to take to become the new testament church. Theology in service to the new testament church, family of God, would be one that addresses the sociocultural mind-sets and life of our people that in many ways are similar to those of NT Christians. It would equip their *sensus fidelium* to tackle faith problems as Spirit-filled people without waiting for theologians or the "church" (meaning the hierarchy) to tell them what to do.

Pope Francis defines the *sensus fidelium* as what the members of the church possess "by the gift of the Holy Spirit, the 'sense of the faith,'" "a kind of 'spiritual instinct,' which permits us to 'think with the Church' and discern what is consistent with the apostolic faith and the spirit of the Gospel."[15] This makes for mature Christians.

Without exception, all Christians by virtue of their baptism are called to be and proclaim the gospel. How consciously aware of this vocation are our people? Do our church structures (cf. *LG*, no. 3) give them opportunity to exercise their charisms in the church? Are our theologies in service to the

---

[15] Francis X. Rocca, "Sensus fidelium doesn't mean 'majority opinion,' Francis says," www.catholicherald.co.uk/, address to the International Theological Commission, December 9, 2013; www.vatican.va.

people promoting this awareness, or do we theologize for ourselves, scholars speaking to scholars? Jesus and the NT church proclaimed the gospel to ordinary people and made them participants of the proclamation.

Ecclesia in Africa, no. 3, treats "inculturation" as essential for becoming church-family of God. Any inculturation of the church not rooted in the Eucharist and its new law is in disservice to the new testament church; it remains a cultural show with gospel trappings but without substantially transforming persons and cultures.

African theologians need to make the call to be Eucharistic church,[16] anchored in the new commandment of love, the soul of their theologizing in service to the church we want to be.[17] We need to help the church hierarchy evolve new practical measures for internalizing this. This requires courageous revision of age-old church structures and the evolution of a new testament ecclesiology and Christology that serve as antidotes to those anti-gospel value systems that infiltrated the church from the empire.

Further, there is need to stay alert to the heresies of our times, especially those that originate from self-interested conceptions of human rights, individualism, and prosperity gospel. Above all, African theologians themselves need to join all God's children in the race to become new testament people, as Paul did (1 Corinthians 9:27).

The new covenant church comes alive when lived. The universal attraction of Pope Francis derives from his witness to the gospel or his Jesus-centered life. Do we truly want to become a church of the New Testament? If so, the way forward is to follow the one who himself is the new testament, "the way, the truth and the life" (John 14:6), Eucharist broken for the life of the world.

Self-giving always requires going forth. Rightly has Pope Francis reminded us that the church is "a church that goes forth" (cf. Matthew 28:16–20). Becoming a new testament church requires us to go forth with the new testament message that believers are God's children, Jesus'

---

[16] Cf. John Paul II, *Ecclesia de Eucharistia* (Vatican City: Libreria Editrice Vaticana, 2003).

[17] See Teresa Okure, "The Eucharist: A Way of Life for Jesus and the Christian according to the Scriptures," in *50th International Eucharistic Congress: Proceedings of the International Symposium of Theology: The Eucharistic Ecclesiology of Communion Fifty Years after the Opening of the Second Vatican II, 6th–9th June 2012* (Dublin: Veritas, 2013), 90–133.

siblings (John 20:17), constituted by God's grace to be Christ in the world so that through our living the new covenant, all may believe in Jesus (John 17:20–21). May we rediscover with excitement this great mystery and with renewed enthusiasm proclaim it everywhere as we march joyfully together toward becoming the new testament church we want to be.

A Theology of Christian Unity
for the Church in Africa

Elochukwu Uzukwu

In the first contribution I made to the Theological Colloquium on Church, Religion, and Society in Africa (TCCRSA), I focused on an African approach to ecclesiology rooted in the Trinitarian *perichoresis*.[1] The "Trinitarian confession" and approach to ecclesiology positively affect ecclesial theory and the sociopolitical life; they carry the potential to transform human social arrangements in a divided world and a divided church. Unlike the pre–Vatican II ecclesiological model that emerged from a pyramidal image of God, the "socio-political monotheism,"[2] the Trinitarian approach adopts an ecclesiology of the interdependence and communion of churches in imitation of the Trinitarian reciprocity (*perichoresis*). I consider probing this ecclesiological perspective the way to make a contribution to the renewal of models in African theology.

This research orientation also affects this essay on church unity. I argue that since the birthing of the church accords with the plan of the Triune God, this God of communion or reciprocity forms God's own people from the diverse peoples scattered all over the earth, people who are everywhere struggling with the demon of division symbolized in the Tower of Babel. The church as the plan of the Triune God, sacrament of the kingdom, stretches through the ages down to Abel the Just and lives and witnesses to unity in God's own world.[3] It realizes in germ, though imperfectly, the

---

[1] Elochukwu Uzukwu, "Church Family of God: Icon of the Triune God, as Listening Church and Africa's Treasure, Reinventing Christianity and the World," in *Theological Reimagination—Conversations on Church, Religion, and Society in Africa*, ed. Agbonkhianmeghe E. Orobator (Nairobi: Paulines, 2014), 211–29.

[2] Yves Congar, "Le Monthéisme politique et le Dieu Trinité," *Nouvelle Revue Théologique* 103, no. 1 (1981).

[3] See the interesting points made about the plan of God, the kingdom of God, that gathers all peoples divided when left to their own devices (symbolized by Babel) in J.

kingdom. This church struggles to live the prayer of Jesus—that it may be one.

In addressing the "Theology of Christian Unity for the Church in Africa," I note the "scandal of denominational rivalry" despite the faithful observance of "the annual Week of Christian Unity."[4] Are there new ideas African theology can generate to creatively respond to the prayer of the Lord?

African theologians and historians have pioneered research, as pathfinders to Christian unity from various denominational perspectives. Felix Ekechi,[5] Jesse Mugambi and Laurenti Magesa,[6] Ogbu U. Kalu,[7] Kwame Bediako,[8] John Mbiti, and Emefie Ikenga-Metuh,[9] and many others have made significant contributions to the discussion of unity and differentiation among the churches. Broadly speaking, these authors have written or edited books and have contributed essays that draw attention to the rivalry that has bedeviled the Christian churches. Paradoxically, the nerve center of the rivalry is within the execution of the missionary mandate—the essential component of the nature of the church, the bridge toward unity that has become the cause of division. African (Nigerian) delegates to the 1911 meeting of the Christian Council of Nigeria declared, "The great commission we have received from our Lord" is framed within the "express desire that his people should be one." They deprecated the "existence of division" among the Protestant churches "as a source of weakness."[10]

M. R. Tillard, *Church of Churches: The Ecclesiology of Communion* (Collegeville, MN: Liturgical Press, 1992), chapter 1.

[4] This is the prompt sent to me by the coordinator of TCCRSA.

[5] Felix K. Ekechi, *Missionary Enterprise and Rivalry in Igboland, 1857–1914*, Cass Library of African Studies, General Studies (London: Cass, 1972).

[6] J. N. K. Mugambi and Laurenti Magesa, eds., *The Church in African Christianity— Innovative Essays in Ecclesiology* (Nairobi: Acton, 1998).

[7] Ogbu Kalu, *Divided People of God: Church Union Movement in Nigeria, 1875–1966* (New York: NOK, 1978).

[8] Kwame Bediako, "Christian Witness in the Public Sphere: Some Lessons and Residual Challenges from the Recent Political History of Ghana," in *The Changing Face of Christianity: Africa, the West, and the World*, ed. Lamin O. Sanneh and Joel A. Carpenter (New York: Oxford University Press, 2005), 117–32.

[9] Emefie Ikenga Metuh, *The Gods in Retreat: Continuity and Change in African Religions (the Nigerian Experience)* (Enugu, Nigeria: Fourth Dimension, 1985).

[10] Kalu, *Divided People of God*, 5. Of course, Roman Catholics were not included in the council; they were the enemy.

Some African theologians argue that the indigenous religions of Africa open the wealth of the African religious cultural "values of harmony and solidarity" to provide new ideas that help engineer new ecumenical relationships in the post-missionary era of the church.[11]

Focus and Limit of this Essay

The effort of the Christian churches to realize the desire of the Lord that God's people should be one should happen not only in the intimate life of each church and each Christian with the Lord but also in the visibility of ecclesial unity under the guidance of the Holy Spirit. This primary witness to the Lord in a world being transformed by his death and resurrection is the first concern of this chapter. The wise saying of Jesse Mugambi helps clarify the direction of the visible ecclesial unity, the result of the ecumenical effort:

> A divided Church will remain scandalous to the gospel. A differentiated church will manifest the richness of human responses to the gospel, provided that the differences in ecclesiology are mutually recognized and respected.[12]

The insight of Mugambi is not new. The foundational experience of New Testament churches displays diversity that never imperiled communion, koinonia. In this essay, the New Testament canon of koinonia is the first building block in my reflection on church unity in Africa in the image of the Trinity. The dominance of koinonia enabled New Testament churches to avoid the divisiveness that the post-Reformation churches of the West introduced into most of sub-Saharan Africa through missionary Christianity.

The scandal of division is deplored because it departs from the original koinonia; this is being addressed by the churches worldwide and in particular by the churches in Africa. The ecumenical project carefully protects the richness of the differentiated denominational churches not as an encouragement or a justification of division but to display the many colors of the one church of God.

---

[11] J. N. K. Mugambi, "The Ecumenical Movement and the Future of the Church in Africa," in *The Church in African Christianity*, ed. Mugambi and Magesa, 12.

[12] Ibid., 10.

The second point I make concerns the why and wherefore of the divisiveness among churches. It is in the process of carrying out the Lord's missionary mandate of proclaiming and living the kerygma, without which the church is not church, that division became entrenched and manifest to all.

In the Buganda Kingdom, Catholics and Anglicans (even together with Muslims) were martyred (1885–87) because they preferred to witness to salvation in Christ, to integral human wholeness, rather than succumb to the immorality of the Kabaka. Why then should missionary, denominational Christianity in Uganda continue to live in such ferocious antagonism (between Anglicans and Catholics) to the point of pioneering exclusivist political parties?

Third, what should theology and pastoral practice in African Christianity do to enhance the visible unity of the divided people of God? Courageous steps were taken toward unity in the era of missionary Christianity (inspired by or even preceding the Edinburgh conference of 1910); the search for unity in evangelism led to common ecumenical tasks such as the common translation of the Bible. How should one evaluate the initiatives of the Protestant churches and the breath of fresh air introduced into ecumenical dialogue by Vatican II (*Unitatis Redintegratio*)? These initiatives and efforts of the churches confirm their openness to unity.

Finally, and in conclusion, the impact of the wider ecumenism (insight from African indigenous religions) provides new ideas for unity that should not be minimized. Drawing from the resources of indigenous religions of Africa, Christians could intensify their ecumenical efforts and take firmer steps toward realizing visible unity. The values of indigenous African religions, the hospitality they showed to the missionary religions, their nonexclusivist tone, and their readiness to accommodate could encourage Africa's Christian churches to emphasize common zones of unity.

It is important to highlight the unitive force of African indigenous religions and to recognize the authors who labored to open us up to the wealth of these hospitable religions that embody the African cultural values of harmony and solidarity. The values could facilitate ecumenical relationships in the post-missionary era.[13] They challenge Christians (and non-Christians) to mutual discussion and conversation and to move away from violence and division and embrace unity.

---

[13] Ibid., 12.

The One Church of God:
Diversity, Differentiation, and Recognition

The experience of koinonia (communion) presents the ideal of what Tillard calls the "church of churches," the one church of God fully realized in diverse locations.[14] The mutual recognition, respect of difference, singularity, or autonomy of each of the churches as they each realize fully the one church of God (*ekklesia tou Theou*) on earth capture the nature of the New Testament church built on communion. The communion "of the *Ekklesia tou Theou* scattered throughout the whole world and down through the ages" is the face or the very nature of the Catholic Church. Rather than understanding the differentiated churches in their multiplicity as the addition of many churches to form the church of God (the universal church), the true picture is that each local church (in the diocese of Jerusalem, or Lagos, or Rome) is the church of God "having its own characteristics." Consequently, "inculturation" or "contextualization" is not external to Catholicity: "It belongs to the very birth of the Church of God. It is woven into catholicity."[15]

Inculturation or contextualization is revealed in the flesh of the churches the apostles left behind, according to Raymond Brown,[16] but inculturation is not a justification for the scandal of the division of the present-day churches. The churches the apostles left behind (up and until the sub-apostolic period), whether linked to Peter, Paul, or James or closely connected to personal experience of the Lord as in the community of the Beloved Disciple, whether strongly inclined to the Jewish ritual practices (James) or expressing greater freedom in the Spirit (the Hellenists), these churches always retained koinonia and did not experience the type of divisiveness that characterized the postapostolic period and the Western Reformation.

According to Brown, there may have been disagreements between Peter, James, and Paul, but there was no break in koinonia. Indeed, one should not search the New Testament for one ecclesiology binding on all the churches, a "consistent or uniform ecclesiology," the one and only right ecclesiology besides which all the others would be wrong because this would be a

---

[14] Tillard, *Church of Churches*, 14.

[15] Ibid., 15.

[16] Raymond E. Brown, *The Churches the Apostles Left Behind* (New York: Paulist Press, 1984).

fruitless exercise. Rather, Brown insisted, the New Testament writings provide "diverse emphases" effective in "particular circumstances." These emphases are not "isolated and deemed to be sufficient for all times"; nevertheless, they collectively "constitute a remarkable lesson about early idealism in regard to Christian community life."[17]

The lesson today for the divided people of God, especially in Africa, is to appreciate the koinonia of the sub-apostolic church in its rich diversity and as source of self-interrogation, for the "diversity attested to in the New Testament could not be used to justify Christian division today."[18] Rather, they challenge each denomination not to allow the ecclesiological preference of their church to "silence any biblical voice" due to the polemics surrounding church division.[19] Paying close attention to the symphony of these ecclesiologies is a solid point of *ressourcement* for the unity of the churches.

The fact that diversity was the mark of the church of churches and not the foundation for fragmentation must inform the discussion of the search for unity in a divided people of God. The historian Cyrille Vogel, who evaluated the reality of diversity or differentiation, singularity, or autonomy in communion in the third through the fifth centuries, asserted, "Historically, the problem is not to analyze how local churches became autonomous, but rather to find out why they felt the need to regroup under larger units."[20]

The principle of communion, embedded in the New Testament matrix, explains the practice of regrouping differentiated communities into larger groups. For the patristic African ecclesiologist Cyprian of Carthage, the unity of the Catholic Church trumps diverse personal opinions or interests in the churches. Peter and Paul differed in their interpretation of the tradition, but their difference never led to the breaking of koinonia. Rather, their behavior furnished "an illustration to us of both concord and patience."[21]

Augustine, in his very difficult dialogue with the Donatists who claimed to be following Cyprian, argued that the correct interpretation of Cyprian would prefer unity to division. He said:

[17] Ibid., 146–47.
[18] Ibid., 146–48; see also Tillard, *Church of Churches,* 36–37.
[19] Brown, *Churches the Apostles Left Behind,* 150.
[20] Cyrille Vogel, "Unité de l'Eglise et pluralité des formes historiques d'organisation ecclésiastique du 3e au 5e siècle," in *L'Episcopat et l'Eglise universelle,* ed. Yves Congar and B. D. Dupuy (Paris: Cerf, 1962), 601.
[21] Cyprian Epistle LXX: 3 (Oxford ed. LXXI: 3), www.newadvent.org.

[Cyprian] did not sever himself, by refusal of communion, from the others who thought differently, and indeed never ceased to urge on the others that they should "forbear one another in love, endeavoring to keep the unity of the Spirit in the bond of peace." (Ephesians 4:2–3)[22]

The churches implanted in the African continent, following the great missionary movement of the nineteenth century and distinct from the churches of Carthage (or even the Coptic Church of Egypt and the Church of Ethiopia), bear stronger marks of division. They are the "divided people of God."[23] Renewal from the New Testament and patristic resources facilitates the ecumenical effort toward koinonia.

The Why and Wherefore of Divisiveness among the Churches

From the perspective of the African Christian reality, the miracle of Pentecost appears to have had incomplete influence in realizing the ideal of "unity in diversity" within the church of churches. The reasons are social, economic, and political. This was not only the case in the patristic churches of Cyprian and Augustine but also in the churches today in Uganda and Nigeria. Paradoxically, in the process of carrying out the missionary mandate of the Lord, divisions became entrenched. From the postapostolic church, controversies over belief, mission, and life led to divisions that scarred the body of Christ. At times, local and ecumenical councils successfully hammered out agreed-upon statements (creeds and canons) that could exclude those who differed or disagreed.[24]

The political, economic, social, and military realities of the Reformation and the Tridentine and post-Tridentine era of the church were acrimonious to say the least.[25] The nineteenth- and twentieth-century missionary movement

---

[22] Augustine, *On Baptism, Against the Donatists* (Book I), chapter 18:28, www.newadvent.org.

[23] This phrase is taken from the title of Kalu's book: Kalu, *Divided People of God: Church Union Movement in Nigeria, 1875–1966*.

[24] James Stevenson and W. H. C. Frend, *Creeds, Councils, and Controversies: Documents Illustrating the History of the Church, AD 337–461*, 3rd ed. (Grand Rapids, MI: Baker Acadmic, 2012).

[25] See the story of Trent in John W. O'Malley, *Trent: What Happened at the Council* (Cambridge, MA: Belknap Press of Harvard University Press, 2013).

transmitted the Christian message in Africa in all the denominational divisiveness. East Africa and West Africa provide examples of what Kalu described as the divided people of God (the dominant Christian trademark). The denominational churches that emerged from the Western, post-Tridentine and post-Reformation conflict were radically anti-Catholic, on the one hand, and radically anti-Protestant, on the other. The Church of Uganda, for example, is the carbon copy of the Church of England in its pure, "political" Anglicanism, a national church. As of 1982, the Uganda People's Congress party was Protestant while the Democratic Party was Catholic.[26] The bitter rivalry is captured by Michael Komakec:

> Church and State are almost synonymous because of the political and military support from the British against the Catholics during the religious wars in Uganda when missionaries were laying the foundation of the Church in the country. . . . The Anglican affinity with the political leadership of Uganda is another indicator of future danger/conflict should one day a Catholic become the president of Uganda.[27]

This sums up the worst in the antagonism and rivalry that Anglicanism and Catholicism nourished. Although the Anglican-Catholic divide appears unbridgeable, signs of real dialogue and union from unexpected quarters, Anglican-Pentecostal, are appearing. When the Pentecostal churches were suppressed in Uganda under Idi Amin, the Anglican diocese of Kampala gave hospitality to the Pentecostals. This led to a gradual fusion, resulting in the Anglicanization of the Pentecostal Church and the Pentecostalization of the Anglican Church; worship styles and ministerial structures became fused or modified.[28]

When one moves from East Africa to West Africa, the awareness of division is painfully clear at every level of church life, evangelism in particular.

---

[26] Mugambi, "Ecumenical Movement and the Future of the Church in Africa," 17–18.

[27] Michael Komakec, "Making Peace (Peacemaking) in Uganda: Theological Underpinning and Pastoral Ministries," PhD diss., Duquesne University, Theology Department, 2010.

[28] See Rev. Omona Andrew David, "Balancing Ancient and Modern in Kampala: The Ministry of All Saints Cathedral," presented in the consultation World Christianity Project, "New Cities and New Jerusalem," Nairobi, July 2013.

Roman Catholics were the principal opponents and enemies of the Protestants in the mission field. Kalu captured in the following statement the animosity prevalent among members of the Christian Council of Nigeria, Presbyterians, Methodists, and the CMS (Church Missionary Society), gathered for meetings in view of union: "The enemy was Roman Catholicism."[29] Nevertheless, the formation of the Christian Council of Nigeria in 1911 signaled hope for ecumenical dialogue despite the unbridgeable Catholic-Protestant divide. In the council meeting of 1911, "the African delegates representing churches of [the] Eastern Regional section" denounced the "existence of division among us as a source of weakness." They recommended, in urgent terms, that "steps be taken to the consolidation of union among our Churches."[30]

But in the twenty-first century, with the gains recorded thanks to the Vatican II *Decree on Ecumenism*, the need to put an end to division in the proclamation of the gospel of Jesus Christ becomes imperative. Or could it be, as Mugambi suggests, that many on both sides of the aisle (Catholics and Protestants) are totally unaware of the Vatican II *Decree on Ecumenism*?[31]

The denominational churches, while carrying the traditions into which Christians were born or converted, witness to the one tradition, that is, "the *Gospel itself*, transmitted from generation to generation in and by the Church, *Christ himself* present in the life of the Church."[32] Indeed, the one tradition, according to Vatican II (*Dei Verbum*, no. 2) is "Christ, who is both the mediator and the fullness of all revelation."

Tradition is thus wider and more profound than any historical reproduction in the denominational churches, but it cannot be understood or taken to exist as tradition apart from its historical reproduction or transmission.[33] Consequently, the divided people of God who live in traditions that embody the one tradition, the church of churches, need to do more for the

---

[29] Kalu, *Divided People of God*, 6.

[30] Ibid., 5.

[31] Mugambi, "Ecumenical Movement and the Future of the Church," 8.

[32] WCC 1962, *Faith and Order Commission*, my emphasis.

[33] Faith and Order, World Council of Churches, 1962 declaration, "Scripture, Tradition and Traditions," in *The Christianity Reader*, ed. Mary Gerhart and Fabian E. Udoh (Chicago: University of Chicago Press, 2007), 132. See also Vatican II, *Dei Verbum*, 1965, no. 2; *Dei Verbum* states, "Sacred tradition and Sacred Scripture form one sacred deposit of the word of God, committed to the Church," no. 10.

realization of unity to visibly display unity especially in the proclamation of the kerygma that the world may believe.

Enhancing the Visibility of Unity among the Divided People of God

One applauds the courageous but timid steps taken toward unity that came out of the world mission congress of Edinburgh (1910; no African church leader was invited) through the formation of the World Council of Churches.

The event of Vatican Council II, especially the powerful statement of the Decree on Ecumenism (*Unitatis Redintegratio*), challenges ecclesiology world-wide and African ecclesiology in particular. The ideal of the visible unity of the church, as the coming together of diverse peoples thanks to the miracle of Pentecost, addresses the division, disaster, and failure inscribed in the very flesh of humanity symbolized by Babel. Vatican II provides the roadmap:

> All in the Church must preserve unity in essentials.[34] But let all, according to the gifts they have received enjoy a proper freedom, in their various forms of spiritual life and discipline, in their different liturgical rites, and even in their theological elaborations of revealed truth. In all things let charity prevail.[35]

Vatican II captured the memory of a long tradition of the church's witness to its nature as the symbol of unity in a world beset by division of which the denominational churches are not blameless. The witness of communion, no matter how fragile, in the midst of obvious division shows that unity not only "embraces diversity" but is also "verified in diversity."[36] This is the work of God that created the church as symbol of unity from the broken body of Jesus. God gave life to the world in the Spirit through Jesus. Thanks to God's Spirit and the witness of the apostles, the communion among diverse peoples is assured in principle. Tillard talked of the "radically unbreakable" triad that reshapes broken humanity through the witness of the church:

---

[34] This is echoed in the search for unity among the churches of West Africa, especially in Nigeria in 1911.

[35] Vatican II, *Unitatis Redintegratio.*

[36] John Paul II, homily at Mass in Stockholm, June 8, 1989, www.vatican.va.

The Spirit, the apostolic witness which centers on the Lord Jesus Christ, and the *communion* in which the human multitude and its diversity are contained within this unity and where the unity is expressed in the multitude and its diversity.[37]

This is the tall order for the visible unity of the churches in Africa.

The dominant narrative of the divided people of God in the history of Christianity in Africa (e.g., Nigeria) highlights not only the divisions but also the struggle toward unity. True, in Nigeria and West Africa, the union planned for December 1965 never materialized for various reasons—denominational, theological, political, and even personal.[38] But it is important to note that the effort of union initiated by Protestant missionaries and embraced more or less by the local churches was going in the direction of the prayer of the Lord.

In East Africa, there are significant steps taken toward unity despite the fact that on the ground, the actual liturgical celebration (communion) in unity is a rarity. The achievement that merits significant mention is the agreement on rites for the celebration of interchurch marriage.

Mugambi listed other gains in ecumenical dialogue in Tanzania, Kenya, and Uganda: the ecumenical education for students, interseminary discussion in Zambia, and institutions such as the All Africa Conference of Churches and especially the Mindolo Ecumenical Center. While not yet realizing visible unity, these indicate common paths toward union.

The most visible witness of union is the common, vernacular Bible. After Vatican II, ecumenical translations included Roman Catholics; the United Bible Societies (founded in 1946) included in translations the Deuterocanonical books to cater to Catholics.[39]

The return to the sources and the sharing of resources by the churches are helping the common project of the visible unity of the churches. The practice of the Week of Prayer for Unity is therefore not an empty gesture but a way of reclaiming the mission and nature of the one church.

---

[37] Tillard, *Church of Churches,* 8.

[38] Kalu, *Divided People of God,* chap. 5: "The Collapse."

[39] See Peter M. Renju, "United Bible Societies' Strategies for Old Testament Translation in Africa," in *Interpreting the Old Testament in Africa,* ed. Mary N. Getui, Knut Holter, and Victor Zinkurature, Biblical Studies in African Scholarship Series (Nairobi: Acton, 2001).

The Wider Ecumenism— Renewal by Way of Ressourcement from African Indigenous Religious Resources

The wider ecumenism offers new theological ideas that should help churches toward unity in differentiation. The ancestral religions of Africa prioritize harmony and concord. This challenges the churches to shift from denominationalism to peace and amity in the one church of God. *Ressourcement*, going back to the sources, is a self-examination that lays bare one's self before the resources of one's tradition that profoundly challenge every seeker of true unity in church:

> Nothing is as anxiously beautiful as the sight of a people who lift themselves up again through an interior movement, a return to the sources (*ressourcement*) of their ancient pride, by means of a new release of the instincts of their race.[40]

Ressourcement enables African Christians to rediscover Christianity as a religion of peace and concord thanks to African indigenous religions, the invincible resource for renewal.

Historians of African religions Terence Ranger and Isaria Kimambo insist that African religions promote harmony and can affect denominational churches as sources of renovation. Historically, in East and Central Africa, indigenous religious rituals and cults from neighboring communities that were adaptable and malleable were adopted and modified to strengthen sociopolitical institutions. In situations of social or national crises, innovators and charismatic leaders (*nganga*) could call on the authority of the past tradition to introduce ritual novelties in response to changing times.[41]

Religion was not a means of division; rather, existing local practices and theologies were expanded to address novel challenges and to ensure balance or stability. This explains phenomena like the popular "democratic Spirit possession" or the Swezi cult that spread throughout eastern and central African regions during the colonial era.[42]

---

[40] Charles Péguy, cited by Yves Congar, *True and False Reform in the Church*, rev. ed. (Collegeville, MN: Liturgical Press, 2011), 39n35.

[41] Terence O. Ranger and Isaria N. Kimambo, *The Historical Study of African Religion* (1972; Berkeley: University of California Press, 1976), 14–15.

[42] Ibid., 14.

I draw attention to the African indigenous religious template because this template remains always with us all. It is the source of the hospitality shown by one religion to another. It serves as the basis of confronting what the late Kwame Bediako called the "ontocracy" of Christendom,[43] the "all or nothing" of post-Reformation Christianity that in Africa inflamed denominational antagonism rather than promoted ecumenical dialogue and union in differentiation.

The WCC consultation held in Ibadan, Nigeria, in 1973, which had the theme "Christian Involvement in Dialogue with Traditional Thought Forms," stated:

> A primal world view operates in varying degrees within the continuing primal religious traditions, within neo-primal forms, within those who have abandoned the primal inheritance of their fathers and found no new faith, and within those who have adopted some form of Christian or any other religion without shedding their own culture.[44]

To embrace Christianity and to drink from the wells of the invincible sources of our religious cultures enable us to generate theology brewed in "an African pot,"[45] ecclesiology of peace, concord, and relationality that replicates Trinitarian reciprocity. This liberates Catholics and Protestants to appreciate the "zones of communion," the truth that communion comes in degrees (Tillard).[46] We begin to stress our common baptism, the proclamation of the same kerygma, the common Christian witness leading to martyrdom (martyrs of Uganda), and the tasks we all must undertake together for the social and religious transformation of societies and peoples of Africa.

---

[43] Kwame Bediako, "Christian Witness in the Public Sphere: Some Lessons and Residual Challenges from the Recent Political History of Ghana," in *The Changing Face of Christianity: Africa, the West, and the World*, ed. Lamin O Sanneh and Joel A. Carpenter (New York: Oxford University Press, 2005), 122–23.

[44] See John Bernard Taylor, *Primal World-Views: Christian Involvement in Dialogue with Traditional Thought Forms* (Ibadan, Nigeria: Daystar Press, 1976), 5. See also Bediako, "Christian Witness in the Public Sphere," 130n6.

[45] Agbonkhianmeghe E. Orobator, *Theology Brewed in an African Pot* (Maryknoll, NY: Orbis Books, 2008).

[46] See Tillard, *Church of Churches*, 40ff. The efforts in East and West Africa toward union emphasize also these zones of communion.

SCRIPTURE STUDIES AND AFRICAN THEOLOGY

A Critical Overview from an Old Testament Perspective

Paul Béré

Some years ago, I had an informal conversation with two renowned theologians: David Schultenover, SJ, former editor of the American journal *Theological Studies*, and Bénézet Bujo, a leading African moral theologian. My question to the first was about the use of scripture by theologians. His answer at the time (2008) was that almost nobody to his knowledge began his or her theological discourse with an exegetical study of a relevant biblical text.

I asked Bujo a broader question about how African theologians used the Bible in their theologizing. The problem I felt at the time was the gap between some principles Vatican II formulated in the constitution on divine revelation, *Dei Verbum,* in order to facilitate radical ecclesial renewal by reaching deep into its roots (*ad fontes*) and the way those principles have actually been carried out in theology in general, considering Africa as a case in point.[1]

This chapter intentionally narrows the scope to the field of African Old Testament (OT) studies in Catholic theology for two reasons. First, we know that by tradition, Protestant theologizing usually stems from scripture studies. A well-known case in point is David Bosch[2] and his mission theology. Second, the focus of other scholars, like Okure, in this volume on the New Testament (NT) provides that perspective.

---

[1] For the sake of this chapter, I focus on Africa, but a careful assessment of the situation worldwide would show that the problem is universal in the Catholic Church.

[2] See David Bosch's masterpiece, *Transforming Mission: Paradigm Shifts in Theology of Mission* (Maryknoll, NY: Orbis Books, 1991, 2011); it starts from the NT (part 1), moves to history (part 2), and ends with context (part 3).

My perspective is twofold. Under "The Road Traveled Thus Far," I discuss the situation of Bible studies in African theology. After that, I suggest a few steps to help move forward.

Before I step into the arena, some cautions might be useful. The biblical apostolate has been extensively promoted by BICAM (the Biblical Center for Africa and Madagascar). It certainly makes the Word of God nourishment for the people of God whose *sensus fidei* remains the main source of any genuine theology. But whenever I use the phrase "African theology" in this conversation, I will always be referring to what has been produced in and for the academy.

The Road Traveled Thus Far

Principle and Reality: Views of Theologians

African theology is marked by two features that could be identified from its beginning:[3] a reflexive attitude[4] and a conversation.[5] These two events set the agenda for what developed after Vatican II. A few terms will be coined to encapsulate the task: adaptation, inculturation, liberation, contextualization, construction, and so on. A close look at the theological outcome of these trends shows, from a biblical vantage point, that the Bible as a foundational dimension of Catholic systematic theology is a question. As a matter of fact, Charles Nyamiti, notes:

The subject of African theology is closely linked with the question of its sources. This topic was particularly discussed in the late

[3] See the very extensive bibliography provided by Josée Ngalula, *Production théologique africaine, 1956–2010: Bibliographie sélective de 6000 ouvrages et articles des théologiens/nes africains* (Kinshasa: Éditions Mont Sinaï, 2011); see a thematic treatment of African theology in the Anglophone Africa by Benoît Awazi Mbambi Kungua, *Panorama des théologies négro-africaines anglophones* (Paris: L'Harmattan, 2008). An insightful assessment of African theology is provided by Emmanuel Ntakarutimana, "Où en est la théologie africaine?" in Léonard Santedi Kinkupu (dir.), *La théologie et l'avenir des societes: Colloque du Cinquantenaire de la Faculté de théologie de Kinshasa (Avril 2007)* (Paris: Karthala, 2010), 231–47.
[4] Albert Abble, *Des prêtres noirs s'interrogent* (Paris: Cerf, 1956).
[5] Tarcisse Tshibangu and Alfred Vanneste, "Débat sur la théologie africaine," *Revue du Clergé Africain* 15 (1960): 333–52.

1960s and early 1970s. Some suggested that the sources of African theology are the Bible and African traditional religions. Others—especially Catholic writers—claimed that its sources were Christian revelation and African philosophy. Another opinion held that the analysis of sermons by African and non-African preachers in Africa, or the translation of the Bible into African vernaculars, were the right sources.[6]

Nyamiti made his own conclusion and wrote that there were two sources. The first was the Christian: the Bible, which is the soul of all theology, and the authentic tradition of the entire Church—with particular emphasis on the official teaching of the church, the magisterium. The other source was the African sociocultural situation seen in its relation to its past, present, and future, the non-Christian source for African theology.[7]

Emmanuel Ntakaturimana, another African theologian, looking back critically at African theology in its relation to the Bible, writes,

> Wherever African Theology was quite dependent on Western philosophical debates, it becomes important for us now to look back *at Scripture* and its translation into African idioms, in order to rethink the first experience of the encounter with the God who comes to lead us through Jesus Christ to a fulfilling Christification. (Emphasis mine)[8]

The strength of this judgment rests on *Ad Gentes*, a decree of Vatican II that boosted theological work in Africa. The same document has long called

---

[6] Charles Nyamiti, "Jesus Christ, the Ancestor of Humankind: Methodological and Trinitarian Foundations," in *Studies in African Christian Theology*, vol. 1 (Nairobi: CUEA, 2005), 7.

[7] Ibid.

[8] Emmanuel Ntakarutimana, *"Où en est la théologie africaine?,"* 247: *"Là où la théologie africaine a été assez tributaire des querelles philosophiques occidentales, il devient important aujourd'hui de faire un retour sur l'Ecriture et sa traduction en langes africaines pour repenser l'expérience première de la rencontre avec le Dieu qui vient en Jésus-Christ pour nous conduire à un accomplissement de christification."* He further remarks: *"Les instituts de formation théologique en Afrique se trouvent devant le défi de repenser leurs sources, de revoir leurs bibliothèques, de réarticuler leurs programmes, de reconsidérer leurs langes d'enseignement en fonction des communautés qu'ils ont à servir."*

for a theological reflection on "deeds and values revealed by God, and *kept in Holy Scriptures* and explained by the Church and the Magisterium" (no. 22; emphasis mine).

The impression one gets from these witnesses is that despite its centrality, the Bible as a key source of theology has simply been left out of African theology. A question: Is the scholarly work on the Bible in Africa part of "African theology"? In Protestant theology, we would probably get a straightforward answer, for scripture in Protestant theology is its fundamental soul. In the Catholic scholarly environment, the sharp distinction between exegesis and biblical theology has fueled passionate debates. The creation of a specialized institution in 1909[9] with the aim of engaging the Bible scientifically may have been one of the main sources. There is no doubt that the work of those trained by the so-called exegetical programs nourished the mind and judgment of church leaders until Vatican II and beyond. Hence, the call for a theology rooted in "the study of the sacred page" (*Dei Verbum*, no. 24).

The Issue from African Biblical Scholars' Perspective

In his 2011 publication on the Word of God in the plurality of the scholarly readings, Paulin Poucouta, a biblical theologian,[10] discussed the relationship between biblical theology and exegesis. He rightly stated that they should not be separated. Biblical scholars were named under the same appellation, "biblicists," an overriding category that allows Poucouta to discuss the relationship between biblicists and theologians and to conclude,

> In Africa, the rediscovery of the relationship between the Bible and theology was very felicitous. It helps bridge the gap between biblical scholars and theologians. It makes possible for us a cross-fertilization between biblical studies and theology, a cross-fertilization that facilitates the emergence of African readings of the Bible and African theologies.[11]

---

[9] See M. Gilbert, *L'Institut Biblique: Un siècle d'histoire 1909–2009* (Rome: Pontificio Istituto Biblico, 2009).

[10] Paulin Poucouta, *Quand la parole de Dieu visite l'Afrique: Lecture plurielle de la Bible* (Paris: Karthala, 2011) 226–31.

[11] Ibid., 231.

This statement is more of a wish than a reality. Indeed, it tells us what should be done and not what has been done. Biblical scholars have been producing substantial works,[12] but it seems that no consistent theological piece of work in African theology has begun with an in-depth study of the sacred page or an in-depth reading of African exegetical studies on a given issue. The concern has long been expressed and kept on display.[13] André Kabasele, an OT biblical theologian, sounds more radical; he believes that "one must register the *quest for* African Bible reading in the wider horizon of African theology."[14]

Knut Holter, a Norwegian scholar, has dealt with OT scholars of Africa as a topic of research. His studies[15] reveal a striking fact: the first generation of African OT scholars are in conversation with their peers in their respective institutions of training, and the hermeneutical principles they use often simply replicate those of the places where they themselves were educated. One would expect the second generation to dialogue with the first. Unfortunately, this is not the case. As a consequence, a gap appears between African OT scholars themselves and also between all of them and African theologians in their respective fields, including biblical theology, dogmatic and systematic theology, moral theology, and so on.

Summary

To sum up the foregoing overview on the relation between Bible study and African theology, I point out a few facts:

---

[12] For example, see the work of PACE (Pan-African Association of Catholic Exegetes).

[13] See N. Soede Yaovi, *Théologie africaine: Origine, évolution et méthodes* (Abidjan: ICAO, 1995), 54–55; R. L. M. Mika, "Repères éthiques pour un bon usage de l'Ecriture Sainte en théologie morale," in A. Kabasele Mukenge (dir.), *Bible et promotion humaine: Mélanges en l'honneur du professeur P. M. Buetubela Balembo* (Kinshasa: Mediaspaul, 2010).

[14] André Kabasele Mukenge, "La théologie africaine à l'aube d'un nouveau siècle," in *Afrikanistik online* (2005); www.afrikanistik-online.de, 2 (emphasis mine).

[15] See Knut Holter, *Let My People Stay! Researching the Old Testament in Africa* (Nairobi: Acton, 2006); K. Holter, *Old Testament Research for Africa: A Critical Analysis and Annotated Bibliography of African Old Testament Dissertations, 1967–2000*, Bible and Theology in Africa 3 (New York: Peter Lang, 2002).

1. African theology may sometimes use biblical texts in quotes but not a systematic study of the Bible as points of departure. An amazing material fact is the lack of indexes of biblical citations. Very few African theological works with a scholarly brand provide such an index for their readers. Instead, we find indexes on authors and themes.

2. Biblical studies by Africans are well developed, and the work of the Pan-African Association of Catholic Exegetes (PACE) may serve as a case in point. No systematic methodology has so far proven operational for theologians to use, since most African OT scholars—the exceptions are few—work with well-established or mainstream methods.[16]

3. The guild of African OT scholars is made up of two generations, but no conversation seems to be taking place between them. I even doubt that it happens within the same generation. It suffices to check the references.

The awareness we have reached in reviewing African theology from the perspective of the role of the Bible should not leave us lamenting. We should rather devise means of bridging the gaps and hearing the call from *Dei Verbum* to not only quote the Bible here and there to back up this or that idea but also to better let the deep study of the sacred page permeate our theological discourse. We will thus move from a dichotomous perspective on Bible and theology in Africa to a multidimensional understanding of their relationship.

What Does the Expression "Word of God" Refer To?

Some of the unsettled issues in the current theological discussion may come from our struggle to clarify the fact that scripture studies are the soul of theology. What do we refer to when we use the expression "Word of God"? As we know, the word "theology" itself, *theou* and *logos*, may etymologically point to the Word of God through a human, self-disclosing discourse on God. Taken in a subjective sense, we may say that the Word of God refers to any place that one finds God speaking to God's people. Where then do we hear divine utterances? A popular and straightforward answer

---

[16] See Pontifical Biblical Commission, *The Interpretation of the Bible in the Catholic Church* (1993).

usually given narrows the scope of the Word of God to the Bible. The Word cannot be reduced to a book. Happily, in the postsynodal apostolic exhortation *Verbum Domini*, following the 2008 synod on the Word of God in the life and mission of the church, an effort has been made to "unpack" the expression and clarify what it stands for or refers to. There we learn that God speaks through various channels: Jesus Christ, scripture, tradition, cosmos, and conscience.[17]

- *Jesus Christ*: In the proper sense, Jesus is the Word made flesh (see John 1:1ff.). Not only does he reveal by his words and deeds what God has long been telling us (see Hebrews 1:1ff.), but he also explains in human terms, by his whole life, the mystery of God. Through him we hear God speaking.

- *Scripture*: Access to God's words through Jesus is made possible thanks to the written word of the witnesses who lived with him (cf. 1 John), listened to him, and experienced his salvific power in his compassionate ministry. Scripture therefore is the main gate to the person of Jesus, and through him to the unique face of his God. For that reason, scripture plays a special role in Christian life and theology.

- *Tradition:* The concept of tradition points foremost to the soul of a community. What the church has long called tradition has a double understanding: the apostolic tradition, which came down to us exclusively from the apostles (see, for instance, Paul's reference to tradition in 1 Corinthians 11:2; 2 Thessalonians 2:15, 3:6; 2 Timothy 2:2), and the ecclesiastical tradition, which carries with it the effort made by various Christian communities to make the gospel message their own and let it transform and re-create its cultures.[18]

---

[17] This fifth element was not mentioned, but it comes from the theological tradition and has been taken up in the *Catechism of the Catholic Church*, no. 1778, where one reads that the human conscience is the first vicar of Christ. An insight taken from Henry Newman's letter to the Duke of Norfolk, section 5: "Conscience is the aboriginal Vicar of Christ, a prophet in its informations, a monarch in its peremptoriness, a priest in its blessings and anathemas."

[18] If we look at cultures as the mold that shapes humanity, one can hardly separate the experience of God from a genuine process of becoming human. "Long ago," reads Hebrews 1:1, "God spoke to our ancestors in many and various ways" (NRSV);

- *Cosmos:* Nature as God's handiwork speaks on God's behalf: "The heavens are telling the glory of God; and the firmament proclaims his handiwork" (Psalm 19:1 NRSV). Therefore, nobody would find any excuse for not believing in God, as Paul said to the Romans,

> For what can be known about God is plain to them, because God has shown it to them. Ever since the creation of the world his eternal power and divine nature, invisible though they are, have been understood and seen through the things he has made. So they are without excuse. (Romans 1:19–20 NRSV)

- *Conscience:* Finally, human conscience should not be forgotten as we explore places where God's voice can be heard. In accordance with the long theological tradition of the Catholic Church, Henry Newman defined conscience as "the aboriginal Vicar of Christ."[19] The mediatory function of the community through the magisterium should not erase the ultimate place where God's Word becomes a personal calling. The story of Samuel (1 Samuel 3) can be a scriptural case in point.

These five instances, which are not exhaustive, are all sources in which we can hear God speaking. The theological discourse that understands the Word of God as a wide reality that goes beyond the material biblical text can draw from them to make the faith intelligible. The starting point for such a discourse need not necessarily be the Bible; it can be any of the other four elements explained above.

Does scripture therefore lose its specific role? The main function of scripture in the view so far explained could be simply called "canonical" in its etymological sense. It serves as a rule; it portrays for us Jesus, the man who came from God. It equips us with a measure to discriminate

---

this does not hold true only for Israel's ancestors; it is universal. Indeed, each of us can say, "God spoke to my ancestors." The divine words our ancestors have handed to us have been considered stepping-stones. Therefore, through Jesus, we believe that God has fully revealed God's self.

[19] See Henry Newman, "Letter to the Duke of Norfolk," sec, 5. As mentioned above, this sentence has made its way into the *Catechism of the Catholic Church*, no. 1778.

right from wrong in the community (discernment). It teaches us divine grammar so we can decode and interpret God's words through the cosmos or our consciences. If a theological discourse finds God speaking through a particular community experience, it can develop that very word against the witness of scripture, for the God of Jesus cannot contradict God's self. It is also true for the mystic who finds no word to express his or her experience of the divine being.

For the Bible to play such an important role, we have to do more than simply read it; we have to study it in depth. By so doing, the world of the Bible will mold and shape the theologian's worldview and thinking.[20]

The Way Forward

If we want theology in Africa and elsewhere to be molded by an in-depth study of the sacred page, some distinctions have to be made and some cautions respected. The elements I list below are not exhaustive; they are meant to launch the conversation.

Distinction between Biblical Theology and Exegesis

The debate on exegesis and biblical theology has a long history in the Catholic Church.[21] Indeed, it would be counterproductive to separate them. Although it appears irrelevant in today's world of interdisciplinary approaches to reality, we should nevertheless keep sharp the distinction between biblical theology and exegesis because each has its own way of proceeding. We may consider them as steps in the process of receiving the biblical message. Thus exegesis, by "drawing out" of the text the meaning intended by the human author in his or her culture and society, leads to biblical theology, whose task it is to highlight the divine component, namely, that which makes its message a Word of God. This will result in

---

[20] At some stage in African theology, African traditional religion was considered the "OT" of African Christians. We should not forget that the OT is important for us because it provides us with the mental frame of mind and symbols to understand the salvific message of Jesus and to walk in his footsteps. Jesus thus remains the real Word of God in the proper sense.

[21] See Joseph Fitzmyer, *The Interpretation of Scripture: In Defense of the Historical Critical Method* (Mahwah, NJ: Paulist Press, 2008); Gilbert, *L'Institut Biblique.*

providing some responses to faith seeking understanding in dogmatic theology or acting ethically in moral theology.

Exegetical methods are cultural products of a given society.[22] Unless our exegesis is in tune with our cultural and social mind-set, we will not be capable of paving the road for a theology rooted in scripture studies that also speaks to the hearts and minds of our contemporary audience.

Accuracy in the Exegesis of Dei Verbum's *"Let the study of the sacred page be like the soul of sacred theology"*

The avatars of this statement tend to equate the phrase "the study of the sacred page" with other expressions such as "the Word of God" or "the Bible."[23] This lack of precision in itself tells a lot about our way of using the Bible. Despite the strong affinities the OT has with the African world in many aspects (anthropological, social, linguistic, theological, etc.), we should remind ourselves that our Western training gave us Western cultural and hermeneutical lenses with which we read the Bible. We need to deconstruct that mind-set to uncover the specifics on the Bible beyond these cultural conditionings or, better, in a cross-cultural move.[24]

Relevant Exegetical Methods

We need to review the methods we have been using to engage the biblical texts with the questions generated by the exegetical or theological problems we have identified. The relevance I have in mind presupposes that criticism in biblical exegesis applies to the reader of the text and to the text itself. For example, Genesis 2:24 says the man will leave his parents and cling to his wife. It makes perfect sense in some societies in Africa and elsewhere, but in others, the wife should leave her parents and cling to her husband. Depending on where one belongs in a social setting, exegesis

---

[22] See Joseph G. Prior, *The Historical Critical Method in Catholic Exegesis* (Rome: PUG, 2001); John Barton, *The Nature of Biblical Criticism* (Louisville, KY.: Westminster John Knox Press, 2007).

[23] See, for instance, Poucouta, *Quand la parole*, 230, in which he quotes *Dei Verbum* no. 24, and on page 231, one reads, "*si la Parole de Dieu est l'âme de la théologie.*"

[24] See Albert Nolan, *Jesus before Christianity* (London: Darton, Longman and Todd, 1994); Ernest R. Wendland and Jean-Claude Loba-Mkole, *Biblical Texts and African Audiences* (Nairobi: Acton, 2004).

may require moving first out of one's mind-set to properly draw out of the text what it means.

Conversation between Exegetes,
Biblical Theologians, and Theologians in Other Areas

This conversation between exegetes, biblical theologians, and other theologians is badly needed first of all in our respective academic papers, and second, in meetings organized around the theme. PACE has managed to convene its members every two years to reflect on and discuss the same broad theme. The results of all these studies should be considered by theologians in their respective fields and with their proper methods.

This chapter started with a quest: to find out the way African theology used the Bible, particularly the OT. I narrowed the scope to the dialogue between African theologians involved in African OT scholarship. I have reached the conclusion that even the dialogue between African theologians with the Bible in general as requested by Vatican II in *Dei Verbum* no. 24 has not yet started.

African OT scholarship has benefited from a special attention outside Africa, and it became clear to me that many issues have to be clarified first. I have outlined some of them in the second part of this chapter. The task that now faces African theologians and exegetes is to recognize the special character of exegesis and biblical theology and devise creative ways of initiating conversation between biblical scholars and theologians in Africa.

THE COPTIC CHURCH

A Long Heritage with New Challenges

Nader Michel

A Brief History

Tradition tells us that Saint Mark founded the Coptic Church, one of the first churches of Christianity. Throughout its history, the Coptic Church has politically been under the authority of a foreign power—first by the Greeks, then by the Muslims. The name "Coptic" comes from the Greek Αἰγύπτιος / *Aigúptios*. For the Egyptians, fidelity to faith mingled with a sense of belonging to a nation and political resistance was expressed through religious particularity. In this sense, the opposition of the Church of Egypt at the Council of Chalcedon (451) is explained largely by its desire to distinguish itself from the position of the Church of Constantinople and to stake its claim to religious autonomy, considering its inability to free itself from Greek political and military authority.

Although they could not have imagined the extent of the effects of the invasion on the future of their country and their faith in 641, the Egyptian Christians preferred the Arab and Islamic occupation to a Greek one. From the ninth century onward, with both the affirmation and installation of the Islamic regime, Copts revolted against high taxation and vexations by Arab tribes. By the thirteenth century, Christians became a minority, as a major part of the population converted to Islam to save their lives and their properties.[1]

---

[1] Gabriel Hanotaux and Charles Diehl, *Histoire de la nation égyptienne*, tome 3 (Paris: Société de l'histoire nationale et librairie Plon, 1933), 541–57; Gabriel Hanotaux and Gaston Wiet, *Histoire de la nation égyptienne*, tome 4 (Paris: Société de l'histoire nationale et librairie Plon, 1933), 1–80; Divers historiens et archéologues: Gaston Wiet et Henri Munier, *Précis de l'histoire d'Egypte,* tome w (Institut Français d'Archéologie Orientale du Caire [IFAO], 1932); Jacques Tagher, *Coptes et musulmans,* Dar El Maaref (Le Caire, 1952), 1–130.

Under difficult circumstances, and due to its theological choices and orientations, the Church of Egypt saw itself as an island detached from Western Christianity. What was this church going to become, since it existed far from its sister churches and struggling in the middle of an Islamic mass exerting strong pressure on it, enacting a clear and systematic policy of discrimination, as well as oppression and persecution? From its origins, the Coptic Church has been firmly committed to its liturgy as the preferred means of catechesis of the faithful. This liturgy continues to this day, along with the Coptic language in some parts of the Mass, even though the people were arabized in the thirteenth century. Monastic life that began in the fourth century by Saint Anthony continued, not without great difficulties, such as attacks against monasteries in Wadi Natrun desert and Upper Egypt. To this day, in the Coptic mentality, the monk is the model of the Christian life, for he embodies the virtues of sacrifice and selflessness, and demonstrates the ideal of martyrdom for Christ.

Spirituality and Theology

The spirituality that feeds Coptic thought is rather dualistic,[2] although officially it is not Monophysite, as illustrated by the confession of faith at the end of the Coptic Mass according to the rite of Saint Basil, which was recovered and signed by Popes Paul VI and Shenouda III in May 10, 1973, in their common theological statement.[3]

The Coptic Church, probably because of its situation of oppression, consistently looks heavenward. The world is regarded as the place of degradation and temptation, and there is emphasis placed on the spiritual struggle to turn away from earthly things in order to embrace heavenly things. The division between good and evil is situated within the human being, as the soul aspires toward heavenly things, while the body is drawn downward. This is nourished by a theological vision that engulfs the humanity of Jesus in Christ and his glory, as if it were a fleeting moment in the destiny of the eternal Son, while placing the cross at the center of its theology. In this sense, therefore, this spirituality contains a sorrowful tone, and this is reflected in

---

[2] Fadel Sidarouss, *Eglise copte et monde moderne,* Thèse de théologie pastorale, présentée à la Faculté des Sciences Religieuses de l'Université Saint-Joseph (Beyrouth, 1978).

[3] *Osservatore Romano,* May 11, 1973.

the hymns and canticles of the Coptic Church. Present suffering is to be endured with patience and courage, with the hope of a better afterlife.

This lived oppression that is fed by a dualistic spirituality led the Christians of Egypt to a number of difficulties throughout their history. They read this history as a story of glory and fidelity that extends even to martyrdom, and is crowned by a monastic life that is full of models of courage and holiness. In other words, they assume no responsibility for the plight that they face. Without historical-critical considerations, they consider their history as a history dotted with holiness and heroism, and they consider that all of their misfortunes have come at the hands of others—the Chalcedonians, Muslims, and bad governors.

All this has led the Coptic Church to a standstill in its theological thinking, which has not greatly progressed since the fourth and fifth centuries. The Coptic Church depends on repetition as a method of transmission and on the scrupulous preservation of the heritage that was received from its predecessors. Thus, the Coptic Church has preserved its faith over the centuries, despite the rupture with the Christian world and the pressure of Muslim masses around it. It is guided and animated by a clerical hierarchical structure, coated with great sacredness, and it asks the faithful to observe a life of strict obedience and reverence.

Recent History

In recent decades the Coptic Church has been organizing catechesis in its parishes, and this movement has primarily been led by laypeople. The monasteries are experiencing a great revival, and a growing number of young academics are bringing the depopulated monasteries back to life. New monastic centers are being opened. Beginning with Pope Shenouda III (1971–2012), the identity of the Coptic Orthodox Church is being established, notwithstanding the temptation of withdrawal, self-justification, and self-reliance.

The parishes are experiencing a new boom, becoming complexes that serve not only as church buildings but also as conference centers, meeting rooms, computer and audiovisual centers, and bookstores, as well as sports fields. Young people lead the "Sunday schools," whereby every Friday (the weekly holiday in Egypt) they teach the Catechism of the Coptic Orthodox Church. Because religious education in public schools is both rudimentary and superficial, the church takes on the responsibility of instilling faith in its youth. Priests who minister in the parishes, especially in cities, are mostly university lecturers, and a group of at least three priests ministers in each parish. The old eparchies have been rekindled, and young bishops appointed to lead them. The Coptic Orthodox Church comprises fifty-one dioceses and eleven metropolitan cities in Egypt, and also in the vast Coptic Diaspora in the world, which includes many dioceses in the United States, Canada, Australia, and Europe. The Holy Synod is made up of more than 125 bishops and metropolitans.

This vitality has been accompanied by an identity discourse that has presented the Coptic Church as the custodian of true Christian teaching and as the guardian of the faith that was received from Christ, with reference to its doctrine, liturgy, and moral precepts. The church's vision is nourished by a feeling of superiority that discredits the proceedings of Catholic and Protestant churches. This critique extends even to the simplest details of these churches, including the administration of the sacraments, the practice of fasting, and models of prayer. In Sunday schools, young people learn the differences between churches, in order to emphasize the manner in which the Coptic Orthodox Church operates.

Since the coup by the Free Officers Movement on July 23, 1952, which brought the military to power in Egypt (Nasser, Sadat, Mubarak, and, finally, Al-Sissi), the Coptic Church has understood itself as a national church distinct from the church of the West, which is often presented as embroiled in hostile politics against the Arab and Muslim world. However, rare are those Christians with access to the highest offices of government, the judiciary, universities, police, and army.

The reinforcement of the Coptic Church's identity has propelled its withdrawal into itself and has hampered attempts at reconciliation with the Catholic Church. It is obvious that this cloistering benefited the political regime in Egypt that did not want Egyptian Christians to find support and backing from worldwide Christianity, thus keeping the problems they suffered confined to Egypt. Egyptian Christians have remained a minority that is easy to deal with, even to control, and the fate of the Egyptian Christians has been discussed and negotiated with a single person, the pope of the Coptic Church. The government has continued to maintain its hold on the life and destiny of Christians. The Coptic Church has compromised itself, hoping to acquire certain advantages, such as construction licenses for churches and the arrangement of old places of worship. The president of the republic granted these licenses sparingly, keeping the church under his yoke.

If the church remained too closely linked to this regime, it was in part an attempt to gain police protection against Islamic fanaticism, content to proclaim its message of faith within the walls of its churches. Therefore, churches have become places of refuge, assembly, and expression. As indicated above, in the churches, there are formation meetings, youth meetings, workshops of all kinds, and various seminars for students. Social life has revolved around the churches. This has meant that many have withdrawn from political life, leaving the field for Muslims close to the regime or members of the Muslim Brotherhood.

Furthermore, in addition to the large Coptic Orthodox majority (8–10 percent of a population of nearly 90 million) is a Coptic Catholic Church that was founded by Franciscans and Jesuits in the seventeenth century.[4] Its hierarchy has slowly established itself since November 26, 1895, when Pope Leo XIII officially erected the Coptic Catholic Patriarchate. Today, there are 150,000 Catholics in Egypt, and religious congregations from France and Italy have played a large role in the social and cultural influence of this community, especially through its large educational network, consisting of nearly 160 schools and health and social institutions.[5] Since the nineteenth century, British and American Protestant missions have also attracted Coptic Orthodox, and today the spiritual influence of Protestantism is prominent, with over 100,000 Protestant Christians living in the country. In addition, there are small communities that represent the various Eastern Churches, both Orthodox and Catholic.

The political upheavals of January 25, 2011, that brought down President Mubarak caught the Church of Egypt, both Orthodox and Coptic Catholic, off guard. The maneuvers of Mubarak, who was president for thirty years and was preparing the way for his son, Gamal, to succeed him, aroused great dissatisfaction. In addition, there was widespread corruption and systematic exclusion of any political opposition. Although occult forces have fueled this movement, the fact remains that it united a large number of the Egyptian people, especially young people who were disillusioned by the

---

[4] Alastair Hamilton, *The Copts and the West, 1439–1822, The European Discovery of the Egyptian Church*, Oxford-Warburg Studies (Oxford: Oxford University Press, 2006).

[5] *Annuaire de l'Eglise catholique en Egypte* (Le Caire, 2012).

lack of opportunities in the future, and were united around the triple claim of the movement: bread, freedom, and social justice.

Orthodox theology, being more apologetic, focused on defending the doctrines of the Christian faith against the fierce attacks of some Muslims in Orthodox sermons, publications, and media, and has not been able to update its theological discourse, nor truly understand its mission to proclaim and spread the gospel in the Arab-Muslim world. The sociopolitical dimension of the Christian message is missing from its discussions, and the various contributions of anthropology, history, and the humanities remain foreign to Coptic Orthodox thought.

For Muslims, the mysteries of the incarnation and the Trinity are not only unthinkable, but also entirely blasphemous. They violate God's transcendence and uniqueness. The height of the scandal is the Christian cross, because not only did God become flesh, but human beings were able to put God to death. If Christians do not make an effort to present their beliefs to Muslims in a language that takes into account their mentality and their resistance, and if they use terms that are obscure or foreign to the Arab-Muslim culture, the gap between Christian and Muslim populations will continue to widen, and the proclamation of the gospel will suffer. In the twelfth and thirteenth centuries, Christian-Arab thinkers were able to find the appropriate language to defend their faith and express it to Muslims, and they left a great amount of literature.[6] Their example must enlighten and stimulate Arab-Christians today.

Signs of Hope

The political events that took place in Egypt over the last five years have brought about some reconciliation between Orthodox, Catholic, and Protestant Egyptian Christians. They felt that their presence was threatened because of the great change that had taken place in the social bases that ensured stability in the country for almost half a century. They were also threatened by the rise of Islamist movements that advocated a fanatical identity and undertook a project that renounced modernity's contribution to Egypt from the nineteenth century onward. This reconciliation between Christians at the official and popular levels may renew the churches from within.

---

[6] Samir Khalil and Jørgen S. Nielsen, eds., *Christian Arabic Apologetics during the Abbasid Period (750–1258)* (Leiden: Brill, 1993).

Recent social and political changes have led many Christians to emigrate, particularly to Canada and the United States. The churches have had little success slowing this outflow of people. In addition, the same events that shook Egypt have strongly revived the nationalist sentiments of Christians, as they provided opportunities for Christians to participate in the reconstruction of their country. The church and its religious leaders are no longer the only representatives of Christianity, as many Christians have found independent paths away from ecclesial structure and have made their way into the public square by free expression of their opinions. This is a historical novelty.

Christians have enrolled in the new liberal parties that emerged during 2011–2012. The confessional compartmentalization imposed on them has begun to fail. There is now an electoral mass of Christians. This has been recognized in the vote on the two Constitutions drafted after January 25, 2011, the first one prepared by the Muslim Brotherhood (voted on December 15 and 22, 2012), and the second made after the repeal of the first (adopted on January 14 and 15, 2014). For this reason, the political authorities, whether the Supreme Council, Armed Forces, or the Muslim Brotherhood, have created new electoral districts to disperse the Christian vote in the districts where they constitute a substantial minority. Their presence was noticed during mass demonstrations in June 2013 that preceded the removal of President and Muslim Brother Mohamed Morsi, on July 3, 2013. They were at the heart of this movement that protested against the actions of the Muslim Brotherhood, which, by excluding all other political forces, monopolized the country's political rule. They infiltrated all the places where decisions were being made, imposed themselves in the administrative positions in the country, and encouraged radical islamization of Egypt. The majority of Egyptians, both Muslim and Christian, rose against what they saw as an attempt to undermine their country.

Christians have realized that they are a minority with full rights, and have a greater respect of democratic principles, principles of freedom of expression, and of social justice. This swelling nationalism has led Christians to take part in public affairs. Christians, especially the youth, have formed political movements, such as Shabab Maspero (the Young of Maspero),[7] to defend their rights. On October 10, 2012, a number of

---

[7] *Maspero* is the name of a neighborhood where la Maison de la Télévision is located, where the Christian youth meet and gather.

these young people, who were protesting peacefully in front of the Television House, were massacred by military tanks. Around thirty people were killed in the incident.[8] Mina Daniel, an emblematic figure of the movement that began on January 25, 2011, also perished there.

Seeds of New Relationships with the Churches

The last official meeting for the purposes of dialogue between the Catholic Church and the Coptic Orthodox Church took place in 1993. Since 1973, a mixed commission had been meeting nearly every year to discuss doctrinal questions that divided the two churches.[9] The formal relations between the two Coptic churches have remained intact, but a cold atmosphere has characterized the relations between the two communities. On occasion, these relations have turned into open rivalry. The re-baptism that the Orthodox Church requires during mixed/intermarriage is not acceptable to Catholics. Some Orthodox parish priests forbid their faithful to receive communion in the Catholic Church, and even to enter into a church.

After the events of January 25, 2011, prayer meetings bringing together Christians of all denominations were held in churches, and church leaders have taken significant steps to bring the different churches closer together. A Christian spiritual renewal has gained momentum since then, as meetings between Christians of all denominations have had scripture reading and the proclamation of the gospel at the heart of their agendas. We are observing the emergence of a new consciousness of the vitality of the Word of God and its prominent place in the life of Christians, and we perceive a certain thirst for a new religiosity that respects changing attitudes, without denying the theological heritage and liturgy of the Coptic Church. There is an active search for a theological discourse that speaks in the language of today's sense of the faith, the Christian dogmas, and the sacraments. Many young people have a thirst for spirituality that joins them in their reality and helps them discover the presence of God at the heart of their questions and their struggle for life.

In addition, a council of Churches of Egypt came into existence on February 18, 2013, and, since then, representatives of all the

---

[8] http://www.presstv.com/.
[9] http://www.pro.urbe.it.

churches—Coptic Orthodox, Catholic, Protestant, Episcopal, and Greek Orthodox—meet regularly.[10] Pope Tawadross II (2012–present) came to congratulate the patriarch Ibrahim Ishaq, patriarch of the Coptic Catholic Church, at his inauguration on March 12, 2013. It was a historic gesture. Then he went to Rome in May 2013, on the thirtieth anniversary of the visit of his predecessor, Pope Shenouda III to Pope Paul VI in May 1973. He announced his desire to unify the dates of the feast of Passover in the East, and to respect the sacrament of baptism in the Catholic Church and not to require a re-baptism in mixed marriages.

We are certainly witnessing an improvement in the spirit of understanding between Christians, and the fanatical climate has recently waned. This climate, in particular, was hindering positive relationships. We have become more familiar with the spiritual and theological trends from other churches, and we are ready to recognize the beauty and authenticity of these various currents. Fear and doubts of the other, mingled with a sense of self-sufficiency and superiority toward the other, have begun to give way to greater kindness and acceptance.

The reconciliation between the churches, through sociopolitical events, can eventually bring changes in Egyptian Christianity. The initiatives of the Coptic Orthodox Church, which are opening toward Islam, can find support and inspiration from the Catholic and Protestant churches that have an experience of openness and dialogue with Muslims through their social organizations, the Justice and Peace Commission, and educational institutions. Catholics and Protestants, especially in large urban areas, are less familiar with the temptation of isolationism and confinement within their churches.

Coptic figures have appeared on the public stage, and they take part in the political debates in Egypt.[11] The voice of Christians has become more and more audible, and their presence more noticeable. The participation of industrialists and heads of Coptic businesses support these initiatives. Among these notable persons and groups are the Sawiress family, which owns an empire composed of telecommunications, civil constructions, tourist attractions, and industrial establishments. Mr. Naguib Sawiress inau-

---

[10] http://unitedeschretiens.fr.
[11] Thirty-seven Christian deputies out of 450 have succeeded in the parliamentary elections that took place in October–November 2015. It is an unprecedented event.

gurated a political TV station, ONtv, which advocates liberal and open policies for all citizens. In addition, several Christian TV channels have also emerged, such as CTV, Aghaby, MEsat, and Miracle. Their program content is not only religious, but high quality social and political programs.

A New Impetus for Muslim-Christian Relationships

The old Islamic-Christian habit of coexistence, which lasted fourteen centuries, has forged a sense of neighborliness, friendship, mutual support, and collaboration. It is true that these were always tainted by fear of one another, suspicion about people's intentions, and doubts about the sincerity of what one carries in his or her heart. However, in this context, Christians and Muslims shared the same cultural heritage and expressed differently the religiosity common to this Nile country.

Today, civil society organizations bring together Christians and Muslims, allowing them to work together for the protection of women and children. Along with the Islamization guided by the Muslim Brotherhood and Salafis (fundamentalist Muslims) that has marked Egypt since January 2011, there has also been an awakening of a sense of citizenship, which, without denying religious affiliation, believes in and promotes human values of solidarity, respect, and equity. A good number of young people are involved in NGOs working for the social welfare of the society's large marginalized population.

Small groups of spiritual exchange and fellowship have begun to emerge. They are not very noticeable yet, but they are there as leaven in the dough that will make up the whole. A new religiosity is thus created for Christians and Muslims. This religiosity is more internal, personal, socially committed, and open to all. It will push the dialogue between officials to become more honest and authentic. A productive dialogue on social issues to improve the quality of relations between Egyptian Christians and Muslims can then take place, and even influence the direction of government.

In other words, daily dialogue has increased thanks to the joint collaboration in the construction of society and the country. This is the dialogue of action. These two meeting places, namely that of life and action, build the spirit of common citizenship, not as a claim, but in the sense of an authentic common good and the defense of the poor. It is a basis for dialogue that will make things happen at the top, where, one day, a specifically religious or theological dialogue will be able to intervene. However, we are still far away.

These small Christian-Muslim initiatives and acts of reconciliation can promote a dialogue between various Muslim groups. In Islam, there is a great debate between a vision shared by the large majority of Egyptian Muslims, who generally recognize the components of the modern state, and another, led by the Muslim Brotherhood and Salafis, which has nostalgia for a model of government that purportedly existed at the time of the Prophet and the first caliphs. However, the debate quickly turns to confrontation, accusations of infidelity, and mutual exclusion. This leads to the use of violence that cuts short the debate until the losing side finds its strength, and the fighting resumes with greater intensity. It is clear that Muslim societies will not know true peace, security, and prosperity unless dialogue takes place between the various trends in order to purify the Muslim literature that does not match the true message of Islam, but rather, represents a limited interpretation linked to a specific time.

Christians provide educational and health institutions as places for meeting and collaboration between Christians and Muslims. Egyptians of all categories attend these centers and discover one another in their cultural and religious particularity. First, they discover the richness of humanity and the Egyptian specificity that unites them, and, then, they learn to trust and work together for the common good of the country.

The events of January 25, 2011, mobilized the Egyptian youth, both Muslim and Christian. Tahrir Square in Cairo city center was not the only place where a claim for political change was made. Rather there was a convergence of multiple actions to promote understanding and cordiality between Christians and Muslims. Those participating believed themselves to be a new Egypt during the first eighteen days of this movement (from January 25 until Mubarak's resignation on February 11, 2011). The Koran and the cross were flown together. Christians protected Muslims during their prayers, and the voice of Christian chant resounded at the square.

Toward a Kairos?

History has inculcated certain reflexes in the minds of Christians in Egypt, and these reflexes cannot be unlearned in a few months. However, the movement that began on January 25, 2011, represented a tremendous blow that shook the great political pyramid dominating the country for almost sixty years, and has given back to the vox populi its place and force.

The people are more aware of their strength, will, and ability to get things moving in the direction they want. This movement represents a tremendous opportunity for the Church of Egypt to exploit the intellectual and political vitality that animates the country, as well as to benefit from the critical momentum that fills people's minds, and to listen to those who want change. The seeds of change are there, present in the church as a buried seed in the ground. The church ought not look elsewhere for it, for it is near to her.

This is a historic moment, a kairos, in the life of the Church of Egypt to hold onto. It is true that changes are costly and burdensome, as the weight of history is felt, and the temptation is great in Egypt today to return to what we have always done, either in terms of politics or church, and defend the model that we have always known in the name of stability, security, and prosperity. For the survival of the church, changes in attitudes that have been shifting for almost five years must encourage the church to invent a new theological discourse. Otherwise, it runs a double risk: either to produce Christians out of touch with their time and world or to lose a number of its followers who will no longer find themselves in the line with the church's proceedings and ways of thinking.

This implies that a serene reading of recent experience is necessary. The church must stand a safe distance away from political power, and rectify itself in order to open new perspectives in the actualization of the gospel message. This is both a spiritual and intellectual task that awaits the Church of Egypt. It can only be based on true communion that is confident and real between the Orthodox, Catholic, and Protestant churches. This is a call that comes from Christ through the signs of the times. In addition, this transformation will require more courageous commitment by inventive and enterprising Christians in their society, along with their fellow Muslims citizens.

Muslim and Christian Egyptians have an opportunity to write a new page in their history, but will they be able to seize the opportunity offered to them? Will the Coptic Church be able to assume its prophetic task to participate in the reconstruction of a country that can embody the three values of the movement that began on January 25, 2011: bread, freedom, and social justice? The signs say it will—slowly but surely.

Translated from French by Jean-Damascène Bavugayabo, SJ

The Gospel of the Family

From Africa to the World Church

Philomena N. Mwaura

In a thought-provoking article titled "Reconstructing the African Family," Laurenti Magesa aptly observes that "sociological ground work is necessary if any theological reflection on the family is to be realistic and make sense at all."[1] He further notes that such ground work is often ignored, resulting in detrimental consequences when a context (e.g., marriage and family in Africa) is idealized and does not reflect the reality on the ground. There is a tendency in symposiums and theological writings to extol the African family and its virtues without being cognizant of the fact that change has been slowly creeping into Africa, as elsewhere, since the fifteenth century, altering social structures and relations.

In this respect, Magesa further avers that the theology of the family and the ecclesiology of the church as the Family of God, as expounded in the 1994 African Synod in Rome, had inherent weaknesses. For example: it was not based on a proper or deep social analysis of the African context. Such an analysis would have provided the bishops a deeper understanding of the African family and revealed where there was need for deeper evangelization and for dialogue that is demanded by the church in Africa today.[2] Magesa's views are still pertinent, especially considering the fact that church-as-family is still the prevailing ecclesiological model of the church in Africa in the twenty-first century.

In a similar vein, Musimbi Kanyoro, a female African theologian, notes that the African family, as socially and culturally constructed, is a site of struggle for African women, and any discourse on the family

---

[1] Laurenti Magesa, "Reconstructing the African Family," in *Marriage and Family in African Christianity*, ed. A. N. Kyomo and S. G. Selvan (Nairobi: Acton, 2004), 9.

[2] Ibid., 10.

requires separating what is life-affirming, especially to women, from what is not.[3]

Whether traditional or modern, the African family has major flaws that must be noted on sociological and anthropological grounds, and must be theologically evaluated. This article argues for a comprehensive analysis of the African family from anthropological, sociological, religious, economic, and theological perspectives. Only when this comprehensive analysis happens, can the African family be properly understood, appropriate interventions constructed, and challenges and problems addressed. We must ask: What is the African family? How is it to be understood? This article explores the nature, structure, and functions of the family in Africa, the changes that have occurred in the family structure, and the factors behind those changes. It concludes with an exploration of the Catholic Church's view of the family and the markers of a Gospel of the family within the context of the challenges that face the African family today.

Understanding the African Family

The family in Africa is a complex institution, and it cannot be described without getting into the trap of generalizations and reductionism. Nevertheless, the family in Africa is the basic social unit founded on kinship, marriage, and adoption, and other relational aspects. The family may also be patriarchal, matrilineal, patrilineal, multilocal, multigenerational, multiethnic, and multireligious owing to migration, marriage, and conversion. It is also marked by tensions between African cultural values, Christian teachings, secularism, and other ideologies and religions. The family is a unit of production,[4] consumption, reproduction, and accumulation. In its simplest form, it consists of a husband, wife, and children. In its complex and most common form, it is extended to include, as John Mbiti says, children, parents, grandparents, uncles, aunts, brothers, sisters, all who may have their own children and other immediate relatives.[5] Membership in families

---

[3] R. A. Musimbi Kanyoro and Nyambura J. Njoroge, eds., *Groaning in Faith: African Women in the Household of God* (Nairobi: Acton, 1996).

[4] Betty Bigombe and Gilbert M. Khadiagala, "Major Trends Affecting Families in Sub-Saharan Africa," in United Nations, *Major Trends Affecting Families: A Background Document* (New York: United Nations, 2003), 1.

[5] John S. Mbiti, *African Religions and Philosophy* (London: Heinemann, 1969), 107.

varies in different African communities from adopted and fostered children to servants, slaves, and their children.

In the traditional society,[6] polygamy was a common marital practice, and such marriages contributed to the extension of relationships of the family by incorporating many more people. Jomo Kenyatta,[7] John Mbiti,[8] and Aylward Shorter[9] observe that a wider family included the deceased (ancestors or living dead) members of the family, as well as those yet to be born, for the unborn assured the survival of the family. The ancestors played a significant role in the dynamics of the family, since they maintained a relationship with the extended family through rituals of propitiation by the living and partook in certain rites of passage such as birth and naming, initiation, marriage, and death.

Ancestors were regarded as the enforcers of morality, values, and culture. Unity of the family is paramount, and the head of the household is expected to maintain the cohesion of the family and solidarity between its members. The extended family is long-lasting, self- perpetuating, and it can last for several generations. As a general rule, extended families are found in rural, rather than urban, areas. A characteristic feature of the extended family, as Mary Getui observes, is its kinship ties and networks that prevail in the lives of the people. She further observes that kinship "controlled social relationships between people, and it determined the behavior of one individual toward another."[10] The sense of kinship binds together the entire life of the society. Almost all of the concepts connected with human relationships were understood and interpreted through the kinship system. The extended family also provided care for the nonproductive members of the society, such as the sick, elderly, and children.[11]

---

[6] The term *traditional* is here used to refer to precolonial African society. Nevertheless, the author is cognizant of the fact that certain traditional aspects of this culture persist especially in rural areas and communities that have not completely embraced the trappings of modernity.

[7] Jomo Kenyatta, *Facing Mount Kenya: The Tribal Life of the Agikuyu* (Nairobi: Heinemann Educational Books, reprint, 1978).

[8] Mbiti, *African Religions and Philosophy*, 107.

[9] Aylward Shorter, *African Culture, An Overview: Socio-Cultural Anthropology* (Nairobi: Paulines Publications, 1998), 84.

[10] Mary N. Getui, "The Family, the Church and the Development of the Youth," in *The Church in African Christianity: Innovative Essays in Ecclesiology*, ed. J. N. K. Mugambi and Laurenti Magesa (Nairobi: Initiatives, 1990), 75.

[11] Ibid.

While traditional forms of kinship are decreasing in importance because of the continued need for urban and industrialized labor and the consequent increase of labor migration, the strength of kinship ties remain. Extended family forms are well suited for traditional forms of production and exchange where they are found, and they provide personal identity and security. In Africa, an individual is defined by his or her family. Family thus exists within a complex and interconnected network of relationships.

Functions of the Family

The extended family formed, and still forms, the basis of all social cooperation and responsibility. In traditional society, the wider family was the primary place where an individual exercised his or her freedom. The individual existed in connection to a larger group, including his or her family. One acquired one's identity from the group, and he or she depended on the group for his or her physical and social survival. Through various rites of passage, the individual progressively became a fuller member of the society, and took on a role that would ensure the survival of the group through marriage and procreation. Mbiti writes, "In traditional life, the individual does not and cannot exist alone except corporately. He/she owes his/her existence to other people. . . . The community must therefore make, create or produce the individual. . . . Only in terms of other people does the individual become conscious of his/her being, his own duties, his privileges and responsibilities towards himself/herself and towards other people."[12]

The extended family provided the individual with a personal and corporate identity. One was assigned to a particular community with clear roles assigned to them at various stages of life. These were assigned on the basis of age, gender, and social status. The cultural, social, and moral norms of the community that were applied within the extended family helped an individual grow into a productive and respected member of the community. Those norms served as a blueprint for his or her life.

The extended family was, and is, also the first religious community to which an individual belonged. It was through parents, grandparents, and other members that one learned about their religious and spiritual heritage. It was also where one learned about God, spirits, ancestors, and the afterlife. The extended family was, and is, also a means of mutual support. The

---

[12] Mbiti, *African Religions and Philosophy*, 108.

principle that guides relationships is that of *ubuntu,*[13] or, as Mbiti puts it, "you are because we are and because you are we are."[14] The extended family thus becomes a means of social, psychological, moral, material, and spiritual support through thick and thin.

Changes in Family Structures in Africa

African society has recently been undergoing tremendous changes in nearly every facet of its life, including its family structure and marriage. The factors that are hostile to the life and structure of the African family are essentially the result of political, social, economic, religious, and cultural changes. These changes were necessitated by the sudden emergence of independent Africa into the industrialized and urbanized world of the twentieth century. This accelerated change from primal to a modern society upset many traditional family patterns. It is becoming more common for African families to be split or broken. Urban living has affected the extended family, even with regard to its most immediate connections.

The customs of receiving visitors to one's home is still strong, but the custom is greatly strained in urban areas. Houses are too small, visiting relatives cost more to feed, and tensions are greater. With the disintegration of the extended family comes decreased involvement in relatives' and individuals' affairs. In urban informal settlements, in Nairobi, for example, where the majority of the population live,[15] amenities are nonexistent, and poverty is widespread. Hence, poverty is another distinguishing feature of the family in modern Africa. Luis L. Otero aptly captures this dynamic when he asserts: "In the past, the extended family existed, at present it disappears and changes into a small conjugal two generation family. The family was in the past an institution, now it becomes a private companionship."[16]

---

[13] *Ubuntu* (a term found in Bantu languages in East, Central, and South Africa) is a concept that encompasses being human, humane, relational, respectful of the dignity of human beings and other creatures, and aware of the interconnectedness of humanity, the earth, and other life forces.

[14] Mbiti, *African Religions and Philosophy*.

[15] It is estimated that 60 percent of the population in Nairobi live on 5 percent of the land in informal settlements. See National Bureau of Statistics, *National Population Census* (Nairobi: Government Printer, 2010).

[16] Luis Lerere Otero, ed., *Beyond the Nuclear Family Model: Cross Cultural Perspectives* (London: Sage Publications, 1997), 18.

Changes in the structure of the family reflect the enduring tensions between traditional, Christian/religious, and modern values and structures. Although there have been widespread accounts of families abandoning key traditional practices in favor of modern ones, one major trend remains: the creation of marital and familial arrangements that draw on both traditional and modern norms. The dominant feature of African families is their ability for innovation and creativity, being able to make new things out of old, and to draw forth new solutions from the traditional resources of family institutions. Thus, the trend toward modernity has been captured in the gradual transformation of African marital and familial arrangements away from corporate kinship and extended families, moving toward nuclear households, especially in urban areas and among the educated. This shift stems, in part, from the breakdown of collective kinship that is oriented toward systems of production and reproduction.

Despite internal differences between urban and rural settings and among African regions, the slow rates of economic growth and disparity between educational outcomes and labor opportunities have compelled smaller family sizes. Betty Bigombe and Gilbert M. Khadiagala observe that "in most urban areas, factors such as wage labor, the monetized economy and cost of living, have altered the value of children. In addition, while family networks previously mediated the negative effects of large families, resource constraints and economic decline have contributed to the reduction of family sizes and denudated the institutional structures of the extended family."[17]

However, there is a critical continuity in African family patterns that relates to the persistence of polygyny. Hence, the much-anticipated decline in polygamous households by sociologists is still far from a social reality in most African societies. In rural areas, polygyny survives largely due to the imperative established by the gender-based division of labor that marks the sphere of agriculture, whereas, in urban areas, it takes diverse forms like concubinage and serial polygamy.

Magesa also argues that the imposition of the patrilineal system and customs on matrilineal communities in Tanzania, and, by extension, to all such families in Ghana, Zambia, and Namibia, by the missionaries and other

---

[17] Bigombe and Khadiagala, "Major Trends Affecting Families in Sub-Saharan Africa," 8.

agents, caused multiple and complex changes in some important African values. Hence, "by introducing the patrilineal system and through the practice of paying bride wealth, the capitalistic economic system and the concept of nuclear family; the communal responsibility of bringing up children, common in the traditional family setup, was undermined."[18] Children's education, socialization, and protection were a communal responsibility in traditional society in line with the *ubuntu* philosophy. Consequently, there were no cases of orphaned and vulnerable children as we know them today. The phenomenon of street children in urban settings in African cities is a consequence of a society that no longer cares for its young.

Today, children learn from their peers, media (print and electronic), and social media. This has resulted in the undermining of the authority of the family, since children may sometimes be more knowledgeable than their parents.[19] These changes have bred an individualistic culture and have contributed to many social ills among them, such as the disintegration of the family structure, cohabitation, neglect of families left in rural areas, sexual immorality, drug abuse, alcoholism, and child abuse.

Families are now neolocal, living far away from the extended family. The consequence of this is the fragility of marriage, since families no longer have the moral, social, and spiritual support systems from their elders. Separation and divorce are now more frequent.[20]

Another social change that is undermining the kinship-based family structures is the prevalence of single parenthood, particularly among urban women. As increasing numbers of women join the workforce, single- and female-headed households have become a discernible pattern on the African social landscape. These trends reflect the secular changes in educational status, employment, and occupational mobility, and other factors like deaths from HIV/AIDS.

Africa's informal settlements are populated with unmarried single and poor women who face considerable challenges in overcoming social dislocation, migration, poverty, and deprivation. In some countries like Kenya, Ghana, South Africa, Ethiopia, and Zambia, over one-third of the house-

---

[18] Magesa, "Reconstructing the African Family," 13.

[19] George M. D. Fihavango, "Leadership in the Family Structure in the New Testament," in *Marriage and Family in African Christianity*, ed. A. N. Kyomo and S. G. Selvan (Nairobi: Acton, 2004), 185.

[20] Ibid., 187.

holds are female-headed. Others are headed by grandparents and children. In South Africa, apartheid policies in many forms "directly impacted family cohesion and reinforced the destructive influences that migrant labor, urbanization, industrialization had on the family."[21] Thus, the consequence of the legacy of apartheid is the high number of single-parent families, resulting largely from pregnancy outside marriage and from divorce. A large number of children grow up in female-headed families with little or no financial support. It has been argued that the black family in South Africa has continued to suffer greater disintegration than other families on the continent. According to a report by the South African Institute of Race Relations, "only 35 percent of children were living with both biological parents by 2010. Another 40 percent were living with their mothers and 2.8 percent with their fathers. This leaves 22.2 percent of children who were living with neither of their biological parents."[22]

The HIV/AIDS pandemic has also had a tremendous impact on the family in sub-Saharan Africa. This is most striking in the increase in orphans and child-headed families. A study issued by UNICEF in 2010 showed that there were 13,000,000 orphans in sub-Saharan Africa.[23] Their condition is exacerbated by poverty, poor health, and a lack of access to health care, education, housing, and other crucial necessities. These children who are both double and single orphans are usually cared for by older siblings or grandparents. This is particularly more prevalent among black African communities than among other races.

Another challenge related to this is the increase in the number and proportion of absent fathers, resulting in what Pastor Simon Mbevi of Transform Nations calls a "crisis of fatherhood."[24] Scholars argue that boys who grow up in absent-father households are more likely to display "hyper-masculine behavior including aggression. This is also associated with poor educational outcomes, antisocial behavior, delinquency and disrupted employment later in life."[25]

---

[21] Bigombe and Khadiagala, "Major Trends Affecting Families in Sub-Saharan Africa," 12.

[22] Lucy Holborn and Gail Eddy, *First Steps to Healing the South African Family* (Johannesburg: South African Institute of Race Relations, 2011), 3.

[23] Missionaries of Africa, "Orphaned and Alone," missionariesafrica.org.

[24] Pastor Simon Mbevi made this statement during a talk show at Kenyatta University when he addressed the topic "Reconfiguring Masculinities," March 5, 2015.

[25] Holborn and Eddy, *First Steps to Healing the South African Family*, 4.

Fosterage, however, is a characteristic that survives in African family structure where the survival of the urban family is sustained by ties with the urban households. A key feature of this is the channeling of remittances from urban workers to rural relatives through educational and other economic and social support. In much of Africa, migration forms a significant component of the livelihood systems of families. For years, internal migration from rural to urban areas has been the essential mechanism for job opportunities, social mobility, and income transfers. Nearly 32 percent of sub-Saharan Africans lived in urban areas in 1996, up from 11 percent in 1950. The United Nations projects that nearly 50 percent of the sub-Saharan African population will be urban by 2025.

New family structures have emerged due to the phenomenon of migration. Globalization has also fostered new forms of migration, as Africans seek better economic opportunities in Europe, the United States, the United Kingdom, the Middle East, Australia, Canada, South Africa, and Botswana. For the majority of these migrants, migration is part of the struggle against both debilitating poverty and implicit and explicit forms of political oppression. Africa's record of civil war, conflict, and political instability has, to a large extent, contributed to migration and the disintegration of the African family. Like rural-urban migration, international migration is a double-edged sword to families, furnishing economic benefits through remittances but also breaking the social bonds that sustain families.[26] Trafficking in children in cross-border interactions has also affected the African family. Traffickers keep victims in subservience through physical violence, debt bondage, passport confiscation, and threats of violence against their families.

Another scourge that has led to the downward spiral of the African family is domestic violence, a taboo subject, which, despite well-intentioned national, regional, and global legislation, has continued unabated, wrecking families. Gender-based violence affects people of all classes, creeds, races, and ethnicities. The family and home, which are supposed to be the safest spaces for women, men, and children, have become sites of struggle, pain, abuse, neglect, and disintegration. The latest *Kenya Demographic and Health Survey*[27]

[26] Bigombe and Khadiagala, "Major Trends Affecting Families in Sub-Saharan Africa," 11–15.

[27] Kenya National Bureau of Statistics, *Kenya Demographic and Health Survey* (Nairobi: Kenya National Bureau of Statistics, 2014), 60.

observes that 49 percent of women and 9 percent of men have reported being violated by an intimate partner.

Domestic violence in all its forms has been destroying the African family. The different forms of domestic violence—cultural, economic, social, psychological, spiritual, physical, and emotional—are symptoms of a deeper malady. The root cause lies in the patriarchal culture in the society we live in. It is my contention that biblical, African, and contemporary culture, which form the environment in which African women live, have significantly contributed to the objectification of women, thus rendering them vulnerable to abuse and violation. Some cultures even describe wife battering as "discipline," and women are socialized to expect and tolerate it.

Domestic violence has contributed to separation, divorce, and, in extreme cases, death of women, men, and children, thus weakening and destroying families. The church in Africa has a critical responsibility for creating awareness and highlighting the shameful and sinful practice of domestic violence. It should speak out against the violence and develop pastoral and theological responses. I have yet to see a policy on gender-based violence from the church—something I consider a necessity, if appropriate responses are to be developed and made available. If the family is to become a model for church and the basis for the gospel of the family and the theology of the family, it has to be expunged of gender-based violence, and its multifaceted forms must be acknowledged.

However, despite all these challenges, the family support systems continue to be alive in Africa. The family is still the locus for the transmission of values, the acquisition of identity, and it provides a framework of inclusion regardless of one's character, age, status, and so on. A Gikuyu proverb succinctly captures this when it says, "*Mwana muciare ndateagwo*" (once a child is born, he/she cannot be abandoned).

From the above discussion, we must ask: What does a gospel of the family mean under these circumstances? What does the church teach about family? What are the markers of such a gospel? What can African theology contribute to the world church? It is to this that we shall now turn.

Toward a Gospel of the Family

Throughout the centuries, the Catholic Church has constantly taught about marriage and the family. The church considers the family as the starting point, or nucleus, of society through which cultural and spiritual values are laid and transmitted. One of the most profound teachings is captured in the Vatican II document, the pastoral constitution on the church in the modern world (*Gaudium et Spes*). This document devotes a chapter to the dignity of marriage and the family. Marriage is seen as a community of life and love. The family is perceived as a miniature church, and a parish or a congregation is viewed as an extension of the family. It is also a "domestic Church" where the primary principle of relationship is love."[28]

Catholic social teaching holds that the family is the basic social unit of every society, and a society is only as healthy, stable, energetic, and imbued with moral values as its families. The life of the church therefore depends on its families. In the *Letter to Families*, Pope John Paul II describes the family as the "heart of the center of the civilization of love"[29] and says that the family constitutes the basic cell of community. In *Centesimus Annus*, Pope John Paul II depicts the family as the first and fundamental structure for a "human ecology," which is "founded on marriage, in which the mutual gift of self as husband and wife creates an environment in which children can be born and develop their potentialities, become aware of their dignity and prepare to face their unique and individual destiny."[30]

The family is also depicted as a miniature domestic church with a missionary dimension, "which is grounded in the Sacrament of Baptism and achieved by fulfilling one's proper task within the Christian community."[31] The family, by its very nature, is a nurturer of young people, witnessing to them as they make critical decisions in life.

On their part, the Symposium of Episcopal Conferences of Africa and Madagascar (SECAM),[32] in its contribution to the 14th General Ordinary Assembly of the Synod of Bishops on the Family, affirms the social teaching of the church on the family and so too the *Instrumentum Laboris*[33] of

---

[28] *Gaudium et Spes*, nos. 46–52.

[29] John Paul II, *Letter to Families* (Nairobi: Paulines Publications Africa, 1994), nos. 6–7.

[30] John Paul II, *Centesimus Annus* (Nairobi: Paulines Publications Africa, 1991), no. 39.

[31] *Gaudium et Spes*, no. 48.

[32] SECAM, *The Future of the Family, Our Vision: Contribution to the 14th General Ordinary Assembly of the Synod of Bishops on Family* (Nairobi: Paulines, 2015), 41–60.

[33] *Instrumentum Laboris: The Vocation and Mission of the Family in the Church and the Contemporary World* (Nairobi: Paulines, 2015), 39–42.

the XIV Ordinary General Assembly of Bishops (2015) and the report of the Association of Member Episcopal Conferences in Eastern Africa (AMECEA) 18th Plenary Meeting held in Malawi in 2014.[34] They, however, observe that the true essence of the family is being eroded and the status of the family is in a state of crisis. The church, according to the AMECEA bishops, needs to learn lessons from African culture, where the role of the family is considered fundamental and the source of life. The value of the family is also enshrined in constitutions in Africa and in the African Charter of Human Rights, an affirmation of the importance ascribed to it.

SECAM[35] draws attention to the challenges the family is facing today, ranging from pauperization occasioned by anthropological, social, financial, spiritual challenges to social exclusion, poverty, ecological challenges, foreign/secular values, political instability, and ethnic conflicts. This leads to a disregard for the elderly, infirm, widows, orphans, people with disabilities, and children. This crisis, therefore, becomes a kairos moment for the church to safeguard the dignity of the human person and combat practices that do not honor the gospel or African tradition. I agree with the proposal by the Synod Fathers that "recommend(s) that our pastoral challenges develop spiritual, psychological, legal and moral structures for the promotion of rights of widows, orphans and the family of the departed,"[36] especially when widows and orphans are mistreated and deprived of the rights to property when the husband or parent dies. The church must engage other disciplines to be able to develop a responsive theology and to understand issues affecting the African family.

The SECAM report also identifies the challenge of polygamy and calls on African Christians and people "to promote the monogamous dimension of marriage in Africa which is open to the teaching of scripture on the uniqueness and the indissolubility of marriage. . . . The pastoral attitude towards the polygamist must avoid anything that could appear as a recognition of polygamy by the Church."[37] The question is: Does the church in Africa and the church worldwide truly and comprehensively understand

---

[34] Edwin Mauluka, "AMECEA Conference Concludes: African Family is in Crisis," *Malawi Voice,* July 14, 2014.

[35] SECAM, *Future of the Family,* no. 18–28.

[36] Ibid., no. 32.

[37] Ibid., no. 40.

the cultural challenges facing the family today? It is not enough to give pastoral responses to polygamy like those that were provided at the initial evangelization in the nineteenth century. Why has polygamy persisted even among Christians who may, on the surface, be regarded as "model Christians"? It is not enough to ask clergy to "exercise the power that Christ has entrusted them to discern and find appropriate responses to the situation."[38] Such an open attitude is tantamount to giving negligible pastoral guidance and leaving Christians in confusion, as well as with feelings of exclusion and being judged harshly. Nor does it help the clergy to devise appropriate and helpful pastoral and theological responses that are grounded in compassion and mercy, but that are not implemented.

Certain doctrines about marriage within the church are therefore being challenged due to the crises the family is experiencing, while others seem as if they are not viable, since they have not responded to the "signs of the times." Examples of these would include divorce, remarriage, and admission of the divorced, the remarried, and those cohabiting and having relations between spouses within marriage into the sacraments. Cardinal Kasper argues that "while the Church must remain faithful to its teaching on the indissolubility of the Sacrament of marriage, it is vital to help, support and encourage those experiencing difficulties in their family life."[39] While perseverance, commitment, and patience are called for, it is sometimes important to recognize that a marriage environment can be so toxic that it negates the purpose of marriage, and it is not healthy to live in such an environment.

My argument is that nobody enters marriage with the intention of leaving, but circumstances may dictate otherwise. Should a devout person who leaves such an environment be restricted to "spiritual communion" and be denied "sacramental communion" when they have had to choose between life and death? Would the church rather tolerate "ritualization" of the sacraments, rather than promoting the well-being of people trying to raise their families and live a life of faith? Sometimes laws themselves can be an obstacle to experiencing the fullness of life that Christ promises.

A gospel of the family would require a listening, empathetic response to hurting families and a mediation of mercy according to each circumstance,

---

[38] Ibid., no. 42.

[39] Cardinal Walter Kasper, *The Gospel of the Family* (Mahwah, NJ: Paulist Press, 2015), 4.

in a way that resembles Jesus' actions. Again, as Kasper observes, "The doctrine of the Church is not an ideology in the clouds but God wants us to be present, close to His people."[40] The church needs to explain in a new way what the family and matrimony are, in order to help people and, at the same time, remain true to the gospel. It needs to be a listening church that hears the faithful and their cry. This also means a revision of pastoral practices in a manner that is consistent with the myriad challenges the family is facing in its new formations—formations such as single parent families, stepfamilies, child-headed families, and grandparent-headed families. There is an urgent need to provide pastoral care the way Jesus did, and to show divine mercy when responding to families in crisis. There should also be adequate preparation for marriage for young people and continuous marital formation. The tendency of many young people is to seek "church services" for the baptism of their children and other sacraments but to ignore the church in most other aspects of their lives.

The values that still persist in the African family of mutual care, solidarity, marriage, and family as a communal affair and care for the vulnerable are an important first step in the evolution of a Gospel of the family that is relevant for Africa and that could offer a contribution to the world church.

---

[40] Ibid., 32–33.

Part Three
A Church That Goes Forth with
Boldness and Creativity

The Church of the Future

Pressing Moral Issues from Ecclesia in Africa

Emmanuel Katongole

Beginning with a Problem

The reader of this essay could be forgiven for assuming that the expression "pressing moral issues" in this essay's title means that it is an essay about sexuality and sexual ethics. The presupposition that these issues relate to sexuality and sexual ethics poses a fundamental problem. Besides, as some have averred, they are often claimed to not concern Africa.

I have a problem with this way of conceptualizing my task for two main reasons. First, my problem has to do with what I perceive as the tyranny of "the untouchable and contested moral issues" and, more specifically, with how these come to be reduced to the "issues of sexuality, exercise of authority, and abuse in the church." Whereas I have no doubt that these are major challenges facing the global church, I am worried that framing these issues as the most "pressing moral issues" is meant to indicate that they are issues that command the immediate attention of each and every Christian. It is not only the assumed inevitability—everyone must address them—that constitutes the tyranny of pressing moral issues, but it is also the narrow range of what might constitute a valid response. Thus, even when it is assumed that particular social, historical, and cultural contexts may offer unique ways to understand the moral issues, it seems that in responding to them one's answer must fit within one of two positions: a liberal or conservative response.

Thus, in relation to sexuality, the pressing moral question easily gets reduced to whether one is for or against gay rights. Consequently, the African theologian often has really nothing interesting to say, other than to restate the positions already available so as to prove himself or herself relevant to the discussion. Consequently, the overall effect of starting with "pressing moral questions" not only makes a parody of the African voice, it also obscures what might be the more urgent but perhaps less "sexy" issues affecting millions of people around the globe, especially in Africa. In this perspective, one wonders why sexuality is a pressing moral question, while the fact that millions of Africans lack basic necessities like water, food, and shelter is not? Why is sexual orientation a basic right, but drinking water is not?[1] I find the often hidden but limited narrow ideological base behind what constitutes the "pressing moral challenges"[2] very problematic, to say the least. Why pressing, and pressing for whom?

My second, and related, problem with my task in this essay is ecclesiological. Under the pressure of having something meaningful to contribute to the debate on "pressing moral questions," African theologians quite often have nothing *theological* to say. They may of course give some preliminary "theological" or biblical indications, but the conclusions at which they arrive are often quite predictable and have very little biblical or theological reasoning. The assumed universality of the pressing moral challenges means that, while addressing them, one has to abstract oneself from any particular cultural, social, and theological consideration and appeal to some putative "human" ideal, such as "tolerance" or "rights." This observation is confirmed by Elias Bongmba in his recent essay, "Hermeneutics and the Debate on Homosexuality in Africa."[3] Even though Bongmba discusses mostly Protestant responses to the homosexuality debate in Africa, the essay is instructive in a number of ways.

Bongmba begins with a general survey and discussion of recent responses by African church leaders to the homosexuality debate and proceeds to a discussion of Rudolf Bultmann's biblical hermeneutics as a

---

[1] Pope Francis's claim in *Laudato Si'* that water is a right deserves serious attention. Access to safe drinkable water, Francis notes, "is a basic and universal human right, since it is essential to human survival and, as such, is a condition for the exercise of other human rights" (no. 30).

[2] For a more general and theoretical exploration of Africa's moral and existential challenges within a presumed "universal" context that often turns out to be but a limited ideological base of Western economic, cultural, and political interests, see my "Postmodern Illusions and the Challenges of African Theology: The Ecclesial Tactics of Resistance," *Modern Theology* 16, no. 2 (2000): 237–54.

[3] Elias Bongmba, "Hermeneutics and the Debate on Homosexuality in Africa," *Religion and Theology* 22 (2015): 69–99.

recommendation for reading and understanding the injunctions against homosexuality in the Bible. Bultmann's biblical hermeneutics, Bongmba argues, compels African Christians toward a "new kind of demythologization" that confirms that "the biblical record is a cultural text" whose message has to be interpreted in light of the context in which it was written as well as the realities of today. Consequently, in light of the current debates about homosexuality, he writes:

> Historical developments have given the church new information about human sexuality and we know that sexuality is expressed in different ways and there is nothing strange about same sex relationships. . . . With this knowledge, we understand that what others considered a cultural taboo is no longer the case. Christians need to understand homosexuality in today's historical context. An appreciation of history invites us to rethink old essentialism because there is no single meaning for the biblical account that we can hold up and claim that this is the single view on homosexuality for all Africans.[4]

The overall effect of Bongmba's analysis is to recommend "dialogue" and a spirit of "openness" and "tolerance" as a way forward. Within that spirit of love and tolerance, "one can hope that the churches would focus on serving and meeting the needs of all people rather than focus on debates that are exclusionary, not because they are polarizing, but because they demonstrate a lack of love and appreciation for difference."[5]

I draw attention to Bongmba's essay because it confirms that whatever theological preliminaries the theologian may engage in, the conclusion is usually predictable, and is one that does not require, or depend on, any substantive theological account. That is what I mean by the claim that the theologian has nothing theologically interesting to add to the debate. In the end, what Bongmba's essay confirms is that a focus on "the most pressing moral issues" often ends up obscuring the reality of the church in its theological, historical, and social context.

---

[4] Ibid., 86.
[5] Ibid., 95.

An Alternative Starting Point: *Ecclesia in Africa*

The overall import of my critical observations is simultaneously methodological and ecclesiological. It is to suggest that instead of beginning with
the "most pressing moral issues" and seeking an African voice or response to
these, our discussion must begin with a sociological reality of the African
church. Such a starting point, by drawing attention to the African context
within which the church is located, will highlight the pressing social and
existential challenges that confront millions of Africans on a daily basis.
Ultimately, the goal of the description is theological and ecclesiological—
namely, to call the African church into an ongoing self-critical posture and
conversation about the kinds of theologies and modes of pastoral praxis that
are necessary if it is to truly live out its calling as the sacrament of God's
salvation in Africa today.

That is why, in order to prove relevant to this task, the African theologian requires more than skills of analytical judgment and moral casuistry,
but narrative skills, so as to provide "thick" and apt descriptions of the reality
of African society with all its complexity, dynamism, and challenges. But in
this task, theologians will also need to draw attention to biblical and theological visions around which the reimagination of ecclesia in Africa can take
shape in the context of the identified social challenges. At the same time, it
will need to point to concrete experiments and examples where this reimagination might already be under way.

Given this consideration, I would like to frame my reflection not as an
African voice responding to the "most pressing moral challenges" but as a
conversation about pressing social challenges of the African church. Doing
so will not only help blur the unhelpful distinction between the "social" and
"moral" challenges, it will point to the reality and priorities of the church
as Catholic community, a community that is both local and universal. In
this connection, the overall framing of this volume's title, looking toward
"Vatican III," provides a good context for our discussion. Framing our
discussion within a projected ecumenical World Council offers an opportunity not only to focus on the kind of issues, ideas, and resources that the
African churches will be bringing to the table, it will provide opportunities
to explore how the unique challenges arising out of Africa might relate to
issues and challenges faced by other communities around the world. In the
end, it may be that the council may generate something like a list of "the
most pressing issues" affecting the World Church, but such a list would have

emerged out of a real and honest interaction with and conversation among various local communities.

African bishops constituted a small percentage of those at Vatican II, and their influence on the council's proceedings was similarly limited.[6] However, given the growth and dynamism of the church in Africa, it is possible to imagine Accra, or another African city, as a host city for the next council, with African bishops and delegates playing a much more significant role. And while at Vatican II Africa's problems and preoccupations had only an indirect influence, African issues and concerns should occupy a key place on the agenda of Vatican III. Below, therefore, I present seven issues I believe should be presented by the African delegates. My goal is not simply to name key challenges, but to suggest biblical and theological frameworks for their discussion.

A Poor Church

"I have come that they may have life and have it to the full" (Jn 10:10).

Sub-Saharan Africa has the fastest population growth projected between now and 2050. What has not been sufficiently captured, however, is that about 65 percent of the total population of Africa is below the age of thirty-five years, and over 35 percent is between fifteen and thirty-five years—making Africa the most youthful continent. By 2020, it is projected that out of four people, three will be, on average, twenty years old. More than 50 percent of these will be illiterate and unemployed.[7] Representing this mostly youthful, unemployed, and poor population, the African delegates at Vatican III will be facing an essentially ecclesiological challenge—the kind of church that ecclesia in Africa needs to be if it is to be the bearer of good news in this context. In facing this challenge, the delegates will hopefully draw on the ecclesiology of Pope Francis to be the church of the poor, for the poor,[8] as they seek a vision

---

[6] In 1962, Africa was, by and large, a missionary territory. Of the 311 (of 2,625) council fathers who represented Africa, only sixty were native Africans. For a full assessment, see Agbonkhianmeghe E. Orobator, SJ, "After All, Africa Is Largely a Nonliterate Continent," in *Fifty Years On: Probing the Riches of Vatican II*, ed. David Schultenover, SJ (Collegeville, MN: Liturgical Press, 2015), 273–92.

[7] See "A Youthful Continent! Africa's Position on Youth," a report by the Youth and African Union Commission, http://www.africa-youth.org.

[8] See Apostolic Exhortation, *Evangelii Gaudium* (*EG*), no. 198. See also, Pope Francis's address to journalists, March 16, 2013. http://www.zenit.org.

and pastoral praxis that moves beyond two shallow ecclesiological visions prevalent on the continent. On the one hand, they will avoid reducing the church's role and presence in Africa to a mere pastoral and spiritual role, for doing so will simply give the globalized forces of neoliberal capitalism and the free market unquestioned power in shaping the destiny of millions in Africa— forces that are partly responsible for confining millions in Africa to a life of poverty. On the other hand, the delegates will need to confront the growing phenomenon of prosperity churches, which promise the poor, unemployed, and desperate Africans a quick "uplift" and miraculous deliverance from poverty.[9] Resisting these two shallow ecclesiologies, and demonstrating that they are two sides of the same economic fundamentalism, will point to the need for grassroots ecclesial communities and forms of cooperative, as well as productive experiments that reconnect the gospel to economic realities—the kinds of experiments under way at the Kuron Holy Trinity Peace Village, at Maison Shalom, and at St. Jude's Farm.[10]

A Nonviolent Community

And they sang in a mighty chorus: "Worthy is the Lamb who was slaughtered" (Rv 5:12).

The widespread phenomenon of political violence on the continent, which often masquerades as "ethnic" violence, poses a major challenge to the church's identity and mission as sacrament of God's peaceable kingdom.

---

[9] On the explosion of the prosperity gospel in Africa as a synthesis at the intersection of precolonial spiritualities of holistic well-being and the illusory promises of health, wealth, and well-being in postcolonial Africa, see Hermen Kroesbergen, ed., *In Search of Health and Wealth: The Prosperity Gospel in African, Reformed Perspective* (Eugene, OR: Wipf & Stock, 2014). For a very interesting study of charismatic Catholicism in the Philippines, which has a lot of similarities with the growing charismatization of African Catholicism with a prosperity underbelly, see Katharine L. Wiegele, *Investing in Miracles: El Shaddai and the Transformation of Popular Catholicism in the Philippines* (Honolulu: University of Hawai'i Press, 2005).

[10] For a discussion of the small Christian communities, see especially Joseph Healey and Jeanne Hinton, *Small Christian Communities Today: Capturing the New Moment* (Maryknoll, NY: Orbis Books, 2005); for a discussion of Kuron and Maison Shalom as ecclesiological models, see my *The Sacrifice of Africa: A Political Theology for Africa* (Grand Rapids, MI: Eerdmans, 2011). For St. Jude's Farm, see my "Mission and the Ephesian Moment of World Christianity," *Mission Studies* 29 (2012): 183–200.

Recent examples, such as Rwanda, South Sudan, Congo, and Central African Republic (CAR), confirm the extent to which violence has become a perpetual feature of social life in Africa, not because of recalcitrant or "age-old animosities," but as a very modern problem, where "ethnicity" is imagined, reproduced, and exploited to further the political project of Africa's modernity.[11] The widespread participation of Christians in violence raises a major theological and social challenge for the African church. After a visit to the Nyamata memorial in Rwanda, where over 1,000 Tutsi were killed by fellow Rwandan Christians during the Genocide, a friend remarked on the following irony: whereas the church has been clear on a number of issues including the use of contraceptives, it has remained vague on the issue of Christian participation in violence and killing. A full recognition of violence as a major challenge for the church in Africa will involve not only clearer recommendations for "reconciliation" and for peaceful coexistence[12] but also a more explicit vision of the church as a peaceable and nonviolent community in the midst of Africa's violent convulsions. Although this ecclesiological vision may not promise to end violence in Africa, and certainly does not make Christians "safe" in the face of violence, it does provide witness to the possibility and reality of another society founded not on violence, but on self-sacrificing love. Fortunately, the African church is not without resources or stories to draw on in lifting up a vision and pastoral praxis of nonviolent social engagement. The story of the young seminarians of Buta in Burundi who refused to discriminate between Hutu and Tutsi, and thus faced death rather than betray their friends, provides a most inspiring story and example.[13]

Vanguard of a Quiet Revolution in a Noisy Africa

"Be quiet. . . . Come out of him" (Lk 4:35).

Noise pollution constitutes a key theological and social challenge in Africa. Everywhere one encounters noise—from cheap and endless

---

[11] For a more elaborate exploration and argument of this conclusion, see my *Sacrifice of Africa.*

[12] See, e.g., the postsynodal exhortation *Africae Munus,* http://w2.vatican.va.

[13] For the story of Buta, see Zacharie Bukuru, *We Are All Children of God* (Nairobi: Paulines Press, 2015).

entertainment, from the buzz of traffic, from places of worship—making it impossible to find a quiet respite. This reality of a loud Africa was confirmed to me on my recent visit to Kumasi. Staying at a local parish, I found myself unable to sleep, as my room felt like a sound box: the church had a night vigil going; the nearby market hosted a disco; on the other side of the Catholic church, the Assemblies of God had an all-night prayer session. At four o'clock in the morning, the Muslim muezzin joined in with a call to prayer. What particularly irritated and deeply annoyed me was the fact that each of these "congregations" was not content with simply addressing their congregations: their speakers were mounted outside on their sanctuaries, and it was as if each congregation was trying to outshout the other. In fact, what the Kumasi experience confirmed was the reality of postcolonial Africa as a marketplace of competing ideologies, each trying to drown out the other. The effect of this cacophony not only contributes to the noise pollution in Africa, but it also has the effect of shaping loud and aggressive African identities (as being loud and aggressive seems to be the only way to be heard). In the end, noise becomes a serious theological challenge in that it makes it impossible to hear and receive any gentle news—which the good news is. That Mark begins the story of the proclamation of the good news with the story of the healing of the man with an unclean spirit, who Jesus orders to be "quiet," is quite telling (Mk 1:21–28). Not only does the story anticipate the rest of Mark's gospel, it defines what, according to Mark, the proclamation of the good news is about. In this connection, the story is part and parcel of Mark's "messianic secret," through which Jesus' audience is told not to publicize Jesus' identity and miracles. However, the overall effect of this hermeneutic device in Mark is to suggest the gospel as a quiet revolution of righteousness, justice, and shalom. Seeking to live within this quiet revolution, and be both its sign and sacrament in the world, the African church cannot but take as one of its first orders of business the task of commanding quiet—and thereby creating the necessary conditions for the gentle revolution of peace. Without this essential dimension of the proclamation of the good news, the church's own life and ministry simply become just one more loud voice of empty chatter, in an endless sea of empty ideologies.

Rooted in the African Soil

> *"The Lord God took the man and put him in the Garden of Eden to cultivate it" (Gn 2:15).*

In the recent encyclical *Laudato Si'*, Pope Francis has drawn attention to the immensity and urgency of the ecological crisis. The crisis is particularly acute in Africa, where a combination of factors—prolonged civil wars, poor or nonexisting food policies, mass deforestation, lack of energy policy, plus a growing population[14]—have all contributed to bringing Africa to a looming ecological crisis. The effects of this crisis are increasingly obvious in the growing cases of starvation and food insecurity, water poverty, and land disputes, as well as more conflicts and civil wars.[15] At the envisioned Vatican III, African delegates will raise and seek ways to respond to the ecological crisis, not simply in terms of ethical and policy recommendations aimed at mitigating the effects of the ecological crisis, but in terms of reassessing the church's essential relationship with the land. For, as Pope Francis notes, at the base of the economic, social, cultural, and political factors that have contributed to the ecological crisis lies a "wound," which has to do with our inability to see and acknowledge our deep connection with the earth: "We have forgotten that we ourselves are dust of the earth" (*Laudato Si'* [LS], no. 2). In practical terms, the "wound" represents our attempt to escape from our vocation to "till the land and take care of it" (Gn 2:15)—an escape that in Africa has taken many forms. At any rate, although the majority of African Christians live and subsist in rural areas, that some never hear a

---

[14] In 1969, Uganda's population was 9.5 million; in 2002, it was 24.5 million; in 2011, 34 million; and by 2014 it was 37.5 million. According to the Ugandan daily, *The New Vision*, of January 23, 2013, with an average population growth rate of 3.1 percent, the population is expected to increase fivefold by 2100, pushing Uganda to the top ten most populated nations in the world (according to the latest world population prospects by the United Nations Social and Economic Affairs Division in New York). The report also points out that the fertility rate of Ugandan women is at 5.9 children per woman, and notes that Uganda has the world's second youngest population after Niger, with the current median age registering at 15.8 (http://www.newvision.co.ug).

[15] See, e.g., Cullen S. Hendrix and Sarah M. Glaser, "Trends and Triggers: Climate, Climate Change and Civil Conflict in Sub-Saharan Africa," *Political Geography* 26, no. 6 (2007): 695–715; see also Muhamed Suliman, *Ecology, Politics and Violent Conflict* (London: Zed Books, 1999).

sermon about the connection between God, the soil, and salvation is quite surprising. This theological silence reflects how, in many ways, the African church is beholden to a modernist but misleading notion of "civilization" and "progress" as a movement away from the land, and all the other "tribal," "native," and "backward" traditions connected with land.[16]

At Vatican III, the African delegates will be exploring ways to recover the vision of Genesis 2: our essential connection with the earth and the vocation to till the land and care for it as an urgent theological and pastoral task. The task will, among other things, call for fresh experiments and education initiatives connected to land but also bring together theology, food production, economics, and ecological consciousness. When thinking about such concrete initiatives, the African church may draw inspiration from historical precedents like the National Catholic Rural Life Conference in America,[17] but it will seek to highlight and offer as models ecclesially informed land-based initiatives under way, for instance, at the Songhai Center in Benin, the Kasisi Agricultural Institute in Zambia, the Jesuit Center for Ecology and Development (JCED) in Malawi, and the Bethany Land Institute in Uganda. These, and other similar experiments, offer refreshing ecclesiological radiations of a church grounded in African soil.

A Community of Servant Leadership

"Anyone who wants to be first must be the very last, and the servant of all" (Mk 9:35).

Writing in 2009, the late Kenyan Nobel Laureate and environment activist, Wangari Maathai, rightly noted that what has held Africa back,

---

[16] See my *Rooting the Church in the African Soil: A Theological Experiment* (forthcoming).

[17] The National Catholic Rural Life Conference (NCRLC) was particularly impressive in its efforts in the 1930s and '40s to spearhead a "green revolution" in rural America by empowering rural communities, supporting small farms and local businesses, promoting responsible land stewardship, and creating a platform to connect rural farmers and enhance their advocacy. For a good introduction and account of these efforts of the NCRLC, see Christopher Hamlin and John T. McGreevy, "The Greening of America, Catholic Style, 1930–1950," *Environment History* 11, no. 3 (2006): 464–99.

and continues to do so, has its origins in a lack of principled, ethical leadership.[18] A number of other commentators have noted that the crisis of leadership in Africa is one of the root causes of the continent's problems. In *The Sacrifice of Africa* I described the predominant forms of "big man," "boss," and "chief" visions of leadership that are shaped at the intersection of precolonial, colonial, and postcolonial dynamics, and whose combined effect is the perpetuation of the self-serving *la politique du ventre* (politics of the belly). Church leadership has, by and large, both mirrored and radiated the same style of leadership, where the bishop, and to a lesser extent the priest, exercises unquestionable lordship over those they lead. Accordingly, church institutions are characterized by the same (and in some cases even worse) forms of corruption and opacity as the nation-state institutions. As the postsynodal exhortation *Africae Munus* notes, "Many decision makers, both political and economic, assume that they owe nothing to anyone other than themselves" (no. 82). Within this context, church leaders find that they lack the moral authority and credibility to question the dictatorship in African politics.

The full context of Jesus' words to the disciples in Mark—"anyone who wants to be first must be servant of all"—is a debate among the disciples as to who was the greatest. Setting a child in their midst, Jesus offers them a distinct way of how they (and the church) are to view leadership. The African delegates at Vatican III will be wrestling with the questions of if and how the African church can display a unique and distinctive form of leadership that can at once interrupt and call into question the self-serving forms of "big man" leadership in Africa. In this search they will find great inspiration in the stories of leaders like the late Archbishop Christophe Munzihirwa of Bukavu,[19] Bishop Djomo of Tshumbe,[20] and Archbishop Odama of Uganda.[21]

---

[18] Wangai Maathai, *The Challenge of Africa* (New York: Pantheon, 2009), 25.

[19] See Deogratias Mirindi Ya Nacironge, *Père Evêque Christophe Munzihirwa Mwene Ngabo, Prophète et martyr en notre temps* (Bukavu, 2003).

[20] See, e.g., James Carney, "'The Bishop Is Governor Here': Bishop Nicholas Djomo and Catholic Leadership in the Democratic Republic of the Congo," in *Leadership in Postcolonial Africa: Trends Transformed by Independence*, ed. Baba G. Jallow (New York: Palgrave Macmillan, 2014).

[21] See my "Performing Catholicity: Archbishop John Baptist Odama and the Politics of Baptism in Northern Uganda," Opening Address, Conference on The Discourse of Catholicity, World Catholicism Week at DePaul's Center for World Catholicism and Intercultural Theology, April 12–13, 2011.

A Women's Church

> *"A woman named Martha opened her home to him. She had a sister called Mary, who sat at the Lord's feet" (Lk 10:38–39).*

In "Of Coffins and Churches," I noted that the African woman is the backbone of African society and the African church. However, as Pope Benedict rightly noted in *Africae Munus,* the dignity and rights of women, as well as their essential contribution to the family and to society, are often not fully acknowledged or appreciated (*AM, no.* 56). The major challenge facing the church is not simply pastoral, namely whether the church can recognize, affirm, and defend the dignity of women, but ecclesiological, namely whether the church can be the space and community where women feel particularly at home, and where their voices and gifts of leadership are welcomed and nurtured. Hopefully at Vatican III the debate about the ordination of women would already have been settled and that the African delegation will already include a few women cardinals, a number of women bishops, and a significant number of women priests and laywomen leaders serving in various capacities in the council secretariat and as auditors and experts. At any rate, African delegates at Vatican III will present spirited theological, pastoral, and pragmatic reasons why the leadership of women in the African church is not only essential but also why this leadership needs to set the pace and be the catalyst for women's leadership in the broad African society. The complementary gifts and postures of the two sisters at Bethany provide a provocative and inspiring model: Martha: outspoken, hardworking, successful, and generous; and Mary: quiet, attentive, intimate, and deep.

An Honest and Truthful Church

> *"All you need to say is simply 'Yes' or 'No'; anything beyond this comes from the evil one" (Mt 5:37).*

If there is one issue that has consistently dogged the African church, it is the issue of clerical celibacy. It is an issue, however, that is rarely publicly discussed, even though it is an open secret that a number of African priests, including bishops, live double lives when it comes to the requirement for priestly celibacy. Unless the gift and challenge of clerical celibacy is openly addressed at various levels of church life, it will continue to undermine the credibility of the church's witness, especially on two fronts. First, on the level of church leadership in general, since church leadership compromised in the area of celibacy will find it hard to speak with credibility and authority in relation to other issues and societal challenges. Second, widespread compromise in clerical celibacy undermines the church's witness and voice on matters relating to the body and human sexuality. The absence of a credible theology and witness in the area of human sexuality will be especially negatively felt in the postmodern context, where not only the meaning and stability of family life, but of sexuality itself, has become uncertain.

At Vatican III, by courageously putting the challenge of clerical celibacy on the agenda and exploring the possibility of married priests, the African delegates will provide an opportunity for transparent and honest dialogue about human sexuality. This may not only encourage conversation around other sex-related concerns within the global church—homosexuality, abuse, marriage, divorce, etc.—it may result in the embracing of new forms of pastoral leadership adequate to meet the needs, challenges, and gifts of the African church.

My goal in this essay has been to shift attention away from the "most pressing moral issues"—issues that often do not reflect the lived reality of the majority of African Christians—so as to generate a more interesting discussion around the social reality of the African church. The effect has been to identify seven pressing challenges and priorities for the mission of the church in Africa. Reflecting on and addressing these challenges is an ongoing process that does not need to wait for a Vatican council, but grows out of the church's call to be an incarnated presence of God's saving work in Africa. However, with this self-reflective conversation of what it means to be the church in Africa underway, the African delegates at Vatican III will not only discover they have something interesting to say to the world church; they might discover that their challenges are not unique. In this way, they may not only draw insights and practical models from other local churches; their own theological visions and models might enrich other local churches, thus contributing to the development of genuine catholicity.

Maternal Well-Being in Sub-Saharan Africa

From Silent Suffering to Human Flourishing

Tina Beattie

The Lord will march out like a champion,
like a warrior he will stir up his zeal;
with a shout he will raise the battle cry
and will triumph over his enemies.

For a long time I have kept silent,
I have been quiet and held myself back.
But now, like a woman in childbirth,
I cry out, I gasp and pant.

(Isaiah 42:13–14, NIV)

I open with these verses from Isaiah, because they offer a vivid image of God speaking in the first person as a silenced woman in childbirth, while the prophet proclaims a warrior Lord of violence and power.

In this essay, I reflect on the silencing of women's voices in the context of poverty and maternal mortality in sub-Saharan Africa. At the Theological Colloquium on Church, Religion, and Society in Africa (TCCRSA) gathering in Nairobi where I first gave this paper, I asked those attending to put their hands up if they had been personally affected by maternal mortality. I discovered that nearly everybody had a female relative or friend who had died in childbirth. Some countries in sub-Saharan Africa have the highest maternal mortality rates in the world,[1] yet maternal death and suffering barely feature in the work of African theologians. Official church teaching is almost entirely silent on the subject, though it has a great deal to say about the gifts, roles, and responsibilities of mothers. Maternal mortality has generated much published research in the social sciences and health and development studies, but these are secularized disciplines that rarely take into account the vast significance of religion for African women. Even when they do, they tend to do so from a sociological rather than a theological perspective.[2]

Underlying these scholarly lacunae is the silence of women whose lives are formed in the nexus of religion, motherhood, and poverty. Their personal stories of suffering and hope do not shape our theological narratives, despite the fact that, as with that quotation from Isaiah with which I started, maternal metaphors are a significant feature of biblical discourse about the nature of God. The God of Isaiah who cries out in childbirth is like a mother who comforts her child (Isaiah 66:13), and who never forgets the child at her breast (Isaiah 49:15). Psalm 91:4 likens God to a mother bird protecting her chicks under her wings, and Jesus takes up this image when he describes himself as a hen who longs to gather her chicks under her wings (Matthew 23:37; Luke 13:34). Jesus' farewell discourse to his disciples in John's gospel is redolent with the language of pregnancy and childbirth (John 16:21). Paul's Letter to the Romans speaks of creation "groaning as in the pains of childbirth" (Romans 8:22, NIV), and Galatians and 1 Thessalonians are also rich in maternal imagery. In Revelation 12, the apocalyptic battle is played out between a woman in childbirth (interpreted as representing the church), and a devouring dragon. All this suggests that, when maternal voices are silenced or appropriated by others, a vital aspect of divine revelation is lacking. We cannot "hear" the voice of God speaking to us through scripture and creation, unless we hear the voices of women made in God's image—including women who suffer and labor to give life, as the God of the Bible does.

---

[1] See *Trends in Maternal Mortality 1990–2013*, estimates by WHO, UNICEF, UNFPA, the World Bank and the United Nations (World Health Organization 2014), Annex 19, http://www.who.int.

[2] Cf. Stephen Obeng Gyimah, Baffour K. Takyi, and Isaac Addai, "Challenges to the Reproductive-Health Needs of African Women: On Religion and Maternal Health Utilization in Ghana," *Social Science & Medicine* 62, no. 12 (June 2006): 2930–44.

What happens to revelation when men appropriate to themselves the exclusive authority to interpret the Word of God and to uphold the traditions of the church? For example, at the two Synods on the Family in October 2014 and October 2015, only a few women were present among nearly three hundred celibate men, and those women were not allowed to vote. It is not possible to arrive at a wise understanding of family life, capable of informing pastoral practice and doctrinal development, when women who in every culture are the primary caregivers and custodians of the family are excluded from the conversation.

This collection of essays looks forward to Vatican III and asks what kind of changes the next council might bring about. The single greatest transformation that needs to happen is the full and equal inclusion of women in the church's theological reflection and decision-making processes. Unless and until that happens, our understanding of what it means to be made in the image of God and to incarnate Christ's love in the world will continue to be distorted by an androcentric exclusivity that refuses to attend to the wisdom and the suffering of women.

In what follows, I approach these issues from three perspectives: the silencing of maternal voices, the facts of maternal mortality, and the teachings of the postconciliar church on human dignity. What would it mean for the church to promote and defend women's human dignity, in situations where poor women and their unborn and newborn children die for lack of access to antenatal and obstetric care? What does women's human dignity mean in contexts where girls and women have little control over their sexuality and their reproductive capacities, and where the children they bear are so often born into situations of poverty and abandonment?

I ask these questions as a theologian and a mother. I was born and brought up in Lusaka, and three of my four children were born in Africa—one in Nairobi and two in Harare. Two of those births involved obstetric emergencies that would probably have resulted in my death if I had been a poor rural woman instead of a white postcolonial. So I feel some sense of kinship with those women in Africa for whom childbirth brings with it the threat of terrible injury or death.

I am also aware that African women generally have a more positive attitude toward motherhood than many of their Western counterparts. While many Western women today remain childless by choice, such a choice would be less common among African women. Explaining her decision to move back to Ghana from England after her baby was born, foreign correspondent Afua Hirsch writes, "I love the ease with which powerful women across the continent are simultaneously seen as mothers, daughters or wives and as presidents, chief prosecutors or chairs of the African Union—all recent examples of new titles taken on by African women." Yet Hirsch also declares herself horrified to discover that "women who have not had children are chirpily described in the press as 'barren.'"[3]

This denigration of childless women is the other side of the valuing of motherhood in Africa, which brings with it the risk that women are valued as mothers more than as persons in their own right. Nigerian theologian Anne Arabome writes:

> The first identity of an African woman is seen as mother and wife, and the roles of motherhood and womanhood are intertwined. However, the church's rush to endorse woman's role as procreator and helpmate often bypasses the positive valorization of the *personhood* of the African woman *in herself.*[4]

With these preliminary observations in mind, let me turn now to the role that silence plays in positioning poor women in the discourses of others.

Silence as a Form of Oppression

When I presented a short version of this paper in Nairobi, I was asked how we might reconcile the virtue of true silence with the silence of being silenced. This is an important question. Silence is a vital aspect of our human capacity to encounter God, but silence is oppressive when it is imposed on people as a way of not having to acknowledge the complex realities of their lives, in order to protect transcendent ideals and dogmas from the messy facts of human existence. Such silence leads to stigmatization and exclusion, while allowing ruling authorities to control the lives of others by way of rigid rules and harsh condemnations.

---

[3] Afua Hirsch, "The Mothers of Africa," *Guardian* (Friday, July 20, 2012), http://www.theguardian.com.

[4] Anne Arabome, "Who Is Christ for African Women?" in *Catholic Women Speak: Bringing Our Gifts to the Table*, ed. Catholic Women Speak Network (Mahwah, NJ: Paulist Press, 2015), 25.

Poor women are particularly vulnerable to this kind of silencing, for they live at the crossroads where the oppressive powers of religious and cultural patriarchy intersect with the no less oppressive powers of the global economic order. This makes them vulnerable to various forms of silencing that can be attributed to different and sometimes conflicting ideologies—religious, cultural, and political.

In his apostolic exhortation *Evangelii Gaudium*, Pope Francis emphasizes the importance of culture as an aspect of revelation. He describes culture as "a dynamic reality which a people constantly re-creates; each generation passes on a whole series of ways of approaching different existential situations to the next generation, which must in turn reformulate it as it confronts its own challenges."[5] Yet the incarnational potential of cultures is often distorted by power relationships, and in particular by patriarchal traditions that refuse to acknowledge the revelatory potential of women's lives.

For example, a survey conducted by the Joint Learning Initiative into HIV/AIDS in sub-Saharan Africa observes that "the voices of women, particularly women living with HIV, seemed subdued within the literature surveyed."[6] The researchers identified a number of factors that might inhibit women and prevent them from accessing HIV and maternal health services, including:

- Experience or fear of stigmatization and discrimination
- Experience or fear of abandonment, abuse, and violence
- Lack of male involvement or support for partners
- Poverty and economic dependence
- Difficulty of access in rural or remote areas
- Cultural influences that make women's health a low priority
- Failure to integrate local services
- Meaningful participation of women living with HIV
- Violence against women *within* health service contexts (coerced or even forced sterilization and being tested for HIV without informed consent or confidentiality).[7]

---

[5] Pope Francis, *Evangelii Gaudium,* Apostolic Exhortation (November 24, 2013), no. 122; http://www.vatican.va.

[6] Joint Learning Initiative on Faith and Local Communities, "HIV and Maternal Health: Faith Groups' Activities, Contributions and Impact" (December 2012), report prepared by Ann Smith and Jo Kaybryn, 17, http://jliflc.com.

[7] Ibid., 28.

The silencing and appropriation of poor women's voices deny those women the right to be, in the words of *Populorum Progressio,* "artisans of their destiny."[8] If, as Paul Ricoeur argues, life is "an activity and a desire in search of a narrative,"[9] then we must have the freedom to make meaning of our own lives, even while acknowledging that we are not in control of all that happens to us. Our meaning-making is therefore always a creative endeavor of seeking coherence and truthfulness within the apparently random and chaotic events that shape us. To quote Ricoeur again, "We learn to become *the narrator of our own story* without completely becoming the author of our life."[10] Arabome quotes a Kenyan proverb—"Nobody can use another person's teeth to smile."[11] In other words, every human being must have the right to tell her own story, to explore and discover the meaning of her own life in a mutually transformative dialogue between her personal circumstances and the cultures, traditions, and communities to which she belongs. A Catholic woman's experience of motherhood is profoundly shaped by church teaching, but she in turn must be able to offer back to the church her own insights gleaned through sometimes painful struggles and learning experiences.

At the Nairobi conference, one participant observed that "we know the position of the church on contraceptives. Yet it is also true that in secret many Catholic women use contraceptives. What do we do? Where do we go with this?" When conformity to church teaching condemns women to secrecy and silence about such vital realities of daily life, that teaching is not a life-giving source of inspiration and meaning but an oppressive and life-denying burden. Another participant spoke of the sterilization of HIV+ women without their consent. All such practices are destructive of the personhood of those who are silenced and denied the opportunity to share their experiences with others and to arrive at a creative and insightful understanding of the meaning of their own lives.

Alongside cultural and religious influences that can have a silencing effect on women, there is also a tendency for African women's lives to be appropri-

---

[8] Pope Paul VI, *Populorum Progressio,* Encyclical on the Development of Peoples (March 26, 1967), no. 65, http://www.vatican.va.

[9] Paul Ricoeur, "Life: A Story in Search of a Narrator," in *A Ricoeur Reader,* ed. M. J. Valdés (New York: Harvester Wheatsheaf, 1991), 434.

[10] Ibid., 437.

[11] Arabome, "Who Is Christ for African Women?" 25.

ated by competing sides in debates about population and development. They thus become objectified in international debates, by those who speak for them and about them while rarely inviting them to speak for themselves.

One heated debate that continues to play out with little grassroots participation concerns the provision of contraception to African women as part of aid and development programs. In 2013 the American Catholic philanthropist Melinda Gates announced her intention to promote voluntary family planning in the world's poorest countries. The Bill and Melinda Gates Foundation website explains the reasoning behind this decision: "Less than 20 percent of women in Sub-Saharan Africa and barely one-third of women in South Asia use modern contraceptives. In 2012, an estimated 80 million women in developing countries had an unintended pregnancy; of those women, at least one in four resorted to an unsafe abortion."[12]

The Nigerian Catholic Obianuju Ekeocha, a biomedical scientist who lives in Britain, wrote an open letter to Gates, challenging her position.[13] Apparently speaking for the whole of Africa, Ekeocha claims, "All I can say with certainty is that we, as a society, LOVE and welcome babies. . . . Amidst all our African afflictions and difficulties, amidst all the socioeconomic and political instabilities, babies are always a firm symbol of hope, a promise of life, a reason to strive for the legacy of a bright future."

Ekeocha points to the "very high compliance with Pope Paul VI's *'Humanae Vitae',"* because "African women, in all humility, have heard, understood and accepted the precious words of the prophetic pope." Rather than funding contraceptive programs, which she argues will encourage promiscuity, infidelity, and disease, Ekeocha urges Gates to sponsor good health care systems, including natural family planning, in response to the "alarmingly high" level of postpartum and neonatal deaths in sub-Saharan Africa (an acknowledgment that sits uneasily alongside her earlier, unqualified celebration of childbearing in Africa), to provide food programs for young children, to fund the promotion of chastity and higher education and micro-business opportunities for women, and to fortify NGOs that protect women from sex-trafficking, arranged marriage, domestic violence, and so on.

[12] Bill and Melinda Gates Foundation, "Family Planning: Strategy Overview," http://www.gatesfoundation.org.
[13] Obianuju Ekeocha, "An Open Letter to Melinda Gates," October 20, 2012, *Catholic Online*, http://www.catholic.org.

There is some substance to Ekeocha's protest. Contraceptive programs are not always effective in reducing birthrates in poor communities for a variety of cultural and economic reasons,[14] and such programs are haunted by the threat of Malthusian population control policies imposed by the wealthy nations on the poor.[15] The most effective way to reduce high birthrates is to educate women and to reduce infant mortality rates.[16] However, the ability to limit the number of children one has still depends on access to reliable methods of birth control, so this does not entirely vindicate the church's emphasis on education and poverty alleviation instead of contraceptive availability. Women surely need both, as well as a culture in which men respect a woman's right to decide whether and when to have sex.

However, to return to the theme of silencing, both Gates and Ekeocha exemplify how powerful elites can silence the voices of women who are poor. In the case of Gates, women's personal narratives of maternal struggle and hope are subsumed within statistics that fail to communicate the textured dynamics of sorrow and love that constitute mothering in its many aspects and contexts. A utilitarian approach that uses statistics as a basis for action risks blanking out vast questions of personal desire, vision, and faith that lend an irreducible diversity to women's reproductive decisions, even when they have some choice in the matter.

Ekeocha has been embraced by conservative Catholic groups that endorse natural family planning and resist programs aimed at promoting women's sexual and reproductive rights.[17] However, she gives no voice to the thousands of African women who are desperate for access to reliable contraception, or who would rather risk death through illegal abortion than carry

[14] Cf. John Bongaarts, "Can Family Planning Programmes Reduce High Desired Family Size in Sub-Saharan Africa?" *International Perspectives on Sexual and Reproductive Health* 37, no. 4 (December 2011), https://www.guttmacher.org.

[15] Cf. Dean Mitchell, "The Malthus Effect: Population and the Liberal Government of Life," *Economy and Society* 44, no. 1 (2015): 18–39; Kalpana Wilson, "Towards a Radical Re-appropriation: Gender, Development and Neoliberal Feminism," *Development and Change* 46, no. 4 (2015): 803–32.

[16] Cf. David Shapiro and Michel Tenikue, "Women's Education, Infant and Child Mortality, and Fertility Decline in Sub-Saharan Africa: A Quantitative Assessment," paper given at Seventh African Population Conference, Johannesburg, November 30–December 4, 2015, http://uaps2015.princeton.edu.

[17] Cf. Ekeocha's biography on the *Culture of Life Africa* website, http://cultureoflifeafrica.com.

an unwanted pregnancy to term. Complex human realities are reduced to competing ideologies, and the bodies of girls and women slip through the linguistic grids of international politics and development discourse.

Maternal Mortality: The Facts

We cannot reduce the multifaceted narratives of human life to statistics, policies, and strategies. However, while statistics must be used with caution, quantitative research can offer a broad overview of progress that has been made and challenges that remain with regard to reducing maternal mortality rates and promoting the well-being of women and thereby of children and families. So let me give a brief statistical summary of recent trends.

In a world in which news relating to poverty and justice often seems unremittingly bleak, statistics relating to maternal mortality show that real progress is possible. The Millennium Development Goals included a resolution to reduce maternal mortality rates between 1990 and 2015 by three quarters. While this goal was not achieved, there has been a worldwide drop in maternal deaths of almost 44 percent since 1990.[18] Globally, the estimated number of maternal deaths every year has declined from 523,000 in 1990 to 303,000 in 2015.[19] Some countries in sub-Saharan Africa have more than halved the number of maternal deaths. In Kenya, First Lady Margaret Kenyatta launched the "Beyond Zero" campaign in 2014, to work with the Kenyan government to reduce maternal and child mortality.[20]

However, 99 percent of maternal deaths still occur in the world's poorest countries, with 66 percent of these in sub-Saharan Africa. Estimates suggest that women in high-income countries face a 1 in 3,300 lifetime risk of dying in childbirth, whereas in Sierra Leone and Chad, a woman faces a 1 in 17 and a 1 in 18 lifetime risk, respectively.[21] Such estimates are inevitably imprecise, but they offer stark evidence of the extent to which poverty, violence, and political instability are linked to high rates of maternal mortality.

Many women who survive complications in childbirth suffer serious long-term injury because of a lack of access to good obstetric facilities. These women are the poorest of the poor, excluded not only in economic terms

---

[18] See *Trends in Maternal Mortality 1990–2013*, ix.
[19] Ibid.
[20] See the Beyond Zero website, http://www.beyondzero.or.ke.
[21] Ibid.

but often socially isolated because of the nature of their injuries and disabilities. Among the most distressing of these are the fistulas that can result from obstructed childbirth. Colleen Carpenter Cullinan describes what this entails:

> The baby usually dies after the first few days, but is only born much later, when the mother's body has been so injured by the unrelenting pressure of the child's body pushing against hers—resulting in a good bit of her living skin and muscle and tissue dying from lack of blood flow—that her body rips apart and frees the dead child at long last. In the best case scenario, the tear opens her bladder and she is left incontinent, unable to contain a constant flow of urine. In the worst case, the tear opens not only her bladder but her rectum, and both feces and urine spill forth from her body in a relentless, unstoppable flow that—without surgical repair—will last for the rest of her life. Some women also have nerve damage and find themselves unable to move their legs properly, or at all. So a child born dead, grievous untended internal injuries, filth, stench, perhaps even paralysis. Of course, this is only the beginning: who would live with such a creature? She smells, she cannot keep herself clean or dry, she is not fit for society and barely fit for work. Her husband leaves her. The other women of the village shun her. Her child is dead.[22]

Such accounts of maternal death and suffering should be a matter of urgent concern to the church, particularly given its emphasis on the importance of family life and, under the leadership of Pope Francis, on focusing attention on the poor and the marginalized. Catholic NGOs and other agencies, often run by religious orders, are in the frontline of providing health care and education to poor women and girls, but as I have already mentioned, maternal mortality does not feature in Catholic social teaching. Moreover, Catholic health care providers have to navigate competing interests and conflicting demands in providing reproductive health care and contraceptive advice to their patients, not least because of the need to uphold church teachings in the policies if not in the day-to-day practices of their institutions.[23] In

---

[22] Colleen Carpenter Cullinan, "In Pain and Sorrow: Childbirth, Incarnation, and the Suffering of Women," *Cross Currents* 58, no. 1 (Spring 2008): 95–96.
[23] Cf. Jill Olivier, "Faith and Health Care in Africa: A Complex Reality," *Open Democracy* (April 18, 2014), https://www.opendemocracy.net.

their influential book on global injustices against women, *Half the Sky*, Nicholas D. Kristof and Sheryl WuDunn point out that Catholic missionaries and organizations like Catholic Relief Services play a crucial role in health care provision in poor societies. They make the point that "local priests and nuns often ignore Rome and quietly do what they can to save parishioners."[24]

These conditions of subterfuge and secrecy create added burdens for those who dedicate their lives to serving the poor yet who cannot speak openly about the nature of the demands on them and the practical responses required. Only when we can bring all these issues into the open for serious theological reflection will we be able to articulate an ethical vision capable of responding to the suffering and needs of the world's poorest women and girls.

With that in mind, I now approach the question of maternal well-being from a perspective that is central to Catholic social teaching—namely, the perspective of human dignity. If we take dignity as our starting point, what might we begin to see with regard to women's sexual and reproductive health?

Maternal Well-Being and Women's Human Dignity

The appeal to human dignity as a modern foundation for politics, law, and ethics is enshrined in the 1948 Universal Declaration of Human Rights. The preamble to that historic document begins with the claim that "recognition of the inherent dignity and of the equal and inalienable rights of all members of the human family is the foundation of freedom, justice and peace in the world."[25]

The principle of human dignity is therefore recognized as the source of all human rights. The Vatican II Pastoral Constitution on the Church in the Modern World, *Gaudium et Spes*, refers to

> a growing awareness of the exalted dignity proper to the human person, since he or she stands above all things, and his or her rights and duties are universal and inviolable. Therefore, there must be made available to all people everything necessary for leading a life truly

---

[24] Nicholas D. Kristof and Sheryl WuDunn, *Half the Sky: How to Change the World* (2009; London: Virago Press, 2010), 158.

[25] The Universal Declaration of Human Rights, United Nations website, http://www.un.org.

human, such as food, clothing, and shelter; the right to choose a state of life freely and to found a family, the right to education, to employment, to a good reputation, to respect, to appropriate information, to activity in accord with the upright norm of one's own conscience, to protection of privacy and rightful freedom even in matters religious.[26]

When viewed from the perspective of women's dignity, that list in *Gaudium et Spes* would be a good starting point. The right to found a family must be protected, particularly when Western states, corporations, and international development agencies might use the threat of overpopulation to justify coercive population control measures. However, the right to choose a state of life freely must include a woman's right to have access to "appropriate information" in order to decide whether or not to have children and how many children to have.

We find the most radical statement on the meaning and implications of the doctrine of intrinsic human dignity in the Vatican II 1965 document on Religious Freedom, *Dignitatis Humanae*. Here is the crucial paragraph, and I have substituted "woman" for "man" in the translation of the Latin "*homo*":

> It is in accordance with their dignity as persons—that is, beings endowed with reason and free will and therefore privileged to bear personal responsibility—that all women should be at once impelled by nature and also bound by a moral obligation to seek the truth, especially religious truth. They are also bound to adhere to the truth, once it is known, and to order their whole lives in accord with the demands of truth. However, women cannot discharge these obligations in a manner in keeping with their own nature unless they enjoy immunity from external coercion as well as psychological freedom. Therefore the right to religious freedom has its foundation not in the subjective disposition of the person, but in her very nature. In consequence, the right to this immunity continues to exist even in those who do not live up to their obligation of seeking the truth and adhering to it and the exercise of this right is not to be impeded, provided that just public order be observed.[27]

---

[26] *Gaudium et Spes*, Pastoral Constitution on the Church in the Modern World, December 7, 1965, no. 26, http://www.vatican.va.

[27] Pope Paul VI, *Dignitatis Humanae*, Declaration on Religious Freedom, December 7, 1965, http://www.vatican.va.

According to this definition of human dignity, women must be free to take ethical responsibility for their own reproductive choices, even when the church believes their choices to be morally wrong or misguided. The insistence that a person's freedom to follow her conscience can only be curtailed if she poses a threat to society has always informed the Catholic understanding of the law. The law cannot be used to regulate personal morality, but only to protect the common good.

If one considers the ways in which the Catholic tradition interprets mothering in relation to religious commitment, then reproductive freedom becomes closely bound up with freedom of conscience and freedom of religion. The religious dimension of mothering means that a woman's decisions concerning her maternal capacities are bound up not only with her natural human dignity but also with the religious freedom that is intrinsic to her dignity. So, for example, there is now abundant evidence that the majority of Catholic women who have the education and freedom to reflect on these issues have decided in good conscience to reject the church's prohibition of artificial birth control.[28] Even if one thinks that they are violating their duty to seek and adhere to the truth, this does not justify violating their freedom to follow their conscience—for example, by using the law to coerce women into compliance with the church's stance against artificial contraception. Space precludes an exploration of the complex moral dilemmas associated with abortion, but I have argued elsewhere that the church's own tradition allows for a distinction between early and late abortion, in a way that might invite a more nuanced moral approach to this personally intimate but also socially significant ethical dilemma.[29]

Populorum Progressio argues that integral human development "involves building a human community in which people can live truly human lives, free from discrimination on account of race, religion or nationality, free from servitude to others or to natural forces which they cannot yet control satisfactorily."[30] For the vast majority of the world's women and girls,

---

[28] Cf. Julie Clague, "Catholics, Families, and the Synod of Bishops: Views from the Pews," in *Catholic Women Speak: Bringing Our Gifts to the Table*, ed. Catholic Women Speak Network (Mahwah NJ: Paulist Press, 2015), 51–56.

[29] Tina Beattie, "Catholicism, Choice and Consciousness: A Feminist Theological Perspective on Abortion," *International Journal of Public Theology* 4, no. 1 (2010): 51–75.

[30] Pope Paul VI, *Populorum Progressio*, Encyclical on the Development of Peoples, March 26, 1967, no. 47, http://www.vatican.va.

freedom from servitude to others and freedom to satisfactorily control the natural forces of pregnancy and childbearing in order to live truly human lives is still a distant and unattainable vision.

In that text from Isaiah with which I began, God identifies with these silenced women in their birth pains, while the prophet shouts to the world about a warrior God. Men of God still do not see that God does not ride out like a warrior to conquer the world. God groans with creation in childbirth, and God shares the anguish of mothers whose birth cries are silenced by the violence and injustice of the powers of this world.

Yet it is not enough just to address material questions of poverty and health care when we speak about such issues—though certainly we must do that. We also have to ask about women's spiritual, social, and psychological well-being—asking not just why women die, but also how women might be fully alive. This means listening to women's stories, allowing them to narrate their lives in ways that express their desires and hopes, their struggles and sorrows. If we are to create a world in which all can flourish, then we must allow those who bear the children of the future to tell their stories—as women, as daughters, as sisters, as mothers, as wives, as persons of dignity made in the image of God. We must recognize that when we stifle their voices, we stifle the voice of the maternal God who groans in childbirth and cannot be heard.

Beyond Vatican II

Imagining the Catholic Church of Nairobi I

Joseph G. Healey

Be Bold and Creative

Agbonkhianmeghe Orobator, the editor of this volume, Jim Keane, the acquiring editor of Orbis Books, and I met to discuss a book that could evolve out of the Theological Colloquium on Church, Religion, and Society in Africa (TCCRSA).[1] In brainstorming about a possible title and cover we tried to think outside the conventional box. We drew a line through the words "Vatican III, Rome" on the cover and wrote "Nairobi I." We could have as easily written "Kinshasa I" or "Lagos I." Going further afield, we could have written "Manila I" or "São Paulo I." The idea was to challenge the natural assumption that the next ecumenical council[2] has to take place in Rome. If the center of gravity of the Catholic Church is moving from the West to the Global South,[3] why not have the successor to Vatican II meet in

---

[1] The spirit and practice of this colloquium is a process or method of African Christian Conversation Theology and African Christian Palaver Theology (more commonly used in Africa); thus I have incorporated the comments and insights from the participants during our discussion and dialogue on this essay. I also invited many pastoral workers and theologians into the "conversation" on this essay and incorporated their comments and insights. Separate volumes on each colloquium were published by Paulines Publications Africa.

[2] There have been twenty-one Catholic ecumenical councils over a period of 1,700 years starting with First Council of Nicaea (part of Asia Minor that roughly corresponds to the Asian part of Turkey) in 325. Most of these councils have taken place in countries in the Middle East and Europe.

[3] The nations of Africa, Central and Latin America, and most of Asia are collectively known as the Global South and include 157 recognized states in the world. This term is preferred to the terms "developing countries" and "Third World countries" that are pejorative and are usually used in a narrow economic sense.

one of the great cities of the Southern Hemisphere? The title we ended up with was *The Church We Want: African Catholics Look to Vatican III*.

I like the words "boldness" and "bold." Listen to the challenge of inculturation and contextualization presented by the German Jesuit theologian Father Karl Rahner, SJ, in 1979 that still rings true today:

> The [Catholic] Church must be inculturated throughout the world if it is to be a World Church. . . . This, then, is the issue: either the church sees and recognizes these essential differences of other cultures for which she should become a World Church and with a Pauline boldness draws the necessary consequences from this recognition, or she remains a Western Church and so in the final analysis betrays the meaning of Vatican II.[4]

Listen to Pope Francis's invitation in 2013 in no. 33 of *Evangelii Gaudium*:

> Pastoral ministry in a missionary key seeks to abandon the complacent attitude that says: "We have always done it this way." I invite everyone to be bold and creative in this task of rethinking the goals, structures, styles and methods of evangelization in their respective communities. A proposal of goals without an adequate communal search for the means of achieving them will inevitably prove illusory. I encourage everyone to apply the guidelines found in this document generously and courageously, without inhibitions or fear. The important thing is to not walk alone, but to rely on each other as brothers and sisters, and especially under the leadership of the bishops, in a wise and realistic pastoral discernment.[5]

---

[4] Karl Rahner, "Towards a Fundamental Theological Interpretation of Vatican II," *Theological Studies* 40, no. 4 (December 1979): 718, 724.

[5] Laurenti Magesa has insightfully commented, "John Paul II's papacy and the nearly eight years of his successor Benedict XVI (2005–2013) saw some practical retrenchment from the theological vision of Vatican II, something which, after Benedict's surprise resignation on 28 February 2013, Pope Francis his successor, has been trying to undo since his election on 13 March 2013." Laurenti Magesa, "Endless Quest: The Vocation of an African Christian Theologian" in *Endless Quest: The Vocation of an African Christian Theologian*, a Festschrift for Professor Laurenti Magesa, ed. Jesse Mugambi and Evaristi Magoti (Nairobi: Acton, 2014), 9.

This is an experience of pastoral accompaniment and walking together (the very meaning of "synod"). In this journey the Catholic Church in Africa has a great deal to contribute to the World Church or Universal Church.

Rethinking the Structures and Styles of Governing and Decision Making in the Catholic Church

How can we respond to Pope Francis's invitation to be bold and creative in this task of rethinking the structures and styles of governing and decision making in the Catholic Church? The Hungarian Jesuit canon lawyer Ladislas Orsy and others say there can be no real reform of the Roman Curia without decentralization of the church's governing structures and its decision-making apparatus. Orsy stresses that the doctrinal role of local and regional bishops' conferences should be developed as should collegiality and synodality.[6]

Let us look at five institutions in the Catholic Church that have the best chance of being given greater authority and carrying out a sound and healthy decentralization with some practical examples:

Pope Francis's Nine-Member Council of Cardinals

Part of the originality of Pope Francis's nine-member Council of Cardinals is its international composition, with representatives of all continents, including Cardinal Laurent Monsengwo, the archbishop of Kinshasa, Democratic Republic of the Congo (DRC). It has already established a new Congregation for Laity, Family, and Life, the Secretariat for the Economy, and the Secretariat for Communications. Presently this council is creating a new dicastery—the Congregation for Charity, Justice, and Peace.

Synod of Bishops

The Synod of Bishops is the perfect place for the doctrine of episcopal collegiality based on synodality and subsidiarity to be put into action. Many think that the two synods (the Third Extraordinary General Assembly

---

[6] Summarized from Robert Mickens, "Can Pope Francis Succeed in Reforming the Curia?" *National Catholic Reporter*, May 26, 2015, http://ncronline.org.

with the title "The Pastoral Challenges of the Family in the Context of Evangelization," in Rome, October 5–19, 2014, and the Fourteenth Ordinary General Assembly of the Synod of Bishops with the title "The Vocation and Mission of the Family in the Church and in the Contemporary[7] World" in Rome, October 4–25, 2015) were a breakthrough and brought back the dynamic Vatican II process.

A new and fresh language is evolving including these expressions/ideas and the theology and pastoral practice behind them:

- Catholic Church not just holding synods but becoming fully synodal
- Connected to the base, to the grassroots
- Directly incorporating collegiality
- Effective collegiality
- Healthy decentralization
- Listening at every level of the Catholic Church
- Making the "synodical model" a permanent feature/the normal way the Catholic Church regularly and routinely decides issues of theology and practice
- More authority to the Post-Synod Council
- More laypeople, especially women, should participate and vote.
- Pastoral window open to new approaches
- Permanent structures for consultation, discernment, and decision making at all levels
- Permanent synodality
- Process of each synod must begin with listening to the faithful
- Reciprocal listening in which each one has something to learn
- Starting point can be a deliberate, not just consultative, vote on important issues
- Synod is a journey
- Synodal church is a listening church, aware that listening is more than hearing
- Synodality of the whole Catholic Church

---

[7] The English word "contemporary" has a more up-to-date, "here and now" meaning than the word "modern."

- Synodal spirit must be at work in parishes and dioceses as well as in the Universal Church
- Way of the Catholic Church in the Third Millennium
- Way of synodality

The *Final Report* (*Relatio Synodi*) *of the Synod of Bishops to the Holy Father, Pope Francis*[8] was published on October 24, 2015, and is forty pages in length. All ninety-four paragraphs of the document were adopted by the assembly with the required two-thirds vote. Pope Francis's apostolic exhortation on the family and marriage, *Amoris Laetitia* (The Joy of Love), was released on April 8, 2016, during the Jubilee Year of Mercy.

Part of this synodal process is a more active role for the ongoing Fourteenth Ordinary Council of the Synod of Bishops made up of fifteen bishops (three bishops elected from each continent and three appointed by the pope). Also known as the Post-Synod Council or the Synod Ordinary Council, it will coordinate the follow-up to the Synod on the Family and marriage and prepare the topic of the next synod, traditionally held after three years. From the viewpoint of Africa there are special concerns. Of the three elected African members—Cardinal Wilfrid Napier from South Africa, Cardinal Peter Turkson from Ghana, and Cardinal Robert Sarah from Guinea—the last two are based in Rome and serving in the Curia. Cardinals in Rome are better known, some even with a celebrity status, and have a better chance of being elected than bishops serving in dioceses in Africa. But how much are they in touch with life in the trenches in Africa. How much of the Catholic Church on the ground in Africa will be represented?

Decentralized Roman Curia

I say "decentralized" Roman Curia because Vatican "business as usual" is fatal for real reform. As a start, might we ask why all the Vatican offices have to be based in Rome? An alternative creative idea could mean having the Office (or Council or Commission) for Environment/Ecology based in Nairobi, Kenya;[9] the Office (or Council or Commission) for Interreligious

---

[8] See the full text at http://www.vatican.va.

[9] This is the logical place because the United Nations Environment Program, the agency of the United Nations that coordinates its environmental activities, has its head-

Dialogue based in a city in Asia; and the Office (or Council or Commission) for Justice and Peace based in a city in Latin America. There should also be more women in leadership positions.

Continental, Regional, and National Bishops' Conferences

In *Evangelii Gaudium*, which he calls a sort of blueprint for his pontificate, Pope Francis says clearly, "I am conscious of the need to promote a sound 'decentralization.'" This means giving greater authority to our bishops' conferences. A dramatic case in point is how the Vatican has usurped authority over liturgical matters such as the Mass and the translation of the Bible into local languages. While being respectful of the Vatican, the Gikuyu-speaking Catholic Bishops in Kenya found it absurd that their professional translation of the Bible into the Gikuyu language had to be approved by the Sacred Congregation of the Liturgy in Rome (whose officials do not know Gikuyu) even to the point of a Gikuyu-speaking Kenyan seminarian studying in Rome vetting the text on behalf of the congregation.

After the universal Synod of Bishops titled "Family and Marriage," meetings (and even local synods) continue on the continental, regional, and national levels. Some initial discussions focused on the role of the local and universal church and the part that episcopal conferences might share. In these debates the focus was on what pastoral issues are best handled at what levels. Here is the perfect place for the doctrine of episcopal collegiality based on synodality and subsidiarity. In this ongoing synodal process and journey the Catholic Church in Africa can share its growing voice and important pastoral experiences of family and marriage and other issues with the Catholic Church worldwide.

In Rome, Cardinal Berhaneyesus Demerew Souraphiel, CM, archbishop of Addis Ababa, Ethiopia, and chairman of AMECEA (Association of Member Episcopal Conferences in Eastern Africa), said:

Pope Francis emphasizes decentralizing, that is, putting into practice the process that had been started in Vatican II, by establishing

---

quarters in the Gigiri neighborhood of Nairobi, Kenya. Pope Francis visited here in November 2015.

national conferences, while respecting the autonomy of each diocese. Then that will give cooperation, national cooperation in the conference, and discuss common issues, for forming solutions together and also regional cooperation. So that is putting into place the Second Vatican Council's decision on ecclesial structures, on church structures. So what Pope Francis is saying is more work on the local level because the church is so different in so many parts of the world. So he was reflecting what was being emphasized during the synod. So give more responsibility to the local bishop and to the local bishops' conference to do more.[10]

Office of Metropolitan Archbishops

Orsy emphasizes that the office of metropolitan archbishops could be reformed with the aim of decentralizing decision making away from Rome. He explains that since the Council of Trent (1545–1563), juridical authority that once was constituent of the metropolitans has all but disappeared, leaving them with the strange woolen band draped over their shoulders and precedence in liturgical processions as the only things that differentiate them from other bishops.

An example of following Pope Francis's rethinking of the structures of evangelization is seen in Eastern Africa: In 2013–2015 AMECEA[11] facilitated small Christian communities (SCCs) workshops in the nine countries of Eastern Africa. After national workshops in Zambia (December 2013), Malawi (December 2013), Ethiopia (March 2014), Kenya (May 2015), and South Sudan (October 2015), the SCCs Eastern Africa Training Team shifted to the more appropriate local-level Metropolitan Workshops in

---

[10] Deborah Castellano Lubov, "Interview: Head of Ethiopian Catholic Church: Human Rights Crises Merit More Attention at Synod," "ZENIT: The World Seen from Rome," October 23, 2015, http://www.zenit.org/.

[11] AMECEA (Association of Member Episcopal Conferences in Eastern Africa) is a service organization for the National Episcopal Conferences of the nine English-speaking countries of Eastern Africa, namely, Eritrea, Ethiopia, Kenya, Malawi, South Sudan, Sudan, Tanzania, Uganda, and Zambia. AMECEA is one of the eight Regional Episcopal Conferences of SECAM (Symposium of Episcopal Conferences of Africa and Madagascar).

Tanzania (dioceses in the Ecclesiastical Province of Mwanza in May 2014) and Uganda (dioceses in the Ecclesiastical Province of Tororo in May 2015).

From the Perspective of SCCs in Eastern Africa

In January 1986 I participated in the South African Missiological Conference in Pretoria, South Africa. The keynote speaker was Swiss theologian Hans Küng. I gave a lecture titled "Basic Christian Communities: Church-Centered or World-Centered?" This lecture was derived mainly from the pastoral experience of SCCs in Eastern Africa. After my talk I received a handwritten message that Küng wanted to see me at the next coffee break. Küng explained that in his latest research he had been studying different paradigms of the church: house churches in the first century, monasteries in medieval times, and the parish in recent centuries. He wondered if the parish model was no longer appropriate in different places in the world, and if the model or paradigm of the future is SCCs.[12]

I have often wondered if this was prophetic. Although the term "small Christian communities" is not mentioned specifically in the documents of Vatican II, some of the great theologians of the council emphasized them in their writings in the 1950s, 1960s, and 1970s. The French Dominican theologian Yves Congar, wrote in *Lay People in the Church* that SCCs are "little church cells wherein the mystery is lived directly and with great simplicity.... The church's machinery, sometimes the very institution, is a barrier obscuring her deep and living mystery, which they can find, or find again, only from below."[13]

In his foreword to the book *Small Christian Communities Today: Capturing the New Moment*, Cardinal Cormac Murphy-O'Connor, the retired archbishop of Westminster, England, quotes Congar and adds:

Congar hit upon an important truth: that renewal in the church has come about, time and time again in its history, in and through

---

[12] See Joseph Healey and Jeanne Hinton, eds., *Small Christian Communities Today: Capturing the New Moment* (Maryknoll, NY: Orbis Books, 2005; and Nairobi: Paulines Publications Africa, 2006), 155.

[13] Yves Congar, *Lay People in the Church* (1953; rev. ed., London: Geoffrey Chapman, 1985), 341.

the inspiration of small communities—monastic, evangelical, missionary, lay communities, communities of women—fired by the Holy Spirit.[14]

Today there are over 180,000 SCCs in the Catholic Church in the nine AMECEA countries. Tanzania has over 60,000 SCCs, and Kenya has over 45,000 SCCs. Since 1973 they have been a key pastoral priority in Eastern Africa as a "New Way of Being (Becoming) Church" and a "New Pastoral Model of Church."[15] The rich experience of the church in Eastern Africa, especially that of pastoral, parish-based SCCs, is contributing to the church in other parts of Africa and to the World Church.

SCCs offer a pastoral model of church integrally connected to the structures, ministries, and activities of the parish. This helps local Catholics feel that "they are the church" and more responsible for church life and decision making (or have "ownership" in the church). Experiments of pastoral restructuring have taken place in Eastern African dioceses such as the Same Diocese in Tanzania.

The then-bishop Josaphat Lebulu of Same (now archbishop of Arusha, Tanzania) and his pastoral coworkers restructured the diocese according to a "Communion of Communities Ecclesiology" in the geographical reality of the northeastern part of Tanzania. The traditional structure of diocese/parish/SCC did not seem to fit the local reality, which includes large, disparate, and unwieldy parishes and a physical geography of many hills and small mountains.

The new structure was diocese/center/SCC. Rather than focusing on the seventeen traditional parishes, they created fifty-five centers (similar to subparishes or outstations) and around 250 SCCs. In this model the diocese is a "Communion of Centers," and the center is a "Communion of SCCs." The pastoral animation and service try to get down to the grassroots where the people live and work. Eight lay ecclesial ministries were started in the SCCs and continue on the center and diocesan levels. These lay ecclesial ministry leaders form a team of coordinators/formators on the SCC, center, and diocesan levels.[16]

---

[14] Healey and Hinton, *Small Christian Communities Today*, xi.

[15] See the Small Christian Communities Global Collaborative website and Facebook page: www.smallchristiancommunities.org.

[16] See Joseph Healey, "Diocesan Structure of Small Christian Communities in

The *Final Report (Relatio Synodi)* on "Family and Marriage," October 24, 2015, mentions SCCs (or their equivalent) three times:

First, under "The Initial Years of Family Life" (no. 60):

The parish is the place where experienced couples may be made available to the younger ones, possibly in conjunction with associations, ecclesial movements and new communities. Strengthening the network of relationships between couples and creating meaningful connections among people are necessary for the maturation of the family's Christian life. Movements and church groups often provide these moments of growth and formation. The Local Church, by integrating the contributions of various persons and groups, assumes the work of coordinating the pastoral care of young families.

Second, under "Accompaniment[17] in Different Situations" (no. 77):

"The Church will have to initiate everyone—priests, religious and laity—into this 'art of accompaniment' which teaches us to remove our sandals before the sacred ground of the other (cf. *Exodus* 3:5). The pace of this accompaniment must be steady and reassuring, reflecting our closeness and our compassionate gaze which also heals, liberates and encourages growth in the Christian life" (*Evangelii Gaudium*, 169). The main contribution to the pastoral care of families is offered by the parish, which is the family of families, where small communities, ecclesial movements and associations live in harmony.

Same," in "Twelve Case Studies of Small Christian Communities in Eastern Africa" in *How Local is the Local Church? Small Christian Communities and Church in Eastern Africa*, ed. Agatha Radoli (Eldoret: AMECEA Gaba Publications, *Spearhead* 126–28, 1993), 59–103.

[17] The *Final Report* has thirteen references to "accompany," eight references to "accompaniment," and four references to "accompanying." The *Instrumentum Laboris* has sixteen references to "accompany," thirteen references to "accompaniment," and eight references to "accompanying." SCC members accompany engaged couples throughout the stages of their marriage and married couples in their first years of marriage.

And third, under "The Family as the Subject of Pastoral Ministry" (no. 90):

May every family, incorporated in the church, rediscover the joy of communion with other families so as to serve the common good of society by promoting policy-making, an economy and a culture in the service of the family through the use of *social networks* and the *media* which calls for the ability to create small communities of families as living witnesses of Gospel values. Families need to be prepared, trained and empowered to guide others in living in a Christian manner. Families who are willing to live the mission *ad gentes* are to be acknowledged and encouraged. Finally, we note the importance of connecting youth ministry with family ministry.

A wide variety of names and terms related to SCCs are used in the document to describe family catechesis, marriage catechesis, and different forms of pastoral ministry connected to the family. The document synthesizes material from previous synods and questionnaires. It affirms the important role of SCCs in pastoral accompaniment of families and married couples. But it does not break too much new ground in providing concrete pastoral solutions to the biggest challenges today.

With the conclusion of the Synod of Bishops on the Family, it is the responsibility of the local churches in Africa to "prepare, train and empower" families for this evangelizing work and to identify where, in the local communities, our families are being called to service. SCCs as a communion of families play a big role.

Pastoral Solutions to the Two Meanings of the Eucharistic Famine in Africa

Pope Francis's challenge to be bold and creative can be applied to the two meanings of the Eucharistic Famine (also called the "Eucharistic Hunger") in Africa: First, due to the lack of priests on any given Sunday, most Catholics in Africa (up to 80 percent in some surveys)[18] rather than

---

[18] American Catholics may not have a sense of the magnitude of this crisis especially as Catholic dioceses in the United States continue to import African and Indian priests.

taking part in a regular Mass, participate in a "Sunday Service without a Priest"[19] (especially in rural areas) where usually there is no Holy Communion. Second, many Catholics in Africa cannot receive communion because they are not officially married in the Catholic Church. In some surveys 60 percent of adult Catholics in Africa have not had their marriages blessed in church (sacramentalized). Other practicing Catholics are divorced and remarried civilly outside the Catholic Church so cannot receive the Eucharist.

Hopefully the ongoing process after the October 2015 Synod of Bishops will find concrete pastoral solutions. Pope Francis in no. 47 of *Evangelii Gaudium* says: "The Eucharist, although it is the fullness of sacramental life, is not a prize for the perfect but a powerful medicine and nourishment for the weak." Two creative pastoral solutions for Africa are discussed in the following sections.

Ordination of Married Community Elders (Married Priesthood)

Providing the Eucharist to all Catholics in Africa is a great need. Malawian theologian Bishop Patrick Kalilombe, who died in 2012, emphasized that the Eucharistic community is the heart of our Christian life. He says that if Christian communities in Africa cannot receive the Eucharist because of the lack of ordained ministers that presently in the Latin Rite are male, celibate priests, then we must rethink our church laws and pastoral practices. For example, we could ordain mature married men of proven leadership skills (*viri probati* in Latin). Then many more people would be able to receive communion and our SCCs would truly be Eucharistic Communities.

The question arises: In reading the signs of the times, is the pastoral solution of married priests an idea whose time has come?

German Bishop Fritz Lobinger, a retired *Fidei Donum* bishop of Aliwal Diocese, South Africa, has written extensively on these topics in *Teams of Elders: Moving Beyond "Viri Probati"* (Claretian Publications, 2007) and *Every Community Its Own Ordained Leaders* (Claretian Publications, Philippines, 2008). He puts forward the case for ordaining

---

[19] Also called "Sunday Celebration in the Absence of a Priest," "Sunday Worship without a Priest," "Sunday Service of the Word with Communion," and "Eucharistic Prayer Service Outside of Mass."

married men in underserved areas. In commenting on the World Church, and particularly in the Global South, Lobinger states: "The priestless communities of the South have already developed a ministry structure of their own. We just have to build on it."[20] "Lay leaders preach, conduct services, conduct funerals, pray for the sick and in some areas they are even authorized to conduct baptisms and marriages. There can be no doubt that they would also be accepted if they were ordained to the ministerial priesthood."[21]

A key for Lobinger is that the ordination of elders would work in vibrant, self-reliant Catholic communities in Africa such as the networks of parish-based SCCs. He admits that some priests view a new path to ordination without formal academic training or the celibacy requirement as a threat that could undermine the traditional priesthood. But Lobinger argues that traditionally trained priests would fit into the new system. "The new local leaders (Married Community Elders) become a leadership team and the priests become formators."[22]

This is similar to the vision of Cardinal Joseph Malula, the late archbishop of Kinshasa Archdiocese in the Democratic Republic of Congo, who died in 1989. He believed very much in the laity and created the lay ecclesial ministry of *Bakambi* (singular *Mokambi*) who were married men who served as responsible parish leaders. They were full-time administrators of parishes empowered to lead communities in everything except in saying Mass. Malula's vision was to have some of these men one day lead Eucharistic communities, that is, celebrate the Eucharist, a vision that met with displeasure at the Vatican and gradually declined. In the church today we have laypeople who can lead Eucharistic communities but can't because of the stringent rules.

The retired Bishop Colin Davies of Ngong Diocese, Kenya, writes:

I am going to advocate the incorporation of the Byzantine Rite into the Roman Rite which has the option of having married priests.

---

[20] Fritz Lobinger, letter to the author dated September 28, 2013.

[21] Fritz Lobinger in Benjamin Soloway, "Brazilian Bishop Urges Ordination of Married Community Elders, *Religious News Service*, November 24, 2014, p. 1. Reprinted in the *Washington Post,* http://www.washingtonpost.com and the *Huffington Post,* http://www.huffingtonpost.com.

[22] Ibid.

Celibacy, a most treasured gift to the Catholic Church, has now become a block to helping to solve the problem, not only of Eucharistic Hunger but also of the Pastoral (Prophetic) Role of Christ active in the Eucharistic Ministry and in the Priesthood of the Laity. I am hoping it will be recognized and discussed as one of the "Signs of the Times" at the Synods of Bishops. I see SCCs as seeds for the growth of Eucharistic Communities with the possibility of mature laymen becoming ordained priests![23]

But many other African bishops differ and want to maintain the present celibate priesthood discipline.

A related twofold pastoral solution to the Eucharistic Famine:[24]

1. Dramatically increase the number of Eucharistic ministers—sisters, brothers, and especially laypeople. More religious sisters and brothers could easily make this part of their pastoral ministry.
2. Build strong, secure churches in the subparishes or Mass centers. Have the Blessed Sacrament reserved in these churches. Then the Eucharist could be given out at all services.

As we journey toward Vatican III, we should have more theological and pastoral research, discussion, and discernment on different forms of ordained and nonordained ministry, including greater leadership for women.

African Stages of Marriage

One intriguing proposal in Africa for many years is to develop an inculturated Rite for the Catechumenate of Christian Marriage (marriage catechumenate) similar to the Rite for the Christian Initiation of Adults (or the adult catechumenate). This could be two years or more depending on the customs and traditions (cultural dimension) of the local ethnic groups

---

[23] Colin Davies, email messages to the author, April 21, 2014, and April 22, 2014.

[24] This solution was developed during discussions in an SCC Workshop in Tororo, Uganda, in May 2015. This could solve the problem of some Catholics in distant rural areas in Uganda (and other African countries) who receive the Eucharist only twice a year.

in Africa. It would integrate the basic elements of consent in the traditional African marriage rituals into the Christian sacrament of marriage.

This would follow the stages of marriage[25] in an African context (also called "marriage in stages") where marriage is a process rather than a single event, and marriage is between two families rather than just between two individuals. The Catholic sacramental and spiritual "moments" (not "moment") would take place during different stages of the marriage process: from the first official meeting and agreement of the two families of the couple to the betrothal (engagement) to the living together to the paying of the dowry or bridewealth (that often takes place slowly over many years) to the wife's pregnancy to the birth of the first child to the civil marriage to the Catholic Marriage Rite (that could be in a Catholic Church or in a SCC) to the wedding celebration.[26]

The couple usually lives together during most of this process—what is commonly called premarital cohabitation. During this period, sometimes called the "trial marriage" or "the test of compatibility" period, the couple test their ability to live together and to get along with their in-laws. In African ethnic groups it is essential for the couple to have successful consummation that leads to procreation. Infertility could be a cause for the breakup of the marriage.

An important dimension is the Ministry of Pastoral Accompaniment that is emphasized in the documents of the two World Synods of Bishops (2014–2015) on "Family and Marriage."[27] SCC members accompany the

---

[25] In an interview with the author in Washington, DC, on October 9, 2014, Orsy mentioned that in the history of the Catholic Church the German tribes had this "gradual" approach to the sacrament of marriage. It was only confirmed after the couple lived together successfully for six months.

[26] I asked a devout Catholic married woman in Iramba Parish in Musoma Diocese, Tanzania, what was the happiest day of her life. She answered: "Not the day of my marriage or the day of the birth of my first child. It was the day my firstborn son was circumcised." For her this symbolized that her son had passed to manhood and the continuance of the family lineage was assured. As a mother she had successfully done her part.

[27] See Kenya Conference of Catholic Bishops (KCCB) General Secretariat, "*Relatio Synodi* 2015—Pastoral Guidelines for a Process of Discussion and Action," Nairobi: Kenya Conference of Catholic Bishops, 2015. Online version: "Family and Marriage in Kenya Today: Pastoral Guidelines for a Process of Discussion and Action," http://www.kccb.or.ke.

engaged couple throughout the stages of marriage. A representative of the
Catholic Church such as a priest or catechist is present at the important cere-
monies and accompanies the couple in the key moments. For example, in
a wedding of a couple of the Sukuma ethnic group in Tanzania, the most
important cultural ceremony is when the father of the groom hands over the
dowry/bridewealth of cows to the father of the bride. This is a large, joyous
event of the two families and the local community that includes the elders
making a careful inspection of the cows themselves and a festive meal with
plenty of food and local beer. In Bunda Parish in Bunda Diocese, the parish
priest participates in this celebration and gives a blessing.[28] Tanzanian theologian Laurenti Magesa suggests that the cultural ceremony of the cows should
be combined/integrated with the Catholic Church marriage ceremony.[29]

A number of African bishops have pointed out how hard it is to achieve
a consensus on marriage rites given the wide variety of African cultural
traditions, customs, and rites. Retired Kenyan Archbishop Raphael Ndingi
Mwana'a Nzeki of Nairobi, Kenya, explained that the 1994 African Synod
appointed him to a Commission on Marriage in an African Context. He
said that our Catholic marriage laws are based on Western law (for example,
German law). The hope was to develop common inculturated guidelines on
marriage that could be used throughout Africa. But the commission failed
and was disbanded.

At the Synod of Bishops on "Family and Marriage" in October 2015
African bishops discerned on the issue of couples cohabiting before
marriage, which legally goes against church teaching. Cardinal Napier
argued that more leniency should be granted couples in Africa, for whom,
he said, living together before marriage is often more a "step" in the marriage
process than a rejection of matrimony or a trial marriage. "Cohabitation in
our case is pro-marriage, not against marriage," he said. "In regard to the
traditional African marriage custom, first of all it's not a marriage between
two individuals but between two families. So there's a whole process of
negotiation," he said. When a dowry is established by the bride's family, the
cardinal said, often it may take a young man a very long time, perhaps years,

---

[28] Based on American missionary Father Bill Vos's several conversations with the
author in 2013 and 2014.

[29] Laurenti Magesa's conversation with the author in Nairobi, Kenya, on March
14, 2007.

to raise the money to cover it. "In the meantime, the families could agree that at a certain point they would start living together as husband and wife, even though the marriage is not yet concluded," he said.

The cardinal said the term "cohabitation" doesn't really fit that African experience. In the West, he said, couples may also live together for economic or other reasons, but it's not the same. He added that it was up to African bishops to make sure that "that particular custom does get incorporated into the sacrament of matrimony." That, of course, would be a major change. The same issue was discussed at the First African Synod, held at the Vatican in 1994, and there's been no significant action on it since. But Napier said he thought that "with Pope Francis's lead," African bishops will have a new impetus for studying the issue.[30] He said sometimes people use the word "arranged marriage" but it is "actually negotiated" in that the bride's family is "to say what the dowry should be." Saving for the dowry can take a long time, the cardinal added, and in the meantime, "the families could agree that they can start living together as husband and wife, even though the marriage is not yet completed." He said it is therefore different from the Western concept of cohabitation, which means moving in together because it's less expensive or for some other reasons, but not necessarily with marriage as an end.[31]

Cardinal Napier is eager to explore the opening toward more local decision making that Pope Francis raised during his speech at the synod when he spoke of a more "synodal" and collegial exercise of authority in the church. According to the US bishops, almost half the couples who come in for marriage preparation courses in local parishes are cohabitating. The figure is really much higher. The rates of cohabitation across Africa are generally much lower, but studies indicate they are increasing in some countries, both as a prelude to marriage and an alternative to marriage.

The synod heard a suggestion, for example, for ritual adaptation to accommodate the stages of traditional African marriage—with the African bishops guiding the discussion. After many years of Rome emphasizing the limits of inculturation, this seems to be a time for new exploration of diversity in the church. Pope Francis, in fact, highlighted this possibility in his final synod speech on inculturation.

---

[30] John Thavis, "Cardinal Napier Has Praise for Synod Process, Pope Francis' Leadership," "The Blog," http://www.johnthavis.com.

[31] See Diane Montagna, "African Bishops Ending Synod with 'Sense of Optimism,'" October 21, 2015, http://Aleteia.org.

On a related family and marriage issue, the pastoral solution to polygamy is an example of "healthy decentralization" that has to be settled locally, that is, in Africa. This was even emphasized by Western bishops at the synod.

Today in Africa there are still many bishops appointed by St. John Paul II and Pope Benedict who have an orthodox, traditional, and cautious style. Now bishops appointed by Pope Francis are emerging; they have simpler lifestyles, are closer to the people, and are more pastorally minded. An example of this diversity is the Catholic Bishops' Conference in South Africa. Following the process of subsidiarity (decentralization) and collegiality, a big question is how a consensus on new pastoral solutions can evolve on the local level in Africa (for example, in a national bishops' conference) on the challenges regarding family and marriage.

Integrating African Process and African Content

One of the goals and objectives of our three theological colloquiums (TCCRSA) was to initiate and experiment with a new way of doing conversational, cross-disciplinary, collaborative, and multigenerational theology. Our unique African theological process or method is African Christian Conversational Theology. This fits very well with Pope Francis's vision of a communal search, not walking alone but relying on each other as brothers and sisters and a wise and realistic pastoral discernment.

This African Christian Conversational Theology is both the name of a process or method of theology and the name of the type of the content of theology (like liberation theology). As we walk together, we continue to integrate African process or method and African content. This African process or method focuses on conversation, active dialogue, intensive listening and learning from each other (described as "listening in conversation"), and consensus. This African content focuses on inculturation and contextualization starting with the concrete, practical pastoral experiences needs of the African people on the grassroots level.

Relevance for the Catholic Church
in North America and Europe

These theological conversations and searches for pastoral solutions are not just for Africa. They are important for the World Catholic Church.

Specifically some of these issues are relevant for the Catholic Church in North America and Europe. Three examples are (1) the married priesthood and the Eucharist; (2) formation: marriage and the priesthood; and (3) restructuring, lay ecclesial ministries, SCCs, and family ministry.

Married Priesthood and Eucharist

The terms "Eucharistic famine" or "Eucharistic hunger" are increasingly being used in North America and Europe and have two meanings. First, because of the shortage of priests, the aging of priests, the clustering of parishes, long distances to the nearby parishes, and elderly people without transportation more and more Catholics cannot go to Mass on Sunday. The so-called circuit rider priest can only get to some of his parishes on a given Sunday, especially in the rural areas. So without the Eucharist some Catholics go spiritually hungry. Opening the door to more types of priests is a priority. More Eucharistic ministers is a priority.

Second, the terms "Eucharistic famine" and "Eucharistic hunger" refer to the many Catholics who are divorced and remarried civilly outside the Catholic Church and thus according to present church laws cannot receive communion. These Catholics may be very devout and have faithfully gone to Mass every Sunday for many years. They desire the Eucharist, the Bread of Life, the Food for the Journey, but they can't receive. The two Synods of Bishops in 2014 and 2015 discussed and debated this challenge extensively. Hopefully creative pastoral solutions on a case-by-case basis can give them permission to receive the Eucharist. Pope Francis's statement that "the Eucharist is a powerful medicine and nourishment for the weak" needs to be emphasized here.

One pastoral solution is local experimentation within a specific context. An interesting proposal comes from England, as an editorial in *The Tablet* states:

> It is estimated that one in 10 priests in diocesan ministry in the Catholic Church in England and Wales began his priestly vocation in the Church of England. Many of them are married. This is very relevant to the question increasingly being raised about the compulsory celibacy of the Catholic priesthood—compulsory except for former Anglican clergy who are given a dispensation. And what

makes it urgent is the growing realization at all levels of the Catholic Church that the shortage of priests is gradually having a profound effect on Catholic parishes who are finding themselves—often with little consultation—being closed, merged, or told to share a priest.[32]

Because of the successful arrangement regarding married former Anglicans, England is uniquely situated to pilot a modest experiment.

Formation: Marriage and Priesthood

The statistics on divorce in Africa are shocking. That 40 percent of Catholic marriages end in divorce is not significantly different from the national average in the United States. What does this say about the effectiveness of our many Pre-Cana, Cana, Marriage Encounter, and Couples for Christ Programs? A provocative question is raised: "Why do candidates for the priesthood spend eight to ten years in formation and studies before ordination to the priesthood (a sacrament in the Catholic Church and a permanent, lifetime commitment) while couples preparing for marriage (also a sacrament in the Catholic Church and a permanent, lifetime commitment) can have as few as three marriage instructions before their wedding in church?"

Religious brothers and sisters undergo rigorous formation and training before temporary and final vows. The American theologian Lisa Fullam draws this parallel. She says that when young people enter a religious congregation, they spend time as a postulant, then at least a year as a novice (two years for some congregations). Only then do they make a commitment of temporary vows—and even that commitment is a temporary, conditional one. Why is it, she asks, that we allow young people to marry (a permanent commitment, at least in theory) with so little preparation or "come and see" time, but allow vowed religious plenty of time to "try it out"?

Restructuring, Lay Ecclesial Ministries, SCCs, and Family Ministry

SCCs have never been center stage in the West, but the Catholic Church in Europe is now being forced to rethink its pastoral strategy as

---

[32] Editorial: "Married Priests: England Can Break New Ground," *Tablet* 268, no. 905 (November 15, 2014), 2, http://www.thetablet.co.uk.

Cardinal Christoph Schönborn, the archbishop of Vienna, Austria, said during the 2012 Synod of Bishops:

> The key idea, which has been extremely present in this synod, is the Small Christian Community. Many, many bishops from around the world have spoken about the Small Christian Communities. We see the need, and we have the desire, not to lose communities but to increase their number. We're forced to reduce the number of parish structures, with all their administration and expenses, but we want to favor a growing number of Small Christian Communities led by laity—laity who aren't full-time, who aren't bureaucrats, but volunteers. These are people living in the field who do what laity in many parishes and other communities already do which is to take responsibility for a large part of the life of the church, the vibrant aspects of community life.
>
> We want to implement more explicitly the great theme of Vatican II: the common priesthood of all the baptized, with the ministerial priesthood at its service, promoting the holiness of the people of God. Laity today—or, I would rather say, the baptized today—are fully capable of being true witnesses to faith in Christ in their daily lives, and therefore in the lives of Small Christian Communities. . . . [In the future] five small parishes in the countryside will form one greater parish. Their facilities, however, could be used to animate some of these Small Christian Communities.[33]

The local churches in North America and Europe and the local churches in Eastern Africa can learn from each other's pastoral experiences in the spirit of the proverb from Uganda and elsewhere: *one hand washes the other,* The Eastern African experience of evolving pastoral structures, lay ecclesial ministries,[34] pastoral, parish-based SCCs, and

---

[33] John L. Allen Jr., "Interview with Cardinal Christoph Schönborn," *National Catholic Reporter,* October 25, 2012, http://ncronline.org.

[34] A list of "Lay Ecclesial Ministries in Small Christian Communities in Eastern Africa" is found as Online Resource No. 4 in the free, online Ebook *Building the Church as Family of God: Evaluation of Small Christian Communities in Eastern Africa* on the Small Christian Communities Global Collaborative Website, http://www.smallchristiancommunities.org.

[35] Eamon Martin, "Irish Church Must Respond Better to Challenges of Family

family ministry described earlier can speak a great deal to the Catholic
Church in the West.

During the Synod of Bishops on "Family and Marriage" in Rome
in 2015, Archbishop Eamon Martin of Armagh Archdiocese, Northern
Ireland, said that he has been struck by the ideas put forward by bishops in
the Philippines and elsewhere (including Eastern Africa) especially about
small Christian communities in which families support one another in times
of need. He compares these to the "paltry efforts I've taken so far in my own
diocese" where he says he'll be looking to do much more at the parish and
diocesan level.[35]

After the synod, Bishop Peter Doyle, the bishop of Northampton,
England, commented on family life in Africa and other parts of the world:

> The point that came across to me is the richness of family life in
> other parts of the world. Here [in England], marriage has become
> very much a privatized industry. What the immigrant community
> can bring is the fact that marriage is more than Jack and Jill but it is
> about their families, their extended families, about the community,
> about the parish communities as well—and that's the sort of rich-
> ness that our immigrant communities are already bringing in our
> parishes. There's much more life, color and joy in their celebrations
> than there can be in ours.[36]

Let Us Journey Ahead Together

As we evolve an agenda for Vatican III—or Nairobi I or any venue in
the world—let us journey ahead together and let us be bold and creative.
Our process or method should be open, flexible, inculturated, contextual,
collegial, decentralized, inclusive, a "big tent" approach to the changes and
developments in the Catholic Church as a World Church. Whether it be
(alphabetically) Eucharist (Communion), family, governing, lay leadership,
liturgy, marriage, pastoral ministry, ordination, restructuring, or SCCs,
it is obvious that one size does not fit all. We need "devolved" authority

Life," Vatican Radio, October 23, 2015, http://en.radiovaticana.va.
    [36] "Elation, But Compromise Too," *Tablet* 269, no. 9124 (October 31, 2015), 8,
http://www.thetablet.co.uk.

structures and decision-making processes. Different pastoral practices will develop in local communities "from below" in different countries and cultures.

Let us follow the well-known African proverb that is also very popular in Western countries: *If you want to walk fast, walk alone. If you want to walk far, walk together.*

"Advocate for Life!"

A Kairos Moment for the Catholic Church in Africa to Be a Guardian, Sustainer, and Protector of Life

Nontando M. Hadebe

The Theological Colloquium on Church, Religion, and Society in Africa (TCCRSA) set a bold vision for a Vatican III Council in Africa, using that vision as a metaphor for a distinctive theological process, method, and reflection that is inclusive, contextual, and creative, and that responds to the challenges the Catholic Church in Africa faces. Participation was extended to the ecclesial hierarchy of bishops and priests, African laymen and laywomen, theologians, and invited participants from outside Africa who represent the global church. A main component of this process was the search for new visions for the Catholic Church in Africa that would respond in liberating ways to the multiple challenges that confront Africans.

In response to this call to search for new visions for the church, this article proposes a vision of the Catholic Church in Africa as a guardian, sustainer, and protector of life—particularly the lives of vulnerable groups experiencing high levels of violence because their identities are contested in their communities and the church. The article focuses on violence perpetuated against women and sexual minorities,[1] and it interrogates the role of masculinities in acts of violence against these groups, since cultural and religious beliefs are often used by perpetrators to justify their acts of violence. These justifications have created conflicts between culture, religion, and human rights. The muted responses and failure to act in solidarity with women and sexual minorities in Africa presents a theological crisis. There is a disjunction between the principles of Catholic social teaching, which is

---

[1] The term "sexual minorities" is used in this chapter to refer to lesbian, gay, bisexual, and transgender persons (LGBT).

the theological framework this article is built on, and the failure to protect women's and sexual minorities' rights in the face of unrelenting violence.

This is a kairos moment for the Catholic Church in Africa to act decisively in support of life. It is also a time to lament over complicity by churches, which have remained silent in the face of violations of women and sexual minorities. Lament also includes protest against churches by violated members of these groups and their families for the failures of churches to live up to their identity and mission as upholders of the dignity of all human beings. The tradition of lament in the Bible has particular relevance in this context. The article will use three other sources from the African context: lessons drawn from the debates between culture and human rights, confessions by ecumenical leaders responding to the church's role in the HIV/AIDS crisis, and the Kairos Document from South Africa. Accordingly, the rest of the article will proceed by addressing the following issues: the context of violence against women and sexual minorities in sub-Saharan Africa, culture and human rights, Catholic social teaching, women and sexual minorities, the call to lament—a kairos moment for the Catholic Church in Africa—and a conclusion presenting the Catholic Church in Africa as a guardian, protector, and sustainer of all life.

Context of Violence: Women and Sexual Minorities in Sub-Saharan Africa

Violence characterizes the lives of many women and sexual minorities in sub-Saharan Africa. The kidnapping of school girls by Boko Haram in northern Nigeria on April 14, 2014, and the failure of the African Union, international community, United Nations, and the churches to employ every means to rescue these girls expose three aspects of violence perpetuated against women: the social powerlessness of women, the role of masculinities, and the social and religious sanction of violence against women. These experiences can also be applied to sexual minorities. Concrete examples from life in Africa will be used to discuss violence that demonstrates the powerlessness of women and sexual minorities and the role of masculinities in violence. The following examples will be cited: women's vulnerability to HIV infection and intimate partner violence, "corrective rape" of sexual minorities and the criminalization of homosexuality, and two studies on sexual violence related to masculinities.

Violence and Powerlessness Experienced by Women:
HIV, AIDS, and Intimate Partner Violence

Sub-Saharan Africa continues to be at the epicenter of the HIV and AIDS[2] epidemic. Women, for both biological and social reasons, suffer higher rates of infection than men. The powerlessness of women over their bodies is one of the factors driving high infection rates:

> In reality, women and girls face a range of HIV-related risk factors and vulnerabilities that men and boys do not—many of which are embedded in the social relations and economic realities of their societies. These factors are not easily dislodged or altered, but until they are, efforts to contain and reverse the AIDS epidemic are unlikely to achieve sustained success.[3]

The source of powerlessness is twofold: the inequality that is reflected in social relations, which subordinate women to men, and the general lack of economic independence by many women.

Intimate partner violence also illustrates the powerlessness of women in the home. Statistics released in South Africa by the Medical Research Council show that one woman is killed by her intimate partner every eight hours.[4] Further, many women stay with abusive partners because of economic dependency, Christian teachings on submission to husbands, and cultural norms. Sophia Chirongoma, an African theologian, describes how culture keeps women silent about violence perpetuated against them by their intimate partners:

> Culture calls for women to be silent about their pain, especially if speaking out will reveal the bad secrets of the family. The Shona

---

[2] HIV is an acronym for Human Immunodeficiency Virus. It is the name of a retrovirus that gradually attacks and destroys the immune system, resulting in acquired immunodeficiency syndrome (AIDS). AIDS is not a disease but a syndrome, or group of illnesses, referred to as "opportunistic infections" because they take the opportunity afforded by a weakened immune system to attack the body. Without HIV, there would be no AIDS.

[3] Medical Research Council. "Every Eight Hours: Intimate Femicide in South Africa 10 Years Later" (2012), www.mrc.ac.za.

[4] Ibid.

culture is also guided by proverbs emphasizing the significance of safeguarding family secrets such that even when the husband is brutally violent, the wife has to bear it. . . . Two proverbs from Shona culture, *Chafukidza dzimba matenga*, literally "what shields a house is the roof," implying that whatever happens inside the house should be confined within those walls, never to be revealed to those beyond that confinement. . . . And *Nhumbu mukadzi mukuru, hairevi chayadya*, literally, "the stomach is like an elderly woman, it does not reveal what it has swallowed," suggesting that just as the stomach would never reveal to anyone whatever it has swallowed whether sweet or bitter, so a woman should never reveal whatever good or bad she encounters in her marriage.[5]

The entrapment of women in contexts of abuse is legitimated by religion and culture. The Catholic Church in Africa can no longer be silent in the face of these violations.

Violence and Powerlessness Experienced by Sexual Minorities:
"Corrective Rape" and the Criminalization of Homosexuality

There is a widespread belief among many Africans that sexual minorities did not exist in their communities prior to colonization. In his study of homosexuality in Zimbabwe, Marc Epprecht found a consistent denial of homosexuality as "unAfrican": "Many black Zimbabweans maintain that homosexual behaviour is 'un-African,' a foreign 'disease' introduced by white settlers, and that it is principally spread by foreign tourists and ambassadors."[6] The absence of vocabulary for gay, lesbian, transgender, and bisexual persons in Shona—as is also the case in many other Africa languages—demonstrates that homosexuality is foreign to African cultures.[7] This denial has sanctioned violence against sexual minorities in the form of "corrective rape" of lesbians in South Africa, and homophobia is rampant, as homosexuality is criminalized in many countries in Africa.

---

[5] Sophie Chirongoma, "Women's and Children's Rights in the Time of HIV and AIDS in Zimbabwe," *Journal of Theology for Southern Africa* 126 (2006): 48–65.

[6] Marc Epprecht, "The 'Unsaying' of Indigenous Homosexualities in Zimbabwe: Mapping a Blindspot in an African Masculinity," *Journal of Southern African Studies* 24, no. 4, Special Issue on Masculinities in Southern Africa (December 1998): 632.

[7] Ibid., 634.

Corrective rape "is a hate crime wielded to convert lesbians to heterosexuality—an attempt to 'cure' them of being gay."[8] The term has been extended to include the rape of any gay, bisexual, transsexual, intersexual, asexual, or queer person with the intent of "curing" them into heterosexuality. The following excerpt from a BBC news report describes the brutality of one of these rapes:

> In April, Noxolo Nogwaza was raped by eight men and murdered in KwaThema township near Johannesburg. The 24-year-old's face and head were disfigured by stoning, and she was stabbed several times with broken glass. The attack on her is thought to have begun as a case of what is known as "corrective rape," in which men rape lesbians in what they see as an attempt to "correct" their sexual orientation.[9]

The silence by communities and churches to the brutal murder of Nogwaza can only be understood in the context of fear—fear that solidarity and defending the rights of Nogwaza would be interpreted as supporting homosexuality, which many Christians believe is in opposition to the teachings of the church and the Bible. This theology renders the lives of sexual minorities expendable.

The other act of violence against sexual minorities is homophobia, which has resulted in the criminalization of homosexuality. According to a news report from CNN, homosexuality is "illegal in 38 African countries, where most sodomy laws were introduced during colonialism. In Uganda, homosexual acts were punishable by 14 years to life in prison even before the controversial bill was signed into law."[10] According to the journalist Saskia Houttuin the bill "not only outlawed homosexual acts, but also compelled citizens to report suspected homosexual activity to the police, triggering increased levels of prejudice, violence, and discrimination against the gay community."[11] Many Christians who believe that homosexuality is against God's law support this outlook and, justify the use of violence in these cases.

---

[8] http://www.independent.co.uk.

[9] http://www.bbc.com.

[10] CNN, "Homosexuality in Africa," http://edition.cnn.com.

[11] http://www.theguardian.com.

While violence against women and sexual minorities is justified by culture and religion, the perpetration of violence is linked to some expressions of masculinities.

Violence and Masculinities

Men account for 95 percent of physically violent actions globally. There is a direct link between violence and distorted masculinities.[12] However, not all men commit acts of violence. "Masculinity" is a term coined by social scientists to describe the construction of maleness in a given culture or historical context. Robert Connell, the pioneer of masculinity theory, notes several characteristics of masculinity: it is not static, but dynamic; it is contextual, and, therefore, there is no homogenous or singular masculinity, but multiple masculinities in every culture that are governed by a dominant masculinity, which is referred to as hegemonic masculinity. Hegemonic masculinity determines ideas about "what a real man is like" in every culture.[13] Because cultures define "what a real man is," many men are unable to fulfill these ideals. For example, in many parts of Africa, a "real man" is defined as the head of his household who is able to provide for his family. This associates masculinity with the ownership of economic resources. In contexts of unemployment, a crisis in masculinity is often created, and this results in high levels of violence against women. The correlation between the crisis of masculinity and violence against women has been attested by research. In particular, two studies in South Africa and East Africa reflect this correlation.

The first study from South Africa was done by Isak Niehaus and is titled "Masculine Domination in Sexual Violence: Interpreting Accounts of Three Cases of Rape in the South African Lowveld."[14] Niehaus found that, in this context, hegemonic masculinity was defined as *"monna na [man of men]."* Masculinity is idealized as a "household head with access to a steady

---

[12] James B Nelson, "Male Sexuality and the Fragile Planet," in *Redeeming Men: Religion and Masculinities,* ed. Steven Blake Boyd, W. Merle Longwood, and Mark W. Muesse (Louisville, KY: John Knox Press, 1996), 274.

[13] Ibid., 24.

[14] Isak Niehaus, "Masculine Domination in Sexual Violence: Interpreting Accounts of Three Cases of Rape in the South African Lowveld," in *Men Behaving Differently: South African Men since 1994,* ed. Graeme Reid and Liz Walker (Cape Town: Double Storey), 67.

income, the *monna na* supports his wives and children, keeps lovers and always has the final say. He is also brave and decisive, and faces any problem head-on."[15] Men who failed to meet the ideals of hegemonic masculinity experienced a "crisis in representation," which led to other ways of expressing their masculinity, such as sexual violence. The study also found that men who committed rape failed to meet the masculine challenges of their age. For example, one of the rapists was a fifty-year-old man. He failed to meet age-appropriate expectations of masculinity: he had never married, had no formal job, and had fathered four children with different women, and could not support his dependents.[16] There were eight elderly men among the group of rapists. They raped vulnerable girls between the ages of six and nineteen who were related to them. This included their own daughters, granddaughters, nieces, and neighbors.[17]

The second study was from East Africa and was done by Margrethe Silberschmidt. It is titled "Male Sexuality in the Context of Socio-Economic Change in Rural and Urban East Africa,"[18] and it confirms the findings of Niehaus that linked failures to achieve ideals of hegemonic masculinities to dominance over women and sexual violence. This confirmation is summarized in the following quotation: "Where there is social disempowerment of men which erodes their masculinity, sexuality becomes a key expression of male self-esteem and is expressed in multiple-partnered sexual relationships and sexually aggressive behaviour that seem to have become essential to strengthen masculinity and self-esteem."[19]

Responses to violence must target the social scripting of masculinities. The next section will discuss lessons learned from discussions on conflicts between culture and human rights.

Culture and Human Rights

Culture, as noted in the preceding section, is often used as a tool to legitimize violence against women and sexual minorities. The expression of

---

[15] Ibid., 70.
[16] Ibid., 73.
[17] Ibid., 80.
[18] Magrethe Silberschmidt, "Male Sexuality in the Context of Socio-Economic Change in Rural and Urban East Africa," *Sexuality in Africa Magazine* 2 (2005): 5.
[19] Ibid.

masculinity also has the potential to perpetuate violence. What follows is a discussion of lessons learned by conflicts between cultures; it begins with a brief definition of culture, then examines culture's conflict with human rights, and, finally, discusses new developments that helpfully direct us to reverence for life over cultural preservation.

Definition of Culture

Culture can be defined as the "the whole way of life, material and non-material, of a human society. It is essentially social, the product of a society's tradition and its interaction with other societies. Culture is a dynamic, not a static, phenomenon. It is also the product of human history."[20] Interpretations of what constitutes culture can result in conflict. The ambiguity of culture is described by the African theologian Musimbi R. A. Kanyoro as a double-edged sword. Culture is "a creed for community identity on one hand and on the other hand the main justification for difference, oppression and injustice."[21] This mixture of good and evil in culture is its source of conflict with human rights.

Conflict between Culture and Human Rights

According to the preamble of the United Nations Universal Declaration of Human Rights (UDHR), the basis of human rights is the "recognition of the inherent dignity and of the equal and inalienable rights of all members of the human family."[22] In other words: human rights are based on the inherent dignity of every human being, including women and sexual minorities. Most countries in Africa are signatories of the UDHR, and have constitutions that accord equal rights to all citizens.

Despite this apparent supremacy of rights over culture, culture too often remains the arbitrator of laws, and, in cases where there is conflict, culture itself often overrules laws. One of the reasons for this discrepancy is that

---

[20] Alward Shorter, *African Culture, an Overview: Socio-Cultural Anthropology* (Nairobi: Paulines Publication Africa, 2001), 22.

[21] Musimbi R. A. Kanyoro, *Introducing Feminist Cultural Hermeneutics: An African Perspective*, Introductions in Feminist Theology 9 (Sheffield: Sheffield Academic Press 2002), 13.

[22] United Nations Universal Declaration of Human Rights: http://www.un.org.

human rights, according to Abdullahi Ahmed An-na'im, possess a "lack of cultural legitimacy."[23] He defines cultural legitimacy as "being in conformity with recognized principles or accepted rules and standards of a given culture."[24] Consequently, in instances where cultural norms are perceived to be violated by laws or bills of rights, there is often resistance from communities. For example, the granting of equal rights to gays and lesbians in South African law has met strong resistance from communities. This is especially evident in the aforementioned atrocity, "corrective rape."

A Call to Reverence of Life: Charting a New Path

One of the lessons that can be learned from the ongoing debates between culture and human rights is that life should be revered more than cultural preservation. Jeanne Gazel and Pat Naidoo have proposed new questions that place the preservation of life at the center of the debates about culture and human rights. They ask, "What would happen if questions of health and viability—rather than cultural preservation—were at the center of this decision-making process?"[25] and "How do beliefs and practices help or hinder the establishment of healthy people, families, and societies?"[26]

Similarly, S. O. Ilesanmi suggests a hermeneutical shift from a preoccupation with the past to a new focus on the present. This would be "a hermeneutical shift from a nostalgic idealization of the past to a liberative engagement with the present."[27] The central ethos of this new focus is reverence for life rather than reverence for cultural values.[28] Reverence for life is also central to the teachings of the Catholic Church, and particularly to Catholic social teaching.

---

[23] Abdullahi Ahmed An-Na'im, "Problems of Universal Cultural Legitimacy," in *Human Rights in Africa: Cross-Cultural Perspectives,* ed. Abdullahi Ahmed An-Na'im and Francis Mading Deng (Washington, DC: Brookings Institution, 1990), 332.

[24] Ibid.

[25] Jeanne Gazel and Pat Naidoo, "Striking the Rock with Impunity: The Consequences of Gendered Practices in 21st Century Sub-Saharan Africa," *Rockefeller Foundation Working Paper #2802004,* http://www.wid.msu.edu.

[26] Ibid., 2.

[27] S.O. Ilesanmi, "Human Rights Discourse in Modern Africa: A Comparative Religious Ethical Perspective," *Journal of Religious Ethics* 23 (1995): 310.

[28] Ibid., 304.

Catholic Social Teaching in Response to Violence against Women, Sexual Minorities, and Masculinity Crises

I have chosen Catholic social teaching as the theological framework for this article because it did not originate in a lecture hall or library but in response to a particular context—a context characterized by violation of workers' rights, competing ideologies, inequality, and poverty. Pope Leo XIII issued the first papal encyclical on social justice, titled *Rerum Novarum*, in 1891.[29] This encyclical resulted in radical changes for exploited workers in the form of just wages, dignity of work, and the critique of oppressive ideologies. A precedent was set, and subsequent popes wrote encyclicals responding to violations of life and injustices in differing contexts. The latest encyclical in the tradition of Catholic social teaching is *Laudato Si'*, written by Pope Francis in response to global economic systems that exploit the environment and the poor. Together these encyclicals produce principles that have become identified as Catholic social teaching. The list below is taken from Thomas Massaro's book titled *Living Justice: Catholic Social Teaching in Action*. These principles are:

a.   The dignity of each person and human rights
b.   Option for the poor and vulnerable
c.   Solidarity, common good, and participation
d.   Family life
e.   Subsidiarity and proper role of the government
f.   The dignity of work, rights of workers, and support for labor unions
g.   Property ownership in modern society: rights and responsibilities
h.   Colonialism and economic development
i.   Peace and disarmament

These principles are often applied to humanity in general, but, given the context of this article, the litmus test should be how these principles apply to the particularities of the experiences of violence against women and sexual minorities, as well as the perpetration of violence by disenfranchised males. In other words: What would it mean to apply the Catholic social teaching on dignity of the human person, solidarity, preferential option for the poor

---

[29] Thomas Massaro, *Living Justice: Catholic Social Teaching in Action* (Chicago: Sheed & Ward, 2011), 72.

and vulnerable, and the common good in countries that criminalize homosexuality and promote homophobia? Women constitute most of the poor in these contexts. Because this is the case, can a preferential option for women be expressed in principles of justice, subsidiarity, equal dignity, and human rights? What would it mean for men to be defined in terms of their inherent dignity, rather than by other contingent factors? Would such a perspective keep their dignity intact in the case of an economic downturn? This failure to apply these principles in response to the violations against women and sexual minorities, and conceptions of masculinity that perpetuate violence has resulted in a kairos moment, and should cause us to lament for the Catholic Church in Africa.

Call to Lament:
A Kairos Moment for the Catholic Church in Africa

The Kairos Document was produced in 1985 by churches in South Africa in response to the state-instituted violence and oppression of black South Africans. The churches were divided and had no clear consensus of a response that would confront the differing theologies among Christians and create a theology that was liberative in the face of oppression. This document will be a reference point for the definition of kairos and for practicing kairos theology. An understanding of the document is essential:

> The KAIROS document is a Christian, biblical and theological comment on the political crisis in South Africa today. It is an attempt by concerned Christians in South African to reflect on the situation of death in our country. It is a critique of the current theological models that determine the type of activities the Church engages in to try to resolve the problems of the country. It is an attempt to develop, out of this perplexing situation, an alternative biblical and theological model that will in turn lead to forms of activity that will make a real difference to the future of our country.[30]

The repression, discrimination, and state violence against the majority black population in a context of a predominantly Christian nation created a crisis of faith. This crisis was the kairos moment:

---

[30] http://www.sahistory.org.za.

For very many Christians in South Africa this is the KAIROS, the
moment of grace and opportunity, the favorable time in which God
issues a challenge to decisive action. It is a dangerous time because,
if this opportunity is missed, and allowed to pass by, the loss for the
Church, for the Gospel and for all the people of South Africa will
be immeasurable.[31]

The result was a theological process that analyzed different theologies that
were guiding the activities of different churches in response to death and
violence. One example of such theologies was "State Theology." It used the
Bible to support the status quo. Another was "Church Theology," which was
opposed to State Theology, but failed to have an impact, as it is "superficial
and counter-productive because instead of engaging in an in-depth analysis of the signs of our times, it relies upon a few stock ideas derived from
Christian tradition and then uncritically and repeatedly applies them to our
situation."[32] Kairos theologians utilized a prophetic theology that adopted a
"preferential option for the poor and oppressed":

As far as the present crisis is concerned, there is only one way
forward to Church unity and that is for those Christians who find
themselves on the side of the oppressor or sitting on the fence, to
cross over to the other side to be united in faith and action with
those who are oppressed. Unity and reconciliation within the
Church itself is only possible around God and Jesus Christ who are
to be found on the side of the poor and the oppressed.[33]

The kairos process, as reflected in both the confession by church leaders in
Africa in relation to the HIV/AIDS context and in the Kairos Document
of South Africa, is directed toward church theologies and their responses to
death, violence, and oppression. This makes the kairos process particularly
relevant to the violence and oppression experienced by women and sexual
minorities in Africa, but also to the constructions of masculinities that fuel
these forms of violence.

---

[31] Ibid.
[32] Ibid.
[33] Ibid.

However, the kairos process needs to be complemented by lament, because lament "protest[s] and complain[s] about the incoherence that is experienced in the world."[34] Lament establishes ownership of the theological process by enabling individuals and communities to bring their experiences as resources for liberating kairos theologies. The biblical tradition is a rich resource for a theology of lament. This is particularly true of the Psalms. In his commentary on the Psalms, Walter Brueggemann describes the lament tradition as an act of "bold faith because it insists that all such experiences of disorder are a proper subject for discourse with God. There is nothing out of bounds, nothing precluded or inappropriate."[35] In terms of content, lament psalms vary, but they do share a similar outline. This outline consists of two parts: plea and praise.[36] The plea usually consists of the following: an address to God, a complaint or uncensored explicit description of the situation, a petition that "asks God to act decisively,"[37] a motivation for the pleas that is based on God's character, and an imprecation that is "the voice of resentment and vengeance that will not be satisfied until God works retaliation on those who have done the wrong."[38] Praise in the lament tradition represents a surprising turn of events:

> When the psalm makes its next move, it is a surprising one. Things are different. Something has changed. We cannot ever know whether it is changed circumstance or changed attitude, or some of both. But the speaker now speaks differently. Now the sense of urgency and desperation is replaced by joy, gratitude and well-being.[39]

It is the raw, uncensored cry of protest in the plea that opens the way for change and reconciliation with God. People living with AIDS need safe spaces to share their stories and experiences. This was confirmed by research done by the Pietermaritzburg Agency for Christian Social Action (PACSA) in 2004.[40]

---

[34] Walter Brueggemann, *The Message of the Psalms: A Theological Commentary* (Minneapolis: Augsburg Press 1984), 52.

[35] Ibid., 52.

[36] Examples of individual lament psalms include Psalms 13, 35, and 86.

[37] Brueggemann, *Message of the Psalms*, 54.

[38] Ibid., 52.

[39] Ibid.

[40] Pietermaritzburg Agency for Christian Social Action (PACSA) *Research Report: Churches and HIV/AIDS: Exploring How Local Churches Are Integrating HIV/AIDS in*

Furthermore, laments not only bring healing, but they also bring justice. Denise Ackermann, a feminist theologian from South Africa, describes the relationship between lament and justice as follows: "The cry for healing is inseparable from the need for justice."[41] When they are given space to lament, violated women, sexual minorities, and men can participate fully in theologies of liberation, healing, and transformation.

The healing and liberation of individuals requires communal support. This is why laments ought to reflect liberative theological responses to "public issues and problems."[42] Communal lament requires social consciousness on the part of the church. Without this consciousness, communal psalms will have no significance. As Brueggemann notes, "To gain access to these psalms, therefore, we need to think through the public sense of loss and hurt and rage that we all have in common."[43] For example, Psalms 74 and 79 respond to the destruction of the Temple, which, to the nation of Israel, was not just a building. This destruction "was about the violation of the sacred key to all reality, the glue that holds the world together."[44] These psalms represent the plea that "Yahweh cannot afford to be a disinterested party."[45]

There are three consequences of public lament, which can be elaborated on by the work of A. Taljaard,[46] who wrote in the context of the Truth and Reconciliation Commission in South Africa, and also by the call to lament from Denise Ackermann.

First, lament brings awareness of the experiences of those who are violated: "When we publicly voice the remorse, suffering and anxiety of the oppressed, we overcome the silence and the ignorance of the past and the ignorance of existing sufferings. Hearing these truths opens a way in which awareness of different realities could become possible."[47]

The Life And Ministries of the Church and How Those Most Directly Affected Experience These (Pietermaritzburg: PACSA 2004), 11.

[41] D. M. Ackermann, "A Voice Was Heard in Ramah: A Feminist Theology of Praxis for Healing in South Africa," in *Liberating Faith Practices: Feminist Practical Theologies in Context,* ed. D. M. Ackermann and R. Bons-Storm (Leuven: Peeters,1998).

[42] Brueggemann, *Message of the Psalms,* 67.

[43] Ibid., 68.

[44] Ibid.

[45] Ibid.

[46] A. Taljaard, "Of Belonging and Longing," in *Ragbag Theologies: Essays in Honour of Denise M Ackermann: A Feminist Theologian of Praxis,* ed. Miranda Pillay, Sarojini Nadar, and Clint Le Bruyns (Stellenbosch: SunPress, 2009), 45.

[47] Ibid.

Second, lament breaks the silence that separates the violated from their communities and churches, creating authentic solidarity: "Lament for these groups means a movement from a mute or silent space into a 'crying out' where the language at least acknowledges the situation. This awareness and acknowledging of the other lead to a way out of isolation, through the communicating (lament), that could lead to solidarity."[48]

Third, and finally, lament leads to accountability: "Accountability requires awareness. And awareness is the waking-up to the 'other.' It is when we become aware of the reality of the other, and in what ways our apathy or power relations have deeply harmed our neighbour, that we can begin to become accountable."[49]

The lament process, as described by both Brueggemann and Taljaard, creates different spaces for the violated and the church. These spaces become the basis for an authentic solidarity that leads to a relationship of mutual trust. The space that the violated need is a lament of pain and protest—a lament regarding their experiences of violation by individuals, communities, and the church. The church, in turn, needs to see these lamentations as a kairos moment that requires confession, analysis of oppressive theologies that legitimate violence, and a stand of solidarity for the liberation and dignity of those violated. This combination of kairos and lament provides a resource for the Catholic Church in Africa to take up the challenge as the protector, guardian, and sustainer of life.

Violence against women, violence against sexual minorities, and the expressions of masculinity that perpetuate violence are challenges that ought to cause the Catholic Church in Africa to redefine itself as the guardian, sustainer, and protector of all lives. The ethos of reverence for life and the principles of Catholic social teaching in a context of lament provide the resources that can generate prophetic theologies. This is evidenced by the Kairos Document—a document that forever transformed the Catholic Church in Africa, and restored the faith of communities that were violated by both its teachings and its silence in the face of extreme abuse and, in some cases, death. This is the kairos moment for the Catholic Church in Africa!

---

[48] Ibid.
[49] Ibid.

LAUDATO SI', PLANETARY BOUNDARIES, AND AFRICA

Saving the Planet

Peter Knox

The current ecological threat facing humanity is one of the most pressing "signs of the times."[1] Pope Francis published his encyclical, *Laudato Si'*, in order to explore this sign in light of the gospel. He writes:

> [Mother Earth] now cries out to us because of the harm we have inflicted on her by our irresponsible use and abuse of the goods with which God has endowed her. We have come to see ourselves as her lords and masters, entitled to plunder her at will. The violence present in our hearts, wounded by sin, is also reflected in the symptoms of sickness evident in the soil, in the water, in the air and in all forms of life. This is why the earth herself, burdened and laid waste, is among the most abandoned and maltreated of our poor; she "groans in travail" (Rom 8:22). We have forgotten that we ourselves are dust of the earth (cf. Gn 2:7); our very bodies are made up of her elements, we breathe her air and we receive life and refreshment from her waters.[2]

The "sickness evident in the soil, in the water, in the air and in all forms of life" will no doubt worsen if we continue "business as usual." However, because we believe in God's universal salvific will,[3] African Christians find

---

[1] *Gaudium et Spes*, no. 4, tells us that "at all times the Church carries the responsibility of reading the signs of the times and of interpreting them in the light of the Gospel, if it is to carry out its task."

[2] Francis, *Encyclical Letter Laudato Si' on the Care for Our Common Home* (Vatican City, 2015), 2.

[3] Saint Paul expresses this as follows: "[God] wants everyone to be saved and reach

hope even in the face of overwhelming odds. Hope is found in listening to, and being actively informed by, a threefold discourse: Christian, African, and scientific.[4] This hope will only be realized if common sense and modesty prevail. If not, then evil will win out—this evil is the failure of planetary systems, under anthropogenic influences, to support the life that God intended.[5] "Evil" may seem to be a strong term, but the danger is so calamitous that no other language is appropriate. Those who deny this real threat to our planet and to its habitability caused by humans are agents of this evil. As Christians we fail in our religious duty if we do not assume a prophetic stance regarding planetary threats.[6] This stance includes changing our lives in ways that eradicate this evil.

In theological terms, we are looking for "salvation." To this end, this essay examines (1) ecological threats facing our planet and (2) three divergent salvific discourses in response to these threats.

Planetary Threats

When I was growing up, we learned a great deal about "pollution." In those days, in suburban Johannesburg, "pollution" implied that the rivers had too much plastic junk and industrial effluent in them, that the air was full of smoke from coal fires, and that people carelessly threw rubbish out their windows, rather than putting it in rubbish bins. It was simple. Not a lot has changed in this regard: the wrong things are still in the wrong places. But the problem is much more complex than it appeared to be in those days. From a chemical perspective, we have a new appreciation for the dimensions

---

full knowledge of the truth" (1 Tm 2:4, New Jerusalem Bible). The Congregation for the Doctrine of the Faith tells us that this "universal salvific will of God is closely connected to the sole mediation of Christ." See *Dominus Iesus: On the Unicity and Salvific Universality of Jesus Christ and the Church* (Vatican City, 2000), 13.

[4] With Pope Francis, I believe that we have a lot to be grateful to scientists for, especially regarding their attempts to resolve these ecological issues, and we should include their discourse when we do theology. See *Laudato Si'*, nos. 34, 102, 135, 199–201.

[5] I do not judge all natural calamities such as volcanoes, earthquakes, or tsunamis as "evil," since there is no intentionality at work with these. These are merely impersonal forces of nature taking their natural course. It is tragic when (often the poorest) people are caught up in forces beyond human control. However, when calamities such as drought or flooding occur due to human ignorance, greed, or neglect, these enter into the realm of evil, since the calamities might have been avoided if foreseeable precautions had been exercised.

[6] "Woe to us if we do not preach the Gospel!"; cf. 1 Cor 9:16.

of this great challenge. The problem is about the wrong *chemicals* being in the wrong places.

Climate Change

Climate change is the most widely recognized and visibly urgent environmental issue we face today. Even in the deepest rural recesses, many people are aware of the imminent threat of climate change. In the media, we are frequently exposed to the real effects of climate change. Since the beginning of the industrial age, the planet has been warming rapidly. This is because of the burning of fossil fuels—primarily oil and coal. The accumulation of the gaseous products that result from this burning have begun to act as a greenhouse, trapping in atmospheric heat that would otherwise be able to escape. As the temperature of the earth rises (imperceptibly to our human senses), our home—the planet as a whole—has slowly begun to change. Ice is melting on the highest mountains, on glaciers, and at the poles. The result is that this melted water is flowing into the oceans, gradually raising the mean sea level around the world. This is especially a problem for island nations and for cities built on the coasts, as they are constantly being flooded. However, this problem also threatens people all around the globe, as a warmer earth also results in altered weather patterns. Rains fall more heavily and for longer periods in some regions, while other locales are experiencing harmful prolonged droughts. Rivers and lakes are drying up, while other areas are perennially submerged under water. These combined effects are known as "climate change." These phenomena will become increasingly destructive as they continue and are multiplied over the years. Developing countries are already beginning to feel the effects of climate change, and many have begun to respond accordingly.[7]

Planetary Boundaries

If we think that climate change is our worst nightmare, then we haven't even begun to dream yet. Even if politicians around the world effectively encourage every citizen of this planet to actively reverse the causes of climate

---

[7] See Government of Kenya, *National Climate Action Plan 2013–2017 Executive Summary* (Nairobi, 2013). Work is also being done in NGO circles to anticipate the disruptive effects of climate change. See Jesuit Hakimani Centre, *Climate Change and Food Security: Preditictions from the Future* (Nairobi: Jesuit Hakimani Centre, 2014).

change, there are other horrors in store for us. The most recent and comprehensive scientific publication (which has informed *Laudato Si'*) discusses what are called "planetary boundaries."[8] These planetary boundaries are nine human-induced factors that have the potential to make this planet uninhabitable for human beings, or at least highly hostile to the continuation of human life.[9] While scientists generally agree on the identity of these factors, there is no consensus concerning the limits within which humans are physiologically able to survive on a planet hostile to life. For human life to continue, people worldwide—especially as represented by their politicians—must make prudential decisions to attempt to keep these planetary factors within safe habitable boundaries.

As an example of prudential action, the United Nations 1987 Montreal Protocol was a worldwide agreement to significantly halt the production of those gases that are largely responsible for the depletion of the circumpolar ozone layer. Although it will take decades before the levels of ozone are fully restored, this measure will restore the earth's protective barrier against UV-B solar radiation, which is a major cause of skin cancers. This is one of the nine factors identified by the planetary-boundary scientists, and it has, with great concerted political will, been tackled, and a boundary has been designated. Scientists are urging similar steps for the other eight life-threatening factors. There is now broad consensus that in order to avert catastrophic climate change, global atmospheric greenhouse gases must be brought down to 350 ppm, which was their level before the start of the industrial age.[10] Unfortunately, the political force to make this a reality appears to be lacking.

Planetary boundaries require great understanding, if lasting changes are going to be enacted. Many African scientists are at the forefront of

---

[8] Johan Rockström et al., "Planetary Boundaries: Exploring the Safe Operating Space for Humanity," *Ecology and Society* 14, no. 2 (2009).

[9] These interacting factors are: (i) global climate change, (ii) depletion of the ozone layer, (iii) freshwater use, (iv) ocean acidification, (v) loss of biodiversity, (vi) changing land use (deforestation), (vii) novel pollutants such as nanoparticles and radioactivity, (viii) aerosols in the atmosphere, and (ix) flows of nitrogen and phosphorous.

[10] There are still those who deny climate change, who contest scientific theories that say that current global climate change is partially due to anthropogenic factors. So they refuse to comply with proposed drastic cuts in greenhouse gas emissions. Not surprisingly, their interests lie with the continued exploitation and consumption of fossil fuels.

these scientific inquiries.[11] However, there is a "brain-drain" that robs the continent of thousands of qualified personnel and has left Africa largely ill-equipped to face the challenges posed by planetary boundaries.

From Threat to Hope

Planetary-boundary science raises awareness of the acute possibility of real calamity. The traditional Christian response to threats to our well-being is to appeal to God for salvation. It is not, however, Christians alone who appeal to the concept of "salvation." Western science can certainly understand what might be meant by salvation within the framework of the pending ecological crisis, and it can offer some helpful directions for seeking salvation. Similarly, African traditions can offer prescriptions for what to do when "things fall apart."

With *Laudato Si'*, Francis has shown us the importance of breaking down the artificial barriers that exist between various intellectual disciplines. By using the language of the physical sciences, he has given the first papal teaching that reflects the spirit of *Gaudium et Spe*s, no. 36, which calls on Christians to respect the autonomy of earthly affairs. We cannot treat the environment as though it is solely a "scientific," "spiritual," or "theological" issue. None of us lives in an exclusively "scientific," "spiritual," "theological" world. We need a multidisciplinary approach if humanity is to be saved from the current crisis. In our contemporary African Christian context, three discourses can inform our response to the prospect of environmental disaster: a Christian discourse, an African discourse, and a (Western) scientific discourse.[12] Each discourse has its own object and method of inquiry. Informed by the methodology of the Kairos Document,[13] we can glean

---

[11] See, for example, the Council for Scientific and Industrial Research, "Scientists Say Four of Nine Boundaries That Make Earth a Safe and Stable Place to Live, Crossed," *CSIR Media Releases* (2015) (Pretoria, 2015), and Belinda Reyers, "A Planetary Boundary for Biodiversity," http://www.futureearth.org.

[12] In his treatment, Menanga Kizito Yves deals with only two of the worldviews. His work would be considerably strengthened by taking the scientific worldview into account. See Menanga Kizito Yves, "Ecological Crisis: The Quest for a Biblical and Traditional African Ecosophy," *AFER* 53, no. 2 (2011).

[13] This prophetic document juxtaposes "church theology," "state theology," and "prophetic theology," showing how the first two were often used to serve the interest of maintaining the status quo. The third was proposed as a way to help South Africans

insights from these three seemingly contradictory worldviews. By investigating each individually, we can show how each complements the insights of the others. No single discourse is more important than the others. Moreover, no one discourse can dismiss the others as irrelevant. Rather than contradict or undermine each other, they can be synthesized—though not harmonized—to give African Christians a grounding and purpose with which the ecological crisis can be faced. Thus armed, African Christian theologians can help our compatriots to face this kairos.

Salvation

Salvation in the Christian Worldview

It is important to understand the relationship between ecology and theology: The Creator is involved in the happenings of creation. Our tradition does not support the idea of a *deus absconditus* who entrusts us with a perfect planet, dusts off its divine hands, and walks away. Rather, God is constantly creating, saving, and sanctifying anew. We are not modalists who believe that God walks on and off the stage, creating sometimes, saving sometimes, and sanctifying sometimes. Creation did not end on that Sabbath day 13.7 billion years ago when God rested. Nor did salvation happen as a one-off that Easter morning two thousand years ago, when the Son of God rose from the dead. Nor did sanctification cease fifty days later at that first Christian Pentecost. Rather, the economy of creation, redemption, and sanctification is an ongoing activity of the Trinity's self-revealing love. Obviously there is a definitive once-for-all dimension of Jesus' saving death and resurrection (cf. 1 Pt 3:18; Heb 7:27; 9:28; 10:12; Rom 6:9, etc.). The effects of that intervention, however, are also eternal, and are being realized at all times.

When all else seems to fail, we turn to God for help in our crises. The ecological crisis facing humanity is one such occasion when we need divine intervention—salvation—to save us. And so we must ask what is meant by "salvation." First of all, salvation is not just something that happened in

---

escape the shackles of apartheid. See the Kairos Theologians, *The Kairos Document: Challenge to the Church—A Theological Comment on the Political Crisis in South Africa* (Braamfontein, South Africa, 1985). I use a similar approach in Peter Knox, *AIDS, Ancestors, and Salvation: Local Beliefs in Christian Ministry to the Sick* (Nairobi: Paulines Publications Africa, 2008).

the mists of ancient time. We pray: "Our help *is* in the name of the Lord—who made heaven and earth." We must be careful not to reduce salvation to any single dimension of our lives. For example, while political liberation is important, it is not the whole story.[14] It is equally reductionist to maintain that salvation concerns only the eschatological fate of our eternal souls.[15] Similarly, in the ecological crisis we cannot restrict our notion of salvation to "scientific" solutions. However, we should neither dismiss scientific discourse as irrelevant to theology, since there is biblical precedent for calling on God to save people from weather-related catastrophes.

Old Testament

In the Old Testament, the faithful frequently called on God in their moments of distress. Salvation was concrete in these situations. God rescued people from mortal danger—war, enemies, disease, death, slavery (the Exodus story), exile (through King Cyrus), floods (Noah; cf. Gn 7:23 and Ws 10:4), drought (cf. 1 Kgs 17–18), etc. As Colomban Lesquivit and Pierre Grelot note, "According to the nature of the danger, the act of saving manifests itself in protection, liberation, ransom, cure and health, victory, life, peace."[16] Of specific interest to us are the stories of the flood in Genesis 6–9 and the great drought and famine in 1 Kings 17. In both cases, God is intimately involved in climactic crises, and agents of God— Noah and Elijah respectively—communicate the theological significance of these events in each instance.

New Testament

In another equally existential crisis, Saint Paul exclaimed: "Wretched man that I am! Who will rescue me from this body doomed to death?" (Rom 7:24; New Jerusalem Bible). His reply was: "God—thanks be to

---

[14] The Congregation for the Doctrine of the Faith warns of the danger of this kind of reductionism. See its *Instruction on Certain Aspects of the "Theology of Liberation"* (Vatican City. 1984).

[15] As, for example, in the rosary, we pray: "Oh my Jesus, forgive us our sins, save us from the fires of hell, lead all souls to heaven, especially those most in need of your mercy."

[16] Colomban Lesquivit and Pierre Grelot, "Salvation," in *Dictionary of Biblical Theololgy*, ed. Xavier Léon-Dufour (London: Chapman, 1973).

him—through Jesus Christ our Lord!" We read in the gospels, and in the theology developed by Paul, that Jesus is God's definitive salvific outreach.[17] As in the Old Testament, so also in the New: there are a number of plights from which Jesus saves: from sin (Lk 7:47–50), from Satan, from illness, from death, from weather (Mt 6:25, 14:30). He has come to save the lost (Lk 19:10) and the entire the world (Jn 3:17). The prerequisites for benefiting from this salvific action of God are baptism and belief in the Christ whom God has sent (Jn 16:16). We see Jesus' dominance of the elements in calming the storm (Mt 8:23–27) and walking on the sea (Mk 6:47–52).

With Saint Paul, we can appeal to Christ as the firstborn of all creation, the firstborn from the dead, in whom all fullness[18] is to be found, reconciling all things to God (Col 1:15–20). "This reconciliation of the whole universe . . . means not the individual salvation of the whole human race but the collective salvation of the world by its return to the right order and peace of perfect submission to God."[19] This is a very strong notion, which in our tradition has been called "the Cosmic Christ." For centuries Eastern iconography has represented Christ as the *Pantokrator*—the Ruler of all Things—things in heaven and things on earth. For the Western mind, it takes a movement of the imagination to see the risen Christ as Lord not only of individual souls but also of the whole created order.[20]

It is important to note that God does not simply act on God's own accord or utter a *"fiat."*[21] God uses human agents to achieve God's salvific purpose. This was the case with Moses, Cyrus, Jesus, Mandela, and others. Similarly, in the crisis associated with the environment, it is not out of character for God to use scientists or politicians who might guide the world back to a more sustainable course.[22]

---

[17] And this is the point being made in the CDF's *Dominus Iesus* cited above.

[18] For more on Paul's vision of the Christ as the Cosmic Savior and the *plēroma*, see Rom 8:19–22; 1 Cor 3:22, 15:20–28; Gal 4:4; Eph 1:10, 1:23, 4:10; Phil 2:10; Col 2:9.

[19] *New Jerusalem Bible—Standard Edition* (London: Darton, Longman & Todd, 1985), col. 1:20 note h.

[20] This broad imagination of "the risen Christ as the measure of the maturity of all things" can be found in the work of Pierre Teilhard de Chardin. See Francis, *Laudato Si',* no. 83.

[21] Meaning "Let it be done."

[22] Agents of salvation need not act out of explicitly "theological" motives. It is up to believers to detect the hand of God working in history. For example, some might regard Angela Merkel, under considerable international pressure, persuading colleagues

Christian Tradition

Building on this scriptural base, the church has had two millennia in which it has understood the meaning of salvation in Christ. The tradition is surely rich in this regard, but a full investigation exceeds the limits of this essay. Instead, I briefly note Francis's contribution.

Pope Francis outlined the contributions of Popes John XXIII, Paul VI, John Paul II, and Benedict XVI to the tradition of social teaching as it relates to environmental issues.[23] *Laudato Si'* also shows how ecological teaching has been an occasion of unity between various churches.[24] Francis also demonstrates that Saint Francis of Assisi is an icon of creation spirituality for Christians and non-Christians alike.[25] Taking Saint Francis's spirit of sacredness in all creation and humanity's loving connectedness with every creature, we are imbued with a profound respect for nature that will not allow us to objectify, instrumentalize, and control it for our own purposes. Without taking a mystical approach, a first step toward the salvation of our planet must be developing a kindred feeling for the planet and every one of its inhabitants.[26]

Salvation in African Tradition

This sense of relatedness to the whole of creation leads to the second discourse—what is loosely called "African tradition." In African tradition, there is an emphasis on the unity between the living, those who have gone before, those who are still to be born, and the earth on which we all live. In many traditions, Africans have a profound respect for the natural world. This

---

at the G7 meeting in Bavaria in June 2015 to wean the global economy from fossil fuels as a divine intervention.

[23] Francis, *Laudato Si'*, no. 4–6.

[24] In particular, he cites the Ecumenical Patriarch Bartholomew asking us to "replace consumption with sacrifice, greed with generosity, wastefulness with a spirit of sharing, an asceticism which 'entails learning to give, and not simply give up.' " See Francis, *Laudato Si'*, nos. 7–9.

[25] Francis, *Laudato Si'*, nos. 10–12.

[26] This must be held in tension with the "demythologization" of nature of which Pope Francis writes in *Laudato Si'* no. 78. When we see ourselves as distinct from nature, we have the duty to "devise intelligent ways of directing, developing and limiting our power" over nature.

respect has mistakenly been condemned by some missionaries, in monotheistic fervor, as "animism" or "spirit worship." A relevant African theologian, Laurenti Magesa, states the emphasis this way: "All space is sacred because its physical material appearance contains the invisible powers that make life possible: the world of the spirits is integrated into that of space. In space as well as time, sacrifices and offerings are made to strengthen the community's soul. For this reason, some spaces carry more significance than others, with places of worship requiring the greatest respect."[27]

Yet in Africa we see that our earth—this sacred space—is repeatedly and grievously violated, which causes the suffering of millions of people. In his exhortation to Africa, Pope Benedict wrote: "Some business men and women, governments and financial groups are involved in programmes of exploitation which pollute the environment and cause unprecedented desertification. Serious damage is done to nature, to the forests, to flora and fauna, and countless species risk extinction. All of this threatens the entire ecosystem and consequently the survival of humanity."[28]

We need to honor the sense of the sacredness of the earth—our living space—of which Magesa wrote. It is not enough to simply cite an idealized tradition that our ancestors may or may not have implicitly held. Because the earth is the creation through which God communicates goodness to us, Christians assert its sacredness. Africans likewise assert the sacredness of the earth, because it is where the spiritual world is encountered. Quoting Augustine Shutte, Magesa maintains that our every contact with the earth is potentially contact with the spirits inhabiting the earth:

> "When one dies one does not leave the earth but moves deeper towards the centre," where . . . even God is to be found. From birth and ultimately and supremely in death, the earth becomes one's "eternal home." It is therefore "the common property of all people," not to be owned by any one individual.
>
> In death, one's existence is joined to and becomes part of the earth, the vegetation, the animals, the stars, and indeed, the cosmos.

---

[27] Laurenti Magesa, *What Is Not Sacred? African Spirituality* (Maryknoll, NY: Orbis Books, 2013), 58. Although nobody can speak on behalf of the entire continent, what Magesa writes is at least indicative of a tendency found throughout Africa.

[28] Benedict XVI, *Africae Munus: Postsynodal Apostolic Exhortation of the Church in Africa in Service to Reconciliation, Justice and Peace* (Vatican City, 2011), 80.

. . . Thus human interaction with any other being also means possible, or even probable, contact with the spirits of the dead.

In a village, every element of significance to the life of the community is associated with a spirit, often ancestral, but also "natural," or spirits created as such. A well, a lake, a river, a hill, or a forest could be such a place. Significant spiritual legends for each community lie behind this association and enforce judicious use of these resources.[29]

Magesa also asserts, "Morality and spirituality are indivisible and inseparable. 'African ethics arises from the understanding of the world as an interconnected whole whereby what it means to be ethical is inseparable from all spheres of existence.'"[30] African ethics are thus inseparable from African spirituality, which in turn connects us with our location on this earth, the source of all life and our home after death. Because we revere the earth, we must treat creation with the dignity it is due as the source and sustainer of life. The earth warrants immense moral consideration because it is the supporter of life and the home of the deceased.

From this African perspective, when nature goes awry, it may be an indication that there is something askew in the moral-spiritual order. Consequently, Magesa writes:

Rain, floods, drought, famine, or epidemics are natural phenomena; they do not carry much significance apart from how they affect existence. They become a matter of serious and public social, moral, and spiritual consideration when they upset the expected order of things, when the rhythm of seasons changes, causing floods and drought that claim the lives of humans, plants and livestock. Then the interplay of the life forces and human responsibility must be gauged, and appropriate (moral) behavior to restore needed balance determined. Communal ritual activity toward God and the

[29] Magesa, *What Is Not Sacred?*, 89, quoting Augustine Shutte, "*Ubuntu* as the African Ethical Vision," in *African Ethics: An Anthology of Comparative and Applied Ethics,* ed. Munyaradzi Murove (Scottsville: University of Kwa-Zulu Natal Press, 2009), 96.

[30] Magesa, *What Is Not Sacred?*, 43, quoting Munyaradzi Murove, "Beyond the Savage Evidence Ethics: A Vindication of African Ethics," in Murove, *African Ethics,* 28.

ancestral spirits proliferates during these periods for the specific purpose of human flourishing.[31]

This could not be any closer to the phenomena being considered in this essay—the disruption of regular human activity that is to be expected from the transgression of planetary boundaries through climate change. The African approach to crises of this type is to regard them as spiritual-moral aberrations. To save the community, communal ritual action is prescribed that will appease God and the ancestors.[32] In addition, appropriate moral behavior is determined to restore the necessary balance. To use Western categories, the former is a matter of "theology," the latter of "science."

Salvation in the Western Scientific Paradigm

Although it may seem to be from an epistemological universe entirely dissimilar to the Christian and African traditions, Western science can help instruct us as to what "appropriate moral behavior" may be. Informed by the Christian and African sense of the sacredness of all creation, scientists may be convinced of the value of preserving human life in a way that honors the planet on which we live.

As mentioned earlier, planetary boundary theory indicates nine threats to human existence on this planet. Although the scientists engaged in this conversation do not make definite prescriptions, the subtext is clear: to save the human species from ultimate extinction on this planet, we need to keep the effects of human activity within safe boundaries for each of these conditions.[33] This is primarily a scientific determination, and secondarily

---

[31] Magexa, *What Is Not Sacred?*, 55.

[32] Often misfortune is perceived as a cause of the ancestors withdrawing their protection from descendants who may have transgressed moral taboos. In this case, ritual action is prescribed to assuage the anger of the ancestors and to implore them to restore their protective care. It goes without saying that this ritual is accompanied by the resolve (at least) to reform one's action. A fuller discussion of this can be found in my *AIDS, Ancestors and Salvation: Local Beliefs in Christian Ministry to the Sick* (Nairobi: Paulines Publications Africa, 2008), 106–7.

[33] And there is no guarantee that the hoped-for salvation can actually be achieved. For example, it may be too late to reverse rampant climate change. The acidification of the oceans, for example, may already be on an inexorable trajectory beyond the tipping point at which mollusks can no longer build their calcium-based shells.

a political process. Both steps demand unprecedented global cooperation. Salvation of the planet as a safe place for human habitation requires that we:

- Stop using ozone-depleting chemicals
- Use fewer fossil fuels and more renewable energy sources
- Protect fresh water from all kinds of pollution
- Reduce use of nitrogen- and phosphorous-based fertilizers
- Convert no more forest cover to agricultural or horticultural land
- Keep habitats intact, so that biodiversity is not lost
- Stop pumping smog into the atmosphere we breathe
- Reverse the acidification of our oceans
- Release no radioactivity and nanoparticles in the environment

In Africa, ecological salvation translates into establishing successful scientifically informed local initiatives that address environmental concerns within communities. These initiatives are wide-ranging and should include: rehabilitating wetlands, lakes, and rivers; using sustainable sources of energy; cooking on more efficient, less polluting stoves; and stopping the cut-flow-er-for-export industry, which consumes much of the continent's water and arable land. When these concerns are addressed, Africans will find that these issues are local manifestations of a much wider, systemic abuse of the earth.

These prescribed intiatives are all actions that ordinary women and men can take. Moreover, these actions concerning the planetary boundaries must be taken on a concerted, worldwide scale. However, the success of these initiatives is dependent on the activity of individuals, insofar as they have freedom and choice in these matters. Individuals can combine their efforts in a mass of political action in a way that will place pressure on legislators and industrialists. In Magesa's terms, this is all "appropriate moral behavior" that can be prescribed alongside the "communal ritual activity toward God and the ancestral spirits."

Laudato Si' is an example of theology that takes scientific discourse seriously and is neither exclusively Christian nor exclusively African. It exemplifies how the insights from various sciences can—and should— inform Christian moral action. Pope Francis compels African Catholic Christians to address the ecological crisis as a matter of urgency. A fortiori, he issues a clarion call to Christians living in parts of the world that more strongly contribute to the risk of transgressing planetary boundaries. As Christians in Africa, we also take seriously the insights of our ethnic and cultural traditions, which are not unique, but do inform our worldview and morality. Our traditions can all address "salvation," although they might not use this precise term. At this kairos, all Christian theologians must include Western science in our discourse. This will allow us to fashion a culturally aware, relevant, effective, and prophetic response to the ecological crisis facing our common home.

The Church We Want

Ecclesia of Women in Africa?

Marguerite Akossi-Mvongo

Women are the mainstay of the church in Africa and around the world. At gatherings of prayer and Eucharistic celebrations women are heavily represented. Christian women are the ones who take the responsibility to give their children a Christian education; they constitute the majority of catechists in parishes. Everyone is well aware that the sustainability of the church is based on their frail shoulders. Therefore, the two African synods (1994[1] and 2009[2]) have reaffirmed that the church should work to integrate women at different levels of the church. But the church is full of contradictions.

Consider the example of Pope Francis. He makes the insightful comment that Mary is more important than the bishops. In his commentary on the *Ave Maria,* he noted that before the Annunciation, we had never heard of an angel bowing to a human being. If the archangel Gabriel did so to Mary, it meant that he felt she was his superior in her fullness of grace, her familiarity with God, and her future dignity as the mother of God. The new Eve gave credit to the female gender; yet not even Francis has succeeded in reversing the current ecclesiastical arrangement that denies women ministerial equality in the church. The question is not considered worthy of open debate; for the pope, the question is closed.[3] Preventing women from being ordained to the priesthood is one thing, but prohibiting debate on the matter?

When the Anglican Church started ordaining women to the priesthood, on the basis of a new hermeneutics of the scriptures, Pope Paul VI registered his disapproval in unequivocal terms:[4]

---

[1] John Paul II, *Ecclesia in Africa,* no. 121.
[2] Second African Synod, 2009, proposition 47.
[3] Francis, *Evangelii Gaudium,* no. 104.
[4] Paul VI, response to letter to His Grace the Most Reverend Dr. Frederick Donald

Your Grace is of course well aware of the Catholic Church's position on this question. She holds that it is not admissible to ordain women to the priesthood, for very fundamental reasons. These reasons include: the example recorded in the Sacred Scriptures of Christ choosing his Apostles only from among men; the constant practice of the Church, which has imitated Christ in choosing only men; and her living teaching authority which has consistently held that the exclusion of women from the priesthood is in accordance with God's plan for his Church.

The same position and the same arguments were given by John Paul II.[5] Thus in the tradition of the church as understood by ecclesiastical authority, discipleship through ministerial leadership is an exclusively male affair.

However, two thousand years of church history are dotted with traditions and customs that have received different interpretations over time. The only thing unchanged is the good news of the gospel: the death and resurrection of Christ for the salvation of the world, the consequence of which—at least according to Paul—is the equality of the people of God:

Since every one of you that has been baptised has been clothed in Christ. There can be neither Jew nor Greek, there can be neither slave nor freeman, there can be neither male nor female—for you are all one in Christ Jesus. (Galatians 3:27–28 New Jerusalem Bible)

The chapter does not focus on whether it is theologically legitimate and part of God's plan to deny women access to the priesthood; I adopt a slightly different perspective. First, I turn to the Catholic faithful, as did Vatican II in *Lumen Gentium*.[6] What kind of church do Catholics want in the twenty-first century? What church do the people of God in Africa want? How can they receive in their authentic African selves the message of God's love? How can they testify that they have met the resurrected Christ? What do they think? What are their hopes and fears? An important aspect of Vatican

---

Coggan, Archbishop of Canterbury, on the priestly ministry of women, November 30, 1975, *AAS* 68 (1976): 599–600.

   [5] John Paul II, *Ordinatio Sacerdotalis*, no. 4.

   [6] *Lumen Gentium*, no. 28.

II was its desire to announce the gospel to all humanity, taking into account their different backgrounds, times, and cultures.

To explore these questions I conducted a survey in a vibrant parish located in a residential area of Abidjan, Ivory Coast. The results form the basis for my analysis and reflections. It consists of four parts: the issues of the role and place of women, the point of view of Catholics, what the church should face on the ground, and a few lines of reflection as conclusion.

Issue of Women's Roles

There is constant talk of a church in which women could fully play roles as prophets, priests, and kings. Oftentimes this rhetoric uncovers deep contradictions in ecclesial teaching and practice. The church defends the equality of men and women in marriage and society. The church teaches that women should reach the fullness of their potential, and it criticizes the traditions and laws that impede their development. But this is valid only outside the church. According to Pope John Paul II, the new Eve, the mother of God and the church, received neither the mission proper to the apostles nor the ministerial priesthood. Accordingly, the nonadmission of women to priestly ordination cannot mean they are of lesser dignity or that they should be subject to discrimination.[7]

Societies have evolved; nowadays, it is no longer possible to confine women to the roles that had been decided for them. This is the case especially in Africa, where other Christian churches offer women opportunities to live out their faith in all aspects of their daily lives. Catholic parents see their children attending other churches that are allowing them to be Christian, African, and themselves. The consequences of such spiritual migration to other churches could be serious for the Catholic Church. This is no mere academic debate; this is a real issue with repercussions for our families and local churches.

What should change substantially if the Catholic Church goes beyond words and actually grants equal access to all ministries on the basis of vocation rather than gender?

---

7 John Paul II, *Ordinatio Sacerdotalis*, no. 3.

The Point of View of Catholics

What church do we want? I tried to look at this question from the perspectives of consecrated men and women, laypeople involved in church movements, and Catholics who attend Sunday Mass. For this project, I enlisted the assistance of fellow psychologists. As psychologists, we did what we do best: we interviewed people, listened carefully, and gathered their views.

We conducted a survey with a small sample (35 people) constituted on prototypical modes: priests in charge of parishes, young and old parish priests, religious responsible for parish councils, members of church movements, and practicing Catholics who were not members of particular movements. We used an open, semidirective interview type with four questions: What should be the role of women in the church and are there any aspects of church life that should be reserved for men? In a church in which women could be priests, what would fundamentally change? What would be positive and negative? Is it desirable?

Role of Women

All parties believed that women have important, decisive roles to play in the church. But the details of their roles reflect the construction of male and female roles that people have in the family and society. Paradoxically, laymen were the most favorable toward the idea of giving women access to all ministries. They often mentioned the argument of Methodist pastors that everyone should listen with great interest to the "shepherds" of new communities and their life experiences at work and outside the church. The views of women were more diverse; we discovered that they had three main positions regardless of their involvement in church movements. The differences seem rather in relation to the education received (family and social models) and professional experiences.

The first group of women was rather active in the church; they had highly skilled professions and worked in mixed environments. In their view, women should have access to all positions, but they thought that organizational changes should be thoroughly reflected on and carefully planned to preserve the unity of the church. A second group with the same sociological characteristics believed not only that there should be no reserved area but also that the contribution of women priests would make the church more efficient.

A third category included women of varied levels of education and commitment to church activities. They believed God's plan for women was procreation; they felt women must play a role in assisting and advising men, and that specific tasks corresponded to gender roles. They felt priesthood should be reserved for men. This group is quite consistent with the view of the church as expressed, for example, in *Mulieris Dignitatem*.[8]

Many of the priests interviewed hid behind the door of the theological impossibility of ordaining women and reiterated the arguments of the pope. But even here, opinions varied. Some were satisfied with the idea that it was a theological impossibility; for others, the example of the Anglican Church showed that women priests were a possibility despite difficulties, but they obeyed the rule of the Catholic Church on this matter.

Religious women were extremely reluctant to discuss the issue; the most we can say is that the positions were actually very diverse and emotional.

Fundamental Changes Deriving from Women's Access to Ministerial Roles

Faith and mission. The mission of the church would remain basically the same, but here and there, innovative methods and rigor might be required to ensure efficiency if women were ordained. Analyzing the experience of the Anglican Church shows that actually there is no major change. As in many domains, the arrival of women helps everyone rethink some practices, draws attention to some aspects, and promotes a "softer way" of achieving the same goals. Women priests would be expected to exercise more rigor, especially in church financial activities.

The liturgy. There was a general consensus that women priests would not change the liturgy; this was one of few points of agreement. The shared part of the liturgy is centralized and codified in the church, and "no other person, even if he be a priest, may add, remove, or change anything in the liturgy on his own authority" (*Sacrosanctum Concilium,* no. 22). Here and there, with the flexibility introduced by Vatican II, it is possible to some extent to have inculturation of prayers and of the Eucharist celebration. The arrival of women priests would not affect the movement.

Authority. Some difficulties could appear with the hierarchical organization of the church with its rules of subordination. The authority of women

---

[8]   John Paul II, *Mulieris Dignitatem,* August 15, 1988, no. 26, *AAS* 80 (1988).

priests could at times be challenged, but that is also the case for some men. The fundamental changes would not be spiritual; they would affect the structure, the organization, and the logistics of church life and should be reviewed from top to bottom.

Advantages and Disadvantages for the Church

The benefits and positive points of ordaining women are numerous: the number of priests would increase; the female qualities of commitment, dynamism, and organization would be better used; and the practices of the church would be less contradictory. The disadvantages are just as many: the temporal structure of the church should be reviewed thoroughly and deal with the realities on the ground, and the risk of schism could not be excluded.

Is it desirable?

The views on this question were very diverse. Some were fiercely opposed to the idea of women priests, and some were eager to see such a change. Some asked, why not? This is where the real challenge is for the church.

What Challenges Would the Church Face on the Ground?

The real challenge is simply that of large organizational change. If we have women priests, where will they stay? How should we organize parishes and presbyteries? Even those who were able to consider the question of women's ordination linked the point to the necessity of a discussion concerning the overhaul of the status of the priests and their lives, including issues such as the marriage of priests.

Contrary to what happens in the rest of the world, the church in Africa (and particularly in Ivory Coast) does not suffer as much of a lack of priestly vocations. The challenge it faces relates more to motivations of a large number of young people seeking priesthood for reasons other than "the call" (enviable social status, opportunities for studies, shelter from difficulties of lay life, and more).

Regarding organizational restructuring, some people envisaged the possibility of reconstituting the large parish, the current model, into smaller communities supported by a priest (man or woman) living in a rectory with his or her family (like Protestant pastors). But all this does not seem to meet the approval of the Catholic base, which prefers the status quo on some points. Their feeling is that any change would result in less-available priests who would have family matters to take care of. A final concern relates to the challenges posed by a materialist and consumerist society. Briefly stated, how would married priests stay away from the attractions of the world? The history of the church includes episodes we do not want to see repeated.

The church we want is one that announces the gospel and takes care of the poor and destitute, a church that defends equal rights and democracy outside and inside itself. The opportunity for all the baptized who feel the call to access the priesthood can contribute to a greater spread of the gospel. Are those who object basing their objections on the Word of God?

As with any change, the risk of schisms is real. The debate about women priests carries a strong emotional charge among the laity, an emotional charge more pronounced in women than in men. Some women in the sample survey, for example, saw this idea of women priests as directly inspired by the devil and Freemasons to weaken the Catholic Church!

Cultural Dimensions

The role and place of women have certainly changed over time in the Catholic Church, but an analysis of the resistance to greater roles for women shows that some aspects of this resistance have something to do with the Mediterranean and European culture that nurtured the beginnings of Christianity. This outlook was reinforced by the negative portrayal of Eve in creation stories and lodged in the collective (un)consciousness of people. Women are too often viewed as temptresses who cause those who approach them to fall. Some of the resistance today to ordained women is reminiscent of this ancient fear.

Indeed, in West Africa, particularly in Ivory Coast, traditions consider women as being in close and easy communication with nature spirits because of their special role as the bearers of life. In African religion they play a prominent role and are considered in West Africa as the *komians,* priestesses who preside at the sacred rites. During the survey, some women did not like the idea of women priests because that mirrored the practice of African religion. They were convinced that Christianity introduced the phenomenon of male priests.

The debate also brought in concerns about the way catechism is taught—by encouraging fear but not encouraging people to read and understand the Bible, get training in religious matters, and nurture a personal relationship with God.

Pope John Paul II has highlighted the reciprocity and the equality of rights and duties Catholic married couples have.[9] Nevertheless, many Catholic women continue to see any claim to rights as a refusal of God's plan for women. It is therefore appropriate for the church to open up leadership and ministerial space to the faithful; otherwise, it could lead to a blurred vision on fundamental points. The church has to prepare Catholics to adapt and remain steadfast in their faith despite the inevitable changes that will occur in the twenty-first century. Some questions must find answers that go beyond the circles of theologians and reach the faithful at the ground level.

Catechism. What is the role of women vis-à-vis the Bible? Is it only procreation? How can this be related to the occurrence of the successful women we see in diverse occupations in society? How can we manage fears of ancient cults in which women are eminent priestesses? How can we distinguish between everyday culture and rites and the call to follow Christ?

In seeking answers to these questions, efforts should be made to publish and distribute the work of African women Christian theologians, because many Catholics at the base do not read extensively and do not know that there are many African theologians (male and female).

We must also make a real place for female religious, who are often seen as simply housekeepers. Nuns are seen by many Catholics as assuming in the consecrated life the traditional roles of women: educating, caring for, feeding, and helping the poor.

What are the challenges of ordaining women for the structure of the church, and what are the challenges of a married clergy? Discussing matters is the best way to make wise choices.

As a feminist who researches gender issues, I would love to say that women's access to all ministries or a church headed by women would be perfect, but the fact is this will not solve all the problems of the church. However, access for women to the priesthood would not fundamentally alter the faith and spiritual dimension of the church. The fundamental mission of spreading the message of Christ will probably be better done

---

[9] Ibid., no. 15.

with women priests because in the current state, "the harvest is rich but, the laborers are few" (Luke 10:2, NJB).

I think the real obstacles are not spiritual but practical. The ordination of women would be a real upheaval and a challenge to the temporal structure of the church, but it would also be an opportunity to correct matters that do not reflect the face of Christ.

The church we want would be more comfortable when it speaks of equal rights for all humanity. In such a church, the faithful would have to be prepared through real religious education. "My people perish for want of knowledge" (Hosea 4:6, NJB). The people of God must be able to distinguish what belongs to faith in the risen Christ and what concerns the need to manage in a centralized manner such a large number of people from different cultures. Then the debate that could give birth to the church we want could confidently start.

Epilogue

Vade mecum: *Come Walk with Me*

Mercy Amba Oduyoye

The project that gave rise to this volume began in 2013, at Hekima University College's School of Theology and Institute of Peace Studies and International Relations in Nairobi, Kenya. Its primary aim was to inaugurate a conversation about church, religion, and society in Africa, and to conduct joint research on what the last fifty years since Vatican II have meant for both the African church and the church worldwide.

This is a convocation of Catholic scholars, but despite being a Methodist, I received an invitation to come walk with participants. I decided to be a fly on the wall and to learn all that I could from the rich theological conversations. From this vantage position, I consider it a privilege to be with scholars who care deeply about the church and about Africa. Conversation is a process. Naturally, the question arises: What next?

In an interesting way this theological initiative projects into the future to imagine the convocation of a Vatican III. And many of us hope that this will occur in our lifetime and perhaps even on our continent, as Emmanuel Katongole and Joseph Healey indicate in their essays. As a Methodist, I was invited to come walk with Catholic scholars; in return, I extend this invitation to the contributors and readers of this volume: come walk with me. From this point forward, the journey, like a pilgrimage or the Lukan Emmaus journey, is a shared experience. What could this theological project and journey mean for theologians like me, Catholic or not, and for the entire church of Christ in Africa and globally?

To return to the Emmaus story. The two disciples who were walking away from the events of the crucifixion at Golgotha were in a state of despondency. Looking to the future, I am not in a state of despondency, and so my invitation is not in the spirit of past hope, but of present and future hope.

Some might query: *Quo vadis?* And that is a fair and natural question. The path of the journey will tell. Come, let us walk together, because as a proverb says, "We create a path by walking." But the Akan proverb tells us, "If you blaze a trail and nobody follows you, you have lost your keys." That is to say: you are mad. Therefore, my key concern is this: Who will walk after us to make our path a real trail? Theological research and scholarship constitute a path-making enterprise. As theologians we are engaged in making a path, and we aim to walk far. For this reason, we must call others to come walk with us. Theology does not foster or satisfy an isolationist agenda. The theological journey is an invitation to mutual accompaniment: dreaming, thinking, acting as members of the human community redeemed by the risen Christ.

There are rules that govern this journey. We must not strive to walk too fast. Some of those who come to walk with us may be toddlers in theology, and others are of a venerable age, like me, who require a third leg—a walking stick or cane. Whatever our status or condition, we all need to learn from and lean on one another's expertise and gifts. We all need to learn about the breadth and depth of the community called church. Together we can create a path that will be widened and furthered by those who join us. Come walk with me, and together we shall work for the church we need, the church that shares the gospel by word and deed.

The three-year theological journey of the Theological Colloquium on Church, Religion, and Society in Africa began and continues in the currents and paths of the fiftieth anniversary of Vatican II and the trail toward Vatican III. Along with previously published volumes, this present volume is a legacy for posterity as signs of how we have used our time and resources on this journey.

Besides, we can only walk together if we agree to stay together: But can two walk together unless they agree? (Amos 3:3). We can only stay together if we share a common goal—if we can call one another to account and invite others in who would like to walk with us. We are on our way to an ecumenical council that includes Africa and the church to which we happily belong.

In this volume, as in previous ones, contributors have made ample use of the imagery of a family, and I evoke that imagery here as well. We have to be ready to live together as teeth and tongue—as those who fight at times, but can never part company.

What do we intend to discuss on our walk? The toddlers of this theological and ecclesial family will continually need care and direction as they walk with us. I myself was brought into this theological family by women who mentored me into theological competence. We need to bring many more women into this role, who will shape theology for the church. Those who are in this role now keep us conscious of what the church needs in the context of the daily lives of our human community, and with reference to the environment that sustains us and for which God has made us stewards. We need continued and intensified conversations and action about our interconnectedness and hospitality, and a respect for the dignity of the other as we guard, nurture, and protect our own humanity for the sake of the *imago Dei*.

We shall research, talk, and write about religious theologies, but, more than that, we shall join others to seek reconciliation and to further promote tolerance and interreligious harmony. We shall nurture the humility that will allow us to talk and act as people who know that no particular religion can exhaust the universal reach for divinity. As the Akan of Ghana say, "One person's arms cannot surround the baobab tree."

We struggle with sexuality and spirituality. We struggle with the current phase of Christianity manifested in Africa, one that struggles with demons and those who claim to dispense deliverance. All of this and more demands not only that we craft relevant and credible theology for the church but also that we create locations for the church, Christians, and Christian communities to do so. I am particularly concerned that we do something about the creeds we repeat with little understanding, and that we help inspire moving liturgies.

Because theological reimagination does not cease, we need to continue to walk together, modeling a community wherein diversity is truly a gift that focuses on living and sharing the gospel of Jesus Christ.

The hedging of the Lord's table remains a challenge. We need scholars who will not tire of providing honest historical analyses of the roots of today's intractable challenges. We need to privilege the lives of the local church—the small ecclesial communities and families, about which Joseph Healey has written in this volume—because without the local church, the world church remains only a concept. We need to promote serious engagement with the autochthonous religious imagination of Africa, especially in the ways that this imagination shapes our culture and spirituality.

As we walk together, listening and acting and imagining Vatican III, we do so knowing that the future of the church and the entire Christian community is held in God's hands and is, therefore, an unfolding and empowering mystery. As far as our faith moves us, we say that the church shall stand, because humanity needs its mission and ministry. Our duty is to collaborate and strive toward a future of challenges and promises, responding to Pope Francis as he calls us to compassion, mercy, and accountability. This call reminds us to be Christ to the world. It is the sum of theological vocation.

Therefore, I invite you: *Vade mecum.*

Contributors

Marguerite Akossi-Mvongo, from Ivory Coast, is a multilingual psychologist working as a university researcher. She has field experience in human resources management and vocational counseling, including measuring human behavior and how the differences in personality affect various behaviors in everyday life. Akossi's major fields of interest are gender issues (including violence and marital relationships), health, and learning abilities. She is the past governor of Zonta International (a charity for advancing the status of women worldwide). A married Catholic woman, she is involved in different positions in the church. She was the coordinator of the French Catholic community in Nairobi, 2004–2009, and is currently a member of the parish council in Abidjan Bon Pasteur, secretary of the Family Commission, and a member of *Legio Mariae*.

Anne Arabome is a member of the Sisters of Social Service in Los Angeles, California, USA. She holds a doctor of ministry degree in spirituality from Catholic Theological Union in Chicago. She is completing a second doctorate in systematic theology at the University of Roehampton, London. She is the co-founder of Wellspring Africa, an affiliate with Works In New Directions, a nonprofit corporation that operates under the auspices of the Sisters of Social Service. Wellspring Africa assists young African women who live in poverty to move forward with their lives through education and life guidance.

Tina Beattie is professor of Catholic studies and director of the Digby Stuart Research Centre for Religion, Society and Human Flourishing at the University of Roehampton in London. Her research and academic publications are primarily concerned with Catholic sacramentality and gender; Marian theology, art, and devotion; theology and psychoanalysis; and Catholic social teaching and women's human rights. She works widely with religious groups and communities, and is a frequent contributor to the media.

Paul Béré is a Jesuit from Burkina Faso. He holds a doctoral degree in Sacred Scriptures from the Pontifical Biblical Institute (Rome). Since 2008, he has been involved in the Synod of Bishops. In 2009, Pope Benedict XVI appointed him as Consultor to the Secretariat of the Synod of Bishops (Vatican) for five years. Pope Francis appointed him Consultor to the Pontifical Council for Culture beginning July 2014. He teaches Old Testament and biblical languages at the Institut de Théologie de la Compagnie de Jésus (ITCJ) in Abidjan, Ivory Coast, and in other institutions. Dr. Béré's current research focuses on Old Testament exegesis and aural criticism (the aural reception of the written text). His publications cover the areas of exegesis, theology, and ecclesiological issues.

Kevin Dowling, from South Africa, is a member of the Congregation of the Most Holy Redeemer, more commonly known as the Redemptorists. He serves as the bishop of Rustenburg and is co-president of the Pax Christi International Board. He has been chairman of the International Sudan Ecumenical Forum, through which he engaged in the Sudan Peace Process. As a trustee of the Ecumenical Solidarity Peace Trust, he is involved in research of human rights abuses in Zimbabwe.

Nontando Hadebe, from South Africa, is currently a sessional lecturer at Saint Augustine College, Johannesburg, South Africa. Her subject is ministry in the Christian tradition with special emphasis on the South African context. She also presents a regular ninety-minute weekly program on Radio Veritas and is currently working on a seven-part series on the interface between women in the Bible and contemporary women. She is also the coordinator of the Circle of African Women Theologians in Southern Africa (ten countries). Her research areas are HIV and AIDS, particularly the intersection of gender, sexuality, and theology; contextual theology; inculturation; and Vatican II.

Joseph G. Healey, MM, is a Maryknoll missionary priest who lives in Nairobi, Kenya. He teaches a full-semester core course on "Small Christian Communities (SCCs) as a New Model of Church in Africa Today" at Tangaza University College (CUEA) and Don Bosco Salesian Theological College. He facilitates SCC Workshops and animates SCCs in Eastern Africa. He is an ordinary member of the St. Kizito Small Christian Community in St. Austin's Parish in Nairobi Archdiocese.

Stan Chu Ilo is a Catholic priest of Awgu Diocese in Eastern Nigeria. He is a research fellow at the Center for World Catholicism and Inter-Cultural Theology and assistant professor of Catholic studies, world Christianity, and African Catholicism in the Faculty of Liberal Arts and Social Sciences, De Paul University, Chicago. He is the editor of the African Christian Studies Series for Wipf and Stock Publishers, publisher of the website www.africantheology.org, and an Ambassador for Peace for the Universal Peace Federation. His forthcoming publications are "The Poor Church for the Poor in Africa: Living the Message of Pope Francis in the Spirit of the Second African Synod" and "African Catholic Ecclesiology," an entry in the *Oxford Handbook of Ecclesiology*. He is the founder of Canadian Samaritans for Africa, a registered Canadian charity working in four African countries.

Antoine Kambanda, from Rwanda, has been bishop of the Kibungo Diocese in Rwanda since 2013. He holds a doctorate in moral theology from Academia Alfonsiana in Rome and has fourteen years of experience in the formation of seminarians. He has also done social and pastoral ministry as a director of diocesan Caritas and as president of the Justice and Peace Commission in the Archdiocese of Kigali. He is the president of two commissions of the Rwandan Episcopal Conference: Justice and Peace and The Family.

Emmanuel Katongole from Uganda is associate professor of theology and peace studies at the Kroc Institute for International Peace Studies at the University of Notre Dame. His research interests focus on politics and violence in Africa, reconciliation, and Catholicism in the Global South. He earned his PhD in philosophy from the Catholic University of Louvain (Belgium) and a diploma in theology and religious studies from Makerere University in Kampala, Uganda. Professor Katongole, a Catholic priest of Kampala Archdiocese, has served as associate professor of theology and world Christianity at Duke University, where he was the founding co-director of the Duke Divinity School's Centre for Reconciliation. As a major part of his research at the Kroc Institute, Katongole will contribute to "Contending Modernities," a cross-cultural research and education initiative examining Catholic, Muslim, and secular forces in the modern world.

Peter Knox was born and raised in Johannesburg, South Africa. After finishing a degree in chemistry at Cape Town University, he joined the Jesuits. Since ordination in 1996, he has worked as university chaplain, completed a PhD in systematic theology, been the theologian at the Jesuit Institute in South Africa, taught theology at the national seminary and St.

Augustine's College in South Africa, and served as treasurer of the Jesuits in South Africa. Since January 2013, he has been teaching at Hekima University College, the Jesuit school of theology for English-speaking Africa, in Nairobi. He has a lifelong interest in issues of ecology and spends hours birdwatching.

Nader Michel, from Egypt, is a professor of moral theology and medical ethics at the High Institute of Religious Studies and the Coptic Catholic Seminary in Cairo. He is also a visiting professor at St. Joseph University in Beirut. A medical doctor (Cardiology), he holds an MA in theology from Centre Sèvres-Paris, and earned a PhD in Islamic studies from Bordeaux University, France, and a PhD in moral theology from St. Joseph University, Lebanon. Father Nader is currently the president of Collège de la Sainte Famille in Cairo, and assistant for formation in the Near East and Maghreb Province of the Society of Jesus. He has published fourteen books in Arabic in moral theology, medical ethics, and spirituality, and written many articles in different languages.

Professor Laurenti Magesa, from Tanzania, is a priest of Musoma Diocese, where he worked in pastoral ministry for several years. Since 2008, he has taught theology at Hekima University College, Tangaza College, and Maryknoll Institute of African Studies in Nairobi. In 2011/2012, he was an international visiting fellow at Woodstock Theological Centre, Georgetown University, Washington, DC, USA. He has recently published *What Is Not Sacred? African Spirituality* (Orbis, 2013).

Dr. Bienvenu Mayemba, from Kinshasa, Democratic Republic of Congo, is a Jesuit Priest. He holds a PhD in systematic theology from Boston College, USA; an MPhil from the Institut Saint Pierre Canisius, in DRC; and the STL in Theological Anthropology from Weston Jesuit School of Theology, USA. Dr. Mayemba is a professor of systematic theology, African Christian theology and postcolonial theory at Institut de Théologie de la Compagnie de Jésus (ITCJ), Abidjan, Ivory Coast. He is visiting professor of environmental ethics at Loyola University, Chicago, USA, and visiting professor of Trinitarian theology at Centre de Formation Missionnaire d'Abidjan (CFMA), Ivory Coast. During Winter 2012, he was visiting professor of African philosophy and critical theories at Arrupe College, Zimbabwe. In 2010, he received the Donald J. White Teaching Excellence Award at

Boston College and was named Boston College's *The Heights* 2010 Person of the Year. He is the executive director of the BARAZA Chair of African Theology at the Jesuit institute of Theology (ITCJ).

Professor Philomena Njeri Mwaura, from Kenya, earned her PhD from Kenyatta University, Nairobi, where she is an associate professor in the Department of Philosophy and Religious Studies. Professor Mwaura is also the director of the Center for Gender Equity and Empowerment and a former president of the International Association for Mission Studies (IAMS), coordinator of the Theology Commission of the Ecumenical Association of Third World Theologians (EATWOT), Africa Region. She is a member of the Circle of Concerned African Women Theologians and the Ecumenical Symposium of Eastern Africa Theologians (ESEAT). Besides teaching at Kenyatta University, Professor Mwaura has been an adjunct lecturer at Akrofi Christaller Institute of Mission Research and Applied Theology, Ghana, and Hekima University College in Nairobi. She has published extensively on various aspects of African Christianity in refereed journals and books.

Dr. Josée Ngalula, from the Democratic Republic of Congo, is a nun with the Order of Religieuses de Saint André. She has a PhD in theology from the Catholic University of Lyons (France). Dr. Ngalula teaches systematic theology in theological institutions in Kinshasa and is a member of several theological institutions. She is also a researcher in African theology, new religious movements in Africa, ecumenism on the African continent, African theological feminism, and Christian lexicology for the African languages. Dr. Ngalula is co-founder of the Association of African Theologians (ATA) and is the initiator of the collection *Bible et femmes en Afrique.*

Professor Mercy Amba Oduyoye, née Yamoah, from Ghana, is a Methodist and former deputy General Secretary of the World Council of Churches. She holds theological degrees from Legon, Ghana, and Cambridge, UK. She has taught in schools in Ghana and Nigeria and in universities and seminaries in Nigeria, the Netherlands, USA, Canada, and South Africa. Professor Oduyoye has served as plenary speaker in several mega women's events both ecclesial and social. She also initiated the Circle of Concerned African Women Theologians and is currently establishing the Institute of Women in Religion and Culture at Legon, Ghana. Both of these are multireligious. Dr. Oduyoye has been awarded seven honorary doctorates for her contributions to theology and ecumenism.

Professor Teresa Okure (PhD), from Nigeria, is a sister of the Society of the Holy Child Jesus (SHCJ). Professor of New Testament and Gender Hermeneutics at the Catholic Institute of West Africa, Port Harcourt, Nigeria, she has authored many books, chapters in books, and articles in scholarly journals. She continues to lecture globally, conduct research on biblical, African, church, and gender issues; she works with women, youth groups, and religious congregations; and she mentors worldwide. Currently, she is the foundational president of the Catholic Biblical Association of Nigeria (CABAN) and a member of the Anglican Roman Catholic International Commission (ARCIC) representing Catholic Africa, a member of the steering committee of Contextual Biblical Interpretation (CBI) of the Society of Biblical Literature, and a member of the Episcopal Working Committee on Catechetics of the Regional Episcopal Conference of West Africa (RECOWA-CERAO).

Agbonkhianmeghe E. Orobator, SJ, is the Principal of Hekima University College Jesuit School of Theology in Nairobi, Kenya. He is the author of *Theology Brewed in an African Pot* (Orbis, 2008) and the editor of *Reconciliation, Justice, and Peace: The Second African Synod* (Orbis, 2011) and (with Linda Hogan) *Feminist Catholic Theological Ethics* (Orbis, 2014).

Professor Eugene Elochukwu Uzukwu, from Nigeria, has been a priest of the Congregation of the Holy Spirit (C.S.Sp) since 1972. He is the first holder of the Rev. Pierre Schouver, C.S.Sp., Endowed Chair in Mission at Duquesne University. He was rector of Spiritan International School of Theology, Attakwu Enugu, Nigeria (1987–91; 1994–97). He has experience in formation work in Nigeria and Congo, and has been a lecturer/professor in broad areas of theology in Nigeria, Congo, France, Ireland, and the United States. His interest areas include liturgy-sacraments, mission, ecclesiology, and contextual theology (Africa). He is editor of *Bulletin of Ecumenical Theology.*

Index